IMAGES
of America

SALEM

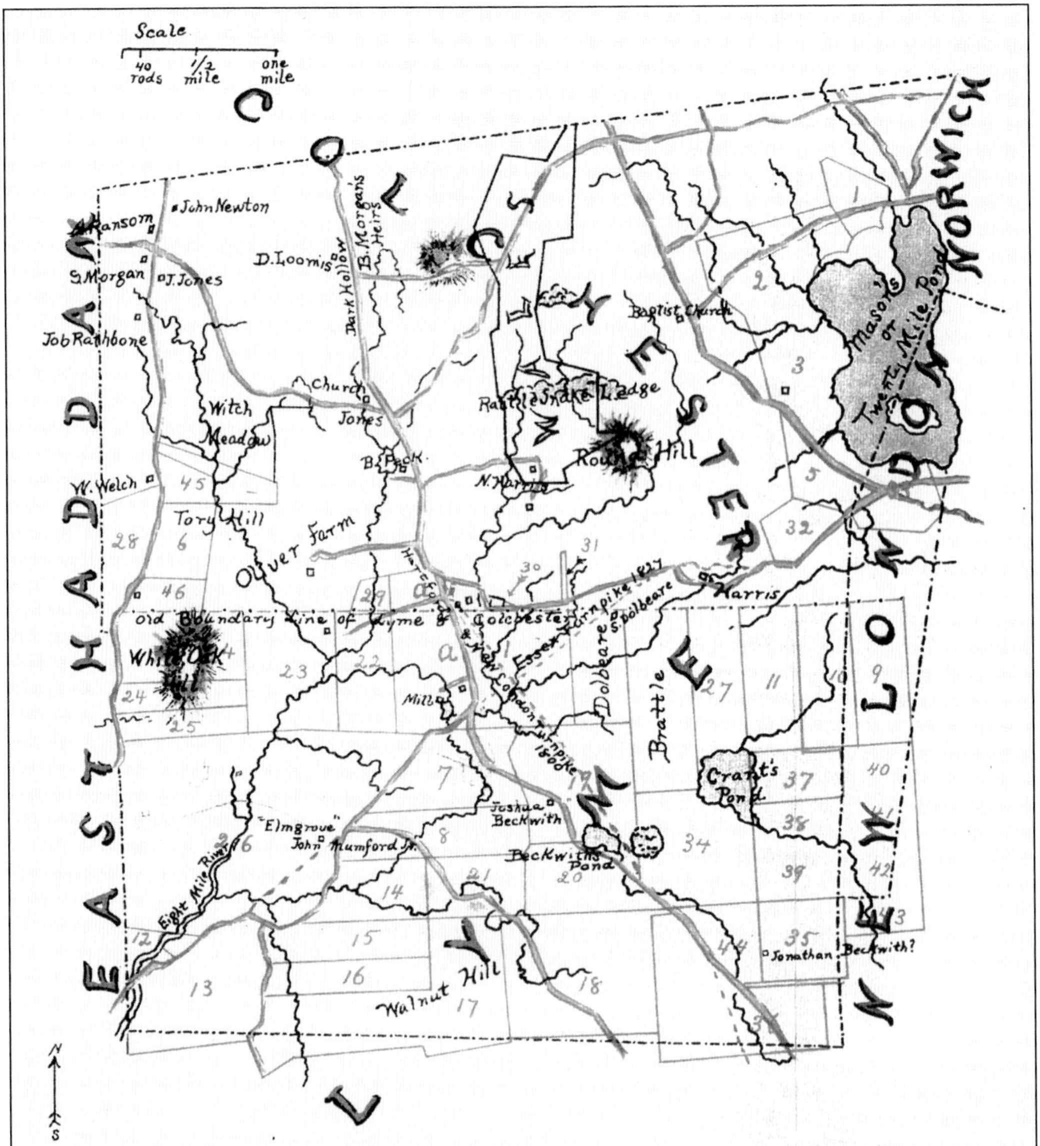

Map of the Confiscated Estate of Col. William Browne of Salem, Mass., in 1780

[*Browne Lands enclosed in red lines, with the Names of Residents on the Estate as far as known at that date, and the sites of the Homes of a few other Residents of the Parish, and the lines of the later Turnpikes. For account of Confiscation see Historical Introduction, and for Deeds see Appendix.*]

This map of the confiscated Salem, Connecticut, estate of Col. William Browne of Salem, Massachusetts, in 1780 was created by Donald Grant Mitchell. Mitchell made the map for Mary E. Perkins for the book *Chronicles of a Connecticut Farm; 1769–1905*. This map shows some of the names of early settlers and their property.

On the cover: Traditionally, Salem has been an agricultural town. In this photograph of Fairy Lake Farm, corn is being gathered. Families, friends, and, in this case, employees of the farm shared the workload. (Courtesy of the Salem Historical Society.)

IMAGES
of America

SALEM

Cindy Lee Corriveau

ARCADIA
PUBLISHING

ISBN 978-0-7385-3945-4

Published by Arcadia Publishing
Charleston, South Carolina

Printed in the United States of America

Library of Congress Control Number: 2005938289

For all general information, please contact Arcadia Publishing:
Telephone 843-853-2070
Fax 843-853-0044
E-mail sales@arcadiapublishing.com
For customer service and orders:
Toll-Free 1-888-313-2665

Visit us on the Internet at www.arcadiapublishing.com

To my son, Quinn

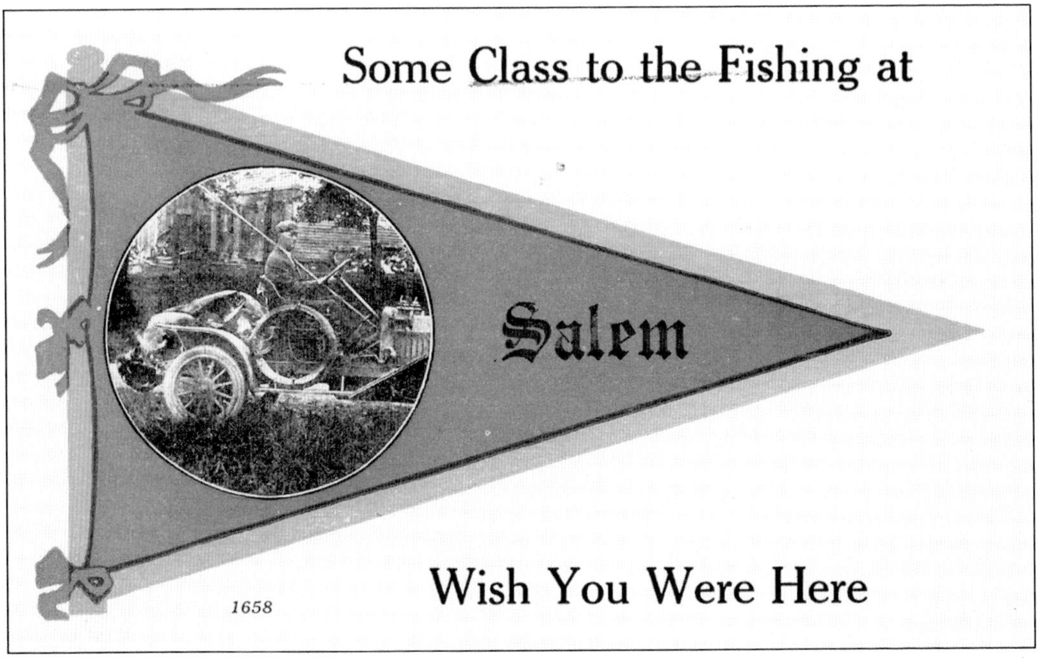

This wish-you-were-here postcard with an old fashioned car was sent in 1915. "Jiggin" with "mousies" in Salem is great!

Contents

ACKNOWLEDGMENTS

It truly was a pleasure to compile this book. A book such as this could not be written without help from the community. It is with the sincerest appreciation that I acknowledge and thank Deanna St. Jean, the town of Salem municipal historian. Deanna and I spent countless hours working on this project and all that it entails. Her incredible knowledge of Salem's history, not to mention her lovely wit and country charm, kept me going and kept me smiling day after day. Salem is a wonderful community, and if you need something, all you have to do is ask. Folks are more than happy to oblige if they can. I gratefully acknowledge those people who showed support by donating photographs, information, and encouragement: Annie and David Bingham, Patricia Crisanti (town clerk), Rev. Timothy Dubeau, Evelyn Cunningham, Charles Dimmock, Stuart Gadbois, Janet Moore Ireland, David Lynn, Alfreda Bingham Shapere, Virginia Day Stevenson, Alfred Wlodarczyk, Helen Kobyluck Woronik, and Andrew and Wilma Zemko. So many people helped me in so many different ways too numerous to mention here. I gratefully acknowledge the information, friendship, and support from the following folks while writing this book: Larry Avery; Robert Kim Bingham; Roberta Bowdler; Jane and Andre Corriveau; Donald Fraser Jr. and Duncan Fraser; Phyllis McCall and Beverly Maynard Davis; Henry Dobrinski; Gail Dukes; Killeen Dwyer and Charles Dwyer; Abraham Abdul Haqq; Lisa Jenkins; Nancy Krissoff; Kerrie O'Connor; Larry Reitz; Ann Pugsley; Carmen and Glen Reeves; Lesley Rogers; Jean Ann and Jack Scaduto; Linda Schroeder; David Wordell; Susan McCusker; Doris McTigre; my parents, Denise and William Zaleski; Folks of the "Fellowship;" and my editor, Dawn Robertson. No act of kindness is ever forgotten. I acknowledge all the ancestors of this town, all the people who created this lovely rural town of Salem that we know of today. To all those of today who will continue the legacy.

While working on this book at the Salem Historical Society, I acknowledge Timothy Molinari, Quinn Corriveau, Bradley Jenkins, and Michael Reeves for making me smile. A special acknowledgment to my husband Daniel and my son Quinn for their endless support and love. Last but not least, thanks to our own personal Images in America: *Salem* mascot, Barnabus Dubeau of Salem, who greeted us each day at the Salem Historical Society and kept the town house yard free of sticks.

Introduction

Welcome to *Salem*. The town of Salem, approximately 30 square miles with a population of 4,000 people, was established in 1819. It is populated by a diverse population of caring, friendly and talented people. In this pictorial history we will traverse the countryside to note various farms and notable folks, and to get a glimpse of the history of this wondeful town.

Salem, the name itself is a derivation of the Hebrew word shalom, or peace. It is a town of peace, a town that promotes and respects education and diversity, as seen by the influx of different nationalities, religions, and cultures with the ever-expanding, consistent population growth. Prior to incorporation of the town in 1819, the land of Paugwonk, once owned by Niantic and Mohegan Native American tribes, had a been a working plantation. The area now known as Salem was attractive to a wealthy merchant named Col. Samuel Browne of Salem, Massachusetts. He purchased a total of 9,500 acres, including parts of Lyme, Colchester, and Montville. Browne established a homestead for one of his three overseers and his African captive families who farmed the land from 1718 to 1781. This homestead later became the first inn in Salem. Salem is only one of the many towns in New England that utilized slave labor. Historical records of the African Captives are minute but some may have later connected with Native American tribes and settled in the area. In all due respect, no history is complete without acknowledging all people who assisted this town in its endeavors. Excavations of captive cemeteries continues as this part of the town's history unfolds in search of a more all inclusive history.

Since Salem was incorporated as a religious parish, we take a look at the churches and the first public buildings in Salem. Community spirit has long been a tradition; people gathering to share news, share joys and sorrow and to help one another as seen here in the places they congregated.

Historically, education has been and still is important to Salemites as seen by six, one room schoolhouses from early in Salem's history. The joy of sharing land and abundance with others in the community is also a reoccurring theme as residents gave of their time and land to help build schools and support programs. As the need arises, some small businesses are openened to help the community. Folks in Salem contributed to wartime as well; sending citizens to defend our country and acknowledging their effort through the monuments on the town green. Salem sees creativity, ingenuity, and diversity as a gift to the community. Higher aspirations, the arts, and education are all appreciated in Salem as we take a look at Music Vale Seminary and Fairy Lake Farm.

Though the roots of agriculture were firmly planted, Salem has always respected Yankee ingenuity and new thinking, reflected in the characters who lived here or migrated to this lush countryside. Prior to the Civil War, Salem boasted seven sawmills, two gristmills, six schools, four churches, a piano factory, an ink factory, and a cotton mill. Rosewood and mahogany pianos with genuine ivory keys and mother-of-pearl inlay and ornamentation were made entirely by hand by the Whittlesey brothers in Salem, later giving birth to a factory located somewhere in the proximity of where the Salem Firehouse exists today. Oramel Whittlesey opened the first normal school of music in the country authorized to confer degrees, Music Vale Seminary. Women from all over the country, Canada, and the West Indies came here to learn music and to become teachers. Descendents of Browne's slaves manned the Concord coaches carrying young women over hill and dale of Salem. Two fires, the second one during a pyrotechnic display during an opera, wiped out the buildings. All that remains is the barn and the two life-size lions that once graced the front entrance of the school. The lions now silently guard the Whittlesey cemetery.

Frederick Rawolle amassed a fortune with his invention of a compact explosive used to fracture oil wells. After moving to Greenwich from New York state in 1918, he purchased 3,000 acres in Salem to fulfill his dream of an elaborate farm complete with the area's first hydroelectric plant. In the area of Fairy Lake, with a view of Long Island Sound, he built a magnificent barn complete with ceramic tiles to house his prizewinning bulls and cows. He used the water flow of Fairy Lake to illuminate his vast estate when only a few towns actually had any electricity. He also built a store in Salem Four Corners, the country store that still stands today, and a store in New London known as the Fairy Lake Store, which sold frozen items from his farm. Due to the fact he had electricity, he was able to freeze food and began delivering frozen food to other areas and businesses. It is said that he also illuminated Fairy Lake to allow hockey players to practice because most were only able to practice at night. This resulted in the team winning a pennant. Rawolle's Yankee ingenuity did not stop there. When he decided he wanted to retire his large houseboat, he used his dynamite-like invention to blast a 5,600-foot channel from Fairy Lake to the road, thus, creating Carr or Stump Pond. Fairy Lake itself is not visible from Route 85; however, the blasted area and the overflow of water sit amongst tree stumps and has an ominous look as one drives by. Yankee ingenuity as its best.

However, in the case of Thomas LeCount, the results were not so fortunate. Back in 1895, LeCount wanted to move his two-and-a-half-story house to a newly acquired lot across the lake. Harnessing up some horses and sliding the house fully furnished across a frozen lake seemed like a great idea. After the project began, misfortune descended as the house itself began to settle into the ice. By morning, the house was half submerged into the lake. Items that could be salvaged were removed, while heavier items such as a sideboard, stove, and piano remained. In time, the house was fully submerged and today still remains at the bottom of Gardener Lake.

In *Salem*, we go on to take a look at some of the local legends and some of the inspirational folks that once lived in Salem. Our own Salem Holocaust war hero Hiram Bingham IV inspires our desire for loftier humanitarian ideals despite the possible repercussions he may have encountered. The history the land, but most of all the people, make Salem what it is. When we see the different types of people that have lived here in Salem, we realize that we can dream and aspire to higher goals. Salem gives a small view of what it was like in the past, how the town progressed historically and how it is today. In this birds eye view, we get a glimpse of the history and mystery of Salem.

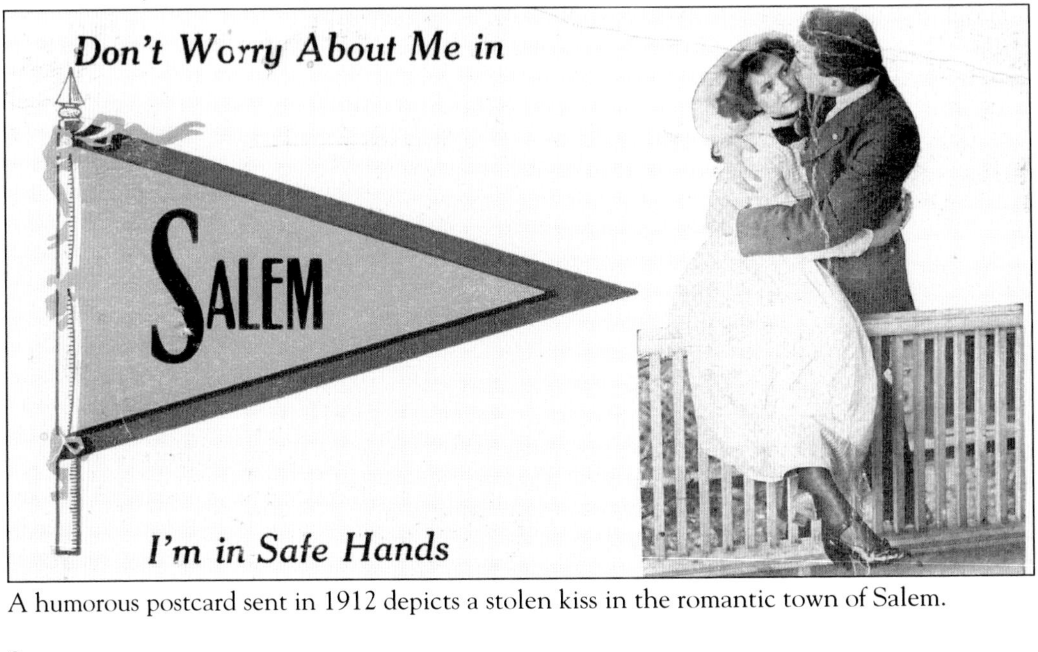

A humorous postcard sent in 1912 depicts a stolen kiss in the romantic town of Salem.

One

Salem Four Corners

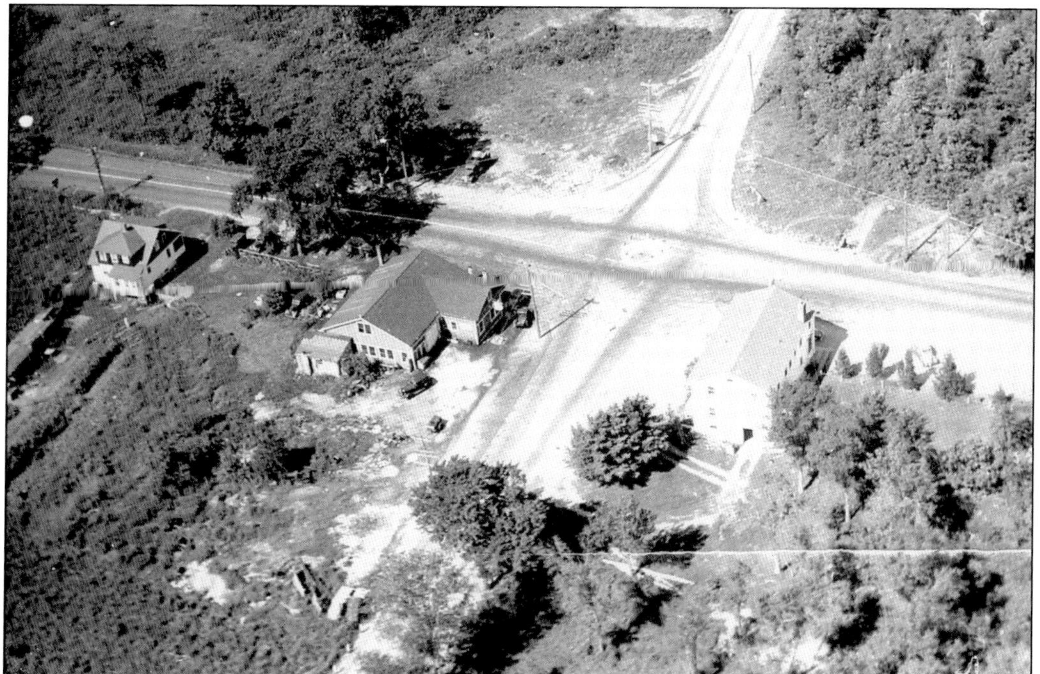

This is an aerial view of the back of the Country Store, Willows Garage, and the McCalls' house. This vertical road is Route 82 heading toward Norwich and the horizontal road is Route 85. Salem Four Corners was established in 1827 when the Norwich Essex Turnpike, now known as Route 82, crossed the Hartford New London Turnpike. The Hartford New London Turnpike, once a Native American trail, was not formally laid out until 1716. It is said that Gov. Gordon Saltonstall used this trail when he went to Hartford to assume his position as governor in 1708. In 1933, by act of the general assembly, it was named Governor's Road. Governor's Road was straightened and moved to the east side of Horse Pond. At one time, the pond went right up along the cliff known as Lover's Leap. The Essex Turnpike was chartered in 1822 provided it operated a ferry over the Connecticut River at the North Cove in Essex, and in 1825, by act of the general assembly, the roads were consolidated. The Salem Norwich Road was created in 1827 from Wharf Bridge in Norwich Landing to Salem. The two became one extended road called the Norwich Essex Turnpike (Route 82).

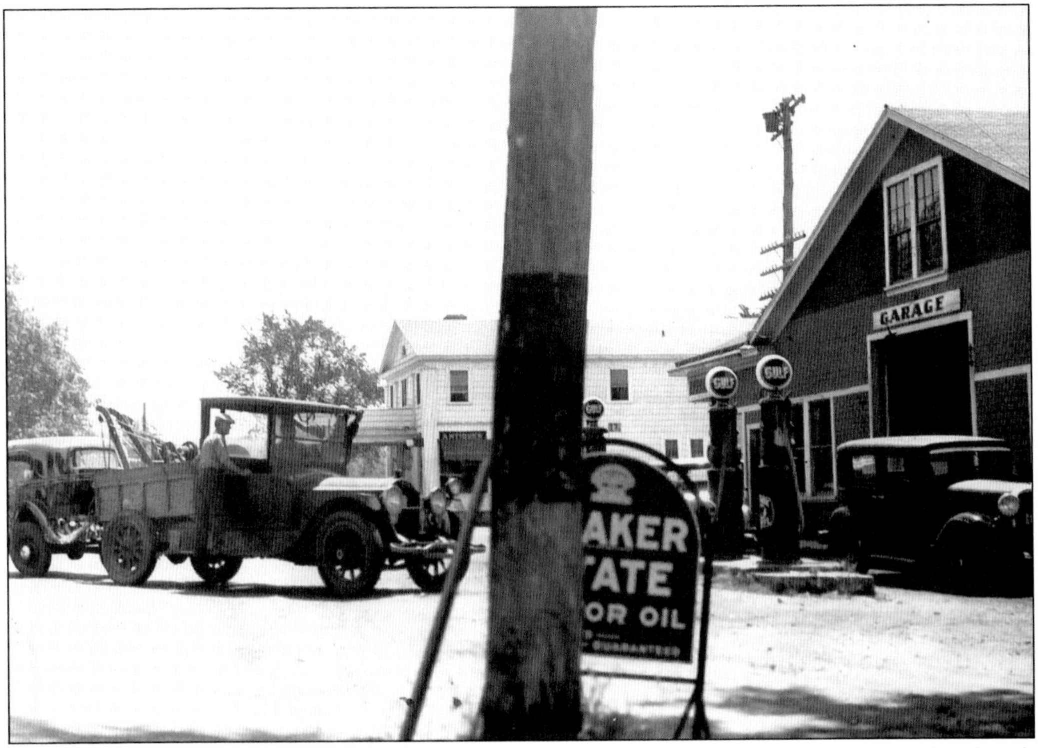

This view features Willows Garage and the Fairy Lake Farm Store, built in 1922 by Frederick Rawolle. The Fairy Lake Farm Store later became known as the Salem Country Store. This photograph was taken in 1934.

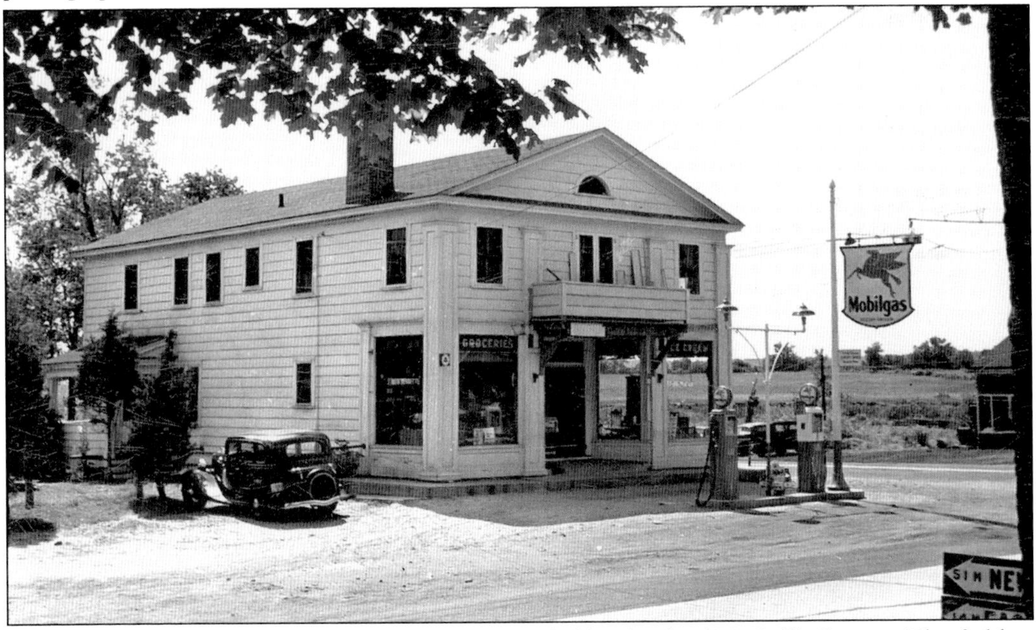

Looking at this photograph, one can see the open field in back of McCall's Garage. The field in back was so marshy that even horses could not get in there for haying. All the hay in back had to be hand cut with a scythe. Whoever got there first got the hay.

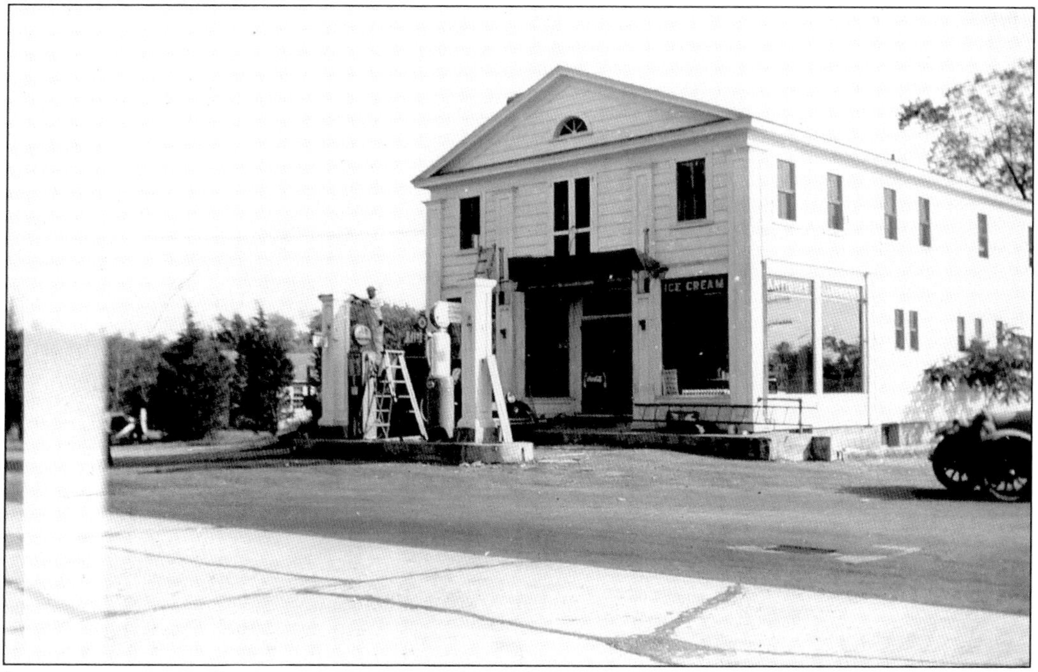

Renovations over the years have given the old Country Store different appearances. In the photograph below, there is an overhang probably to help shield motorists from inclement weather while pumping gas. The old Country Store, in the top photograph, also appears in the 1940s when there was no longer an overhang.

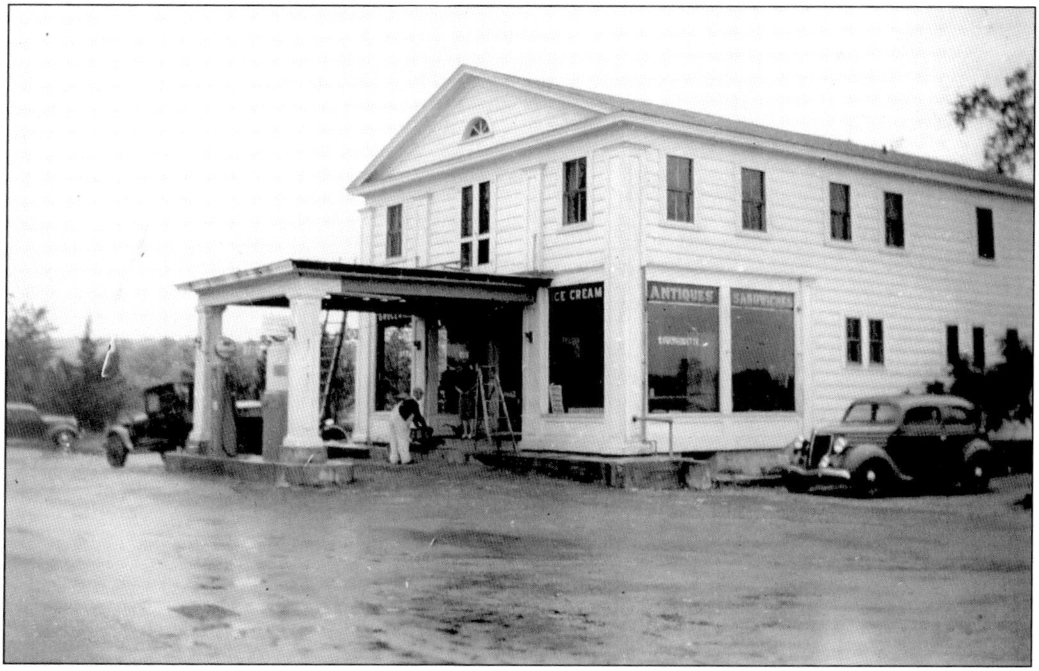

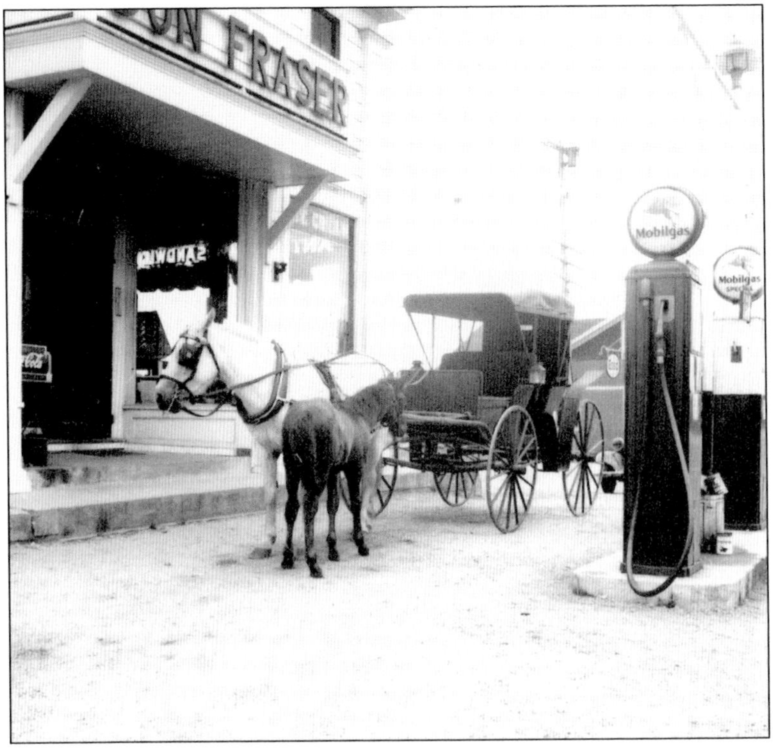

Don Fraser was hired by Frederick Rawolle to run the Firy Lake Farm Store. At some point the name was changed to Don Frasey's Luncheonette. Horse and buggy were still being used even though some folks had automobiles.

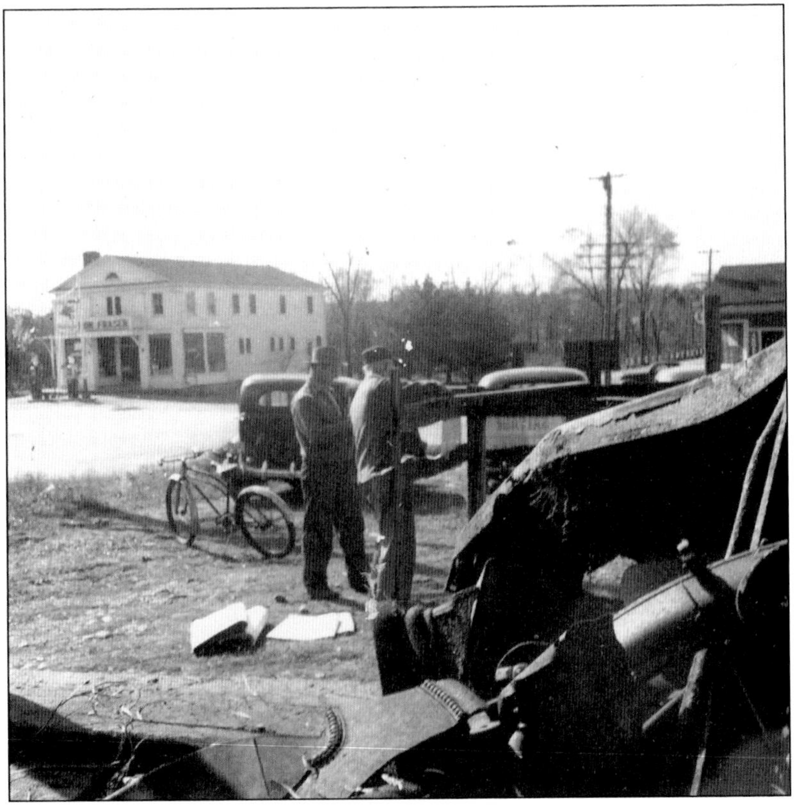

Here is a view taken from the official salvage lot diagonally across Salem Four Corners. The photograph was taken in 1942 or 1943. In the mid- to late 1930s, fireworks were set off in this lot for the Fourth of July.

Fraser's Luncheonette and Soda Fountain menu appears here. This was one of the places to grab a bite to eat—sandwiches, pies, pastries, and ice cream—through Salem. Prices were apparently different during these days. To sit at the fountain was 5¢ cheaper than sitting at a table, and to have a sandwich toasted was 5¢ more.

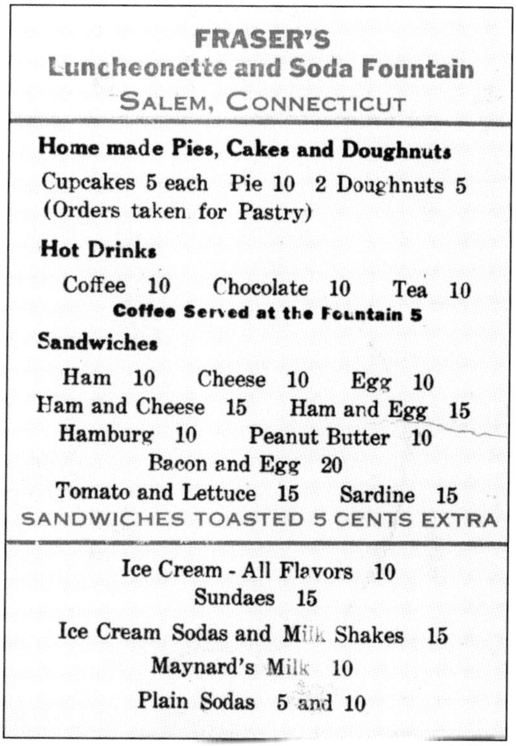

FRASER'S
Luncheonette and Soda Fountain
SALEM, CONNECTICUT

Home made Pies, Cakes and Doughnuts

Cupcakes 5 each   Pie 10   2 Doughnuts 5
(Orders taken for Pastry)

Hot Drinks

Coffee 10   Chocolate 10   Tea 10
Coffee Served at the Fountain 5

Sandwiches

Ham 10   Cheese 10   Egg 10
Ham and Cheese 15   Ham and Egg 15
Hamburg 10   Peanut Butter 10
Bacon and Egg 20
Tomato and Lettuce 15   Sardine 15
SANDWICHES TOASTED 5 CENTS EXTRA

Ice Cream - All Flavors 10
Sundaes 15
Ice Cream Sodas and Milk Shakes 15
Maynard's Milk 10
Plain Sodas 5 and 10

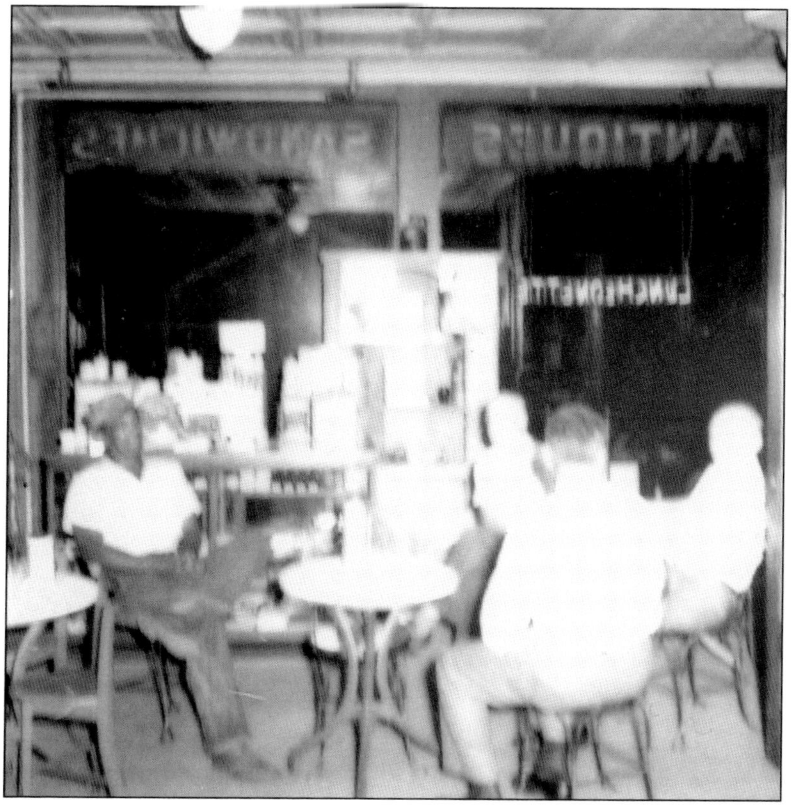

Here are some men having lunch at Fraser's Luncheonette and Soda Fountain (the Country Store). The men shared stories and tall tales, sometimes playing checkers and catching up on the latest gossip.

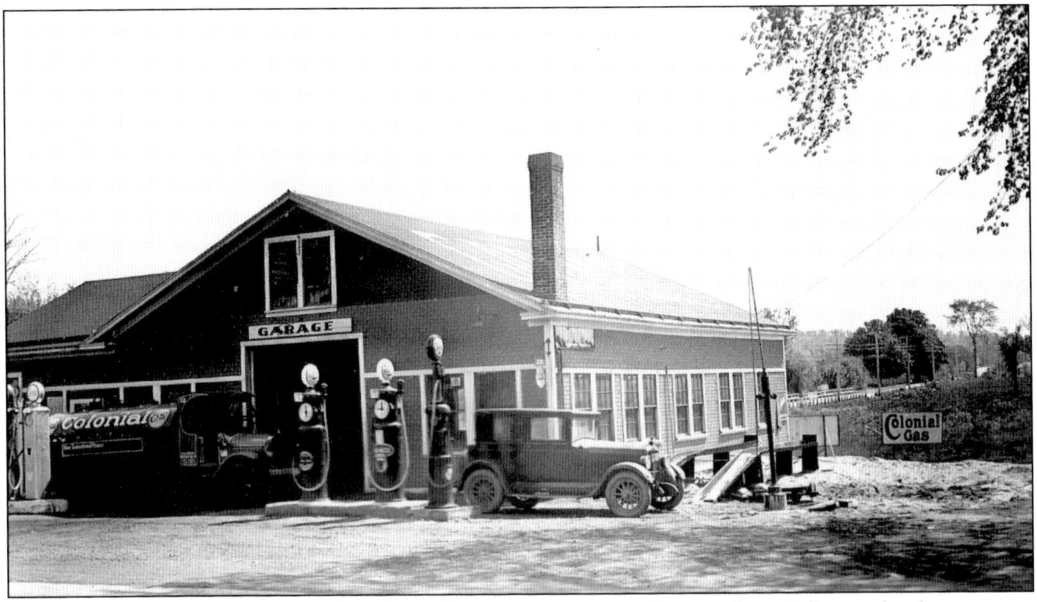

Another hangout for the locals where the men went to play pool and shoot the breeze was here at Willows Garage and gas station as it looked in 1930.The Willows Garage was owned by Calvin McCall Sr. and Ethel McCall. The McCalls lived in the house adjacent to the business. They owned the business for over 75 years.

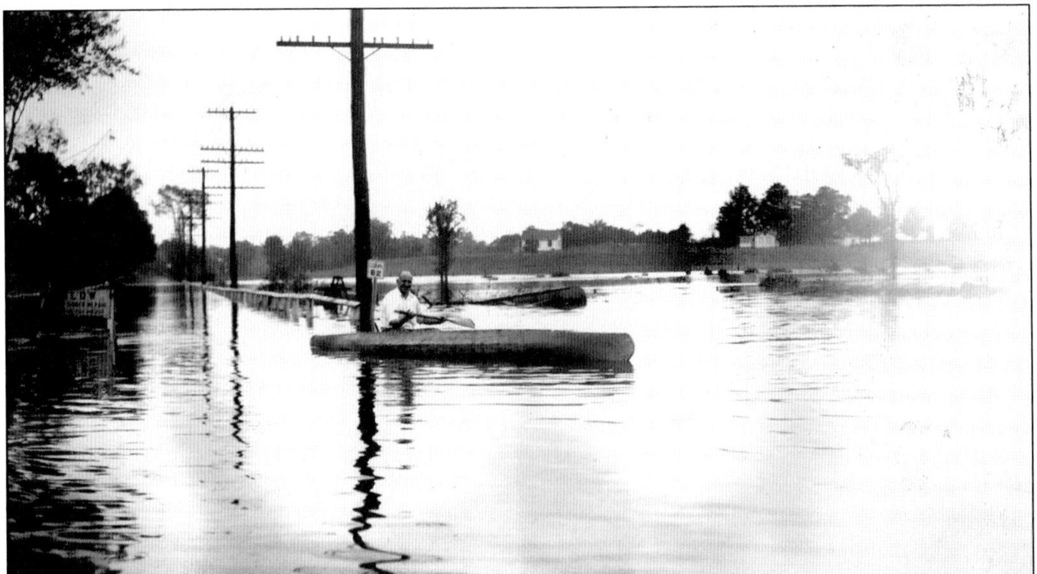

Canoeing through three and a half feet of water through Salem Four Corners after a flood resulting from the Hurricane of 1938, this man is smiling and apparently not exceeding the speed limit.

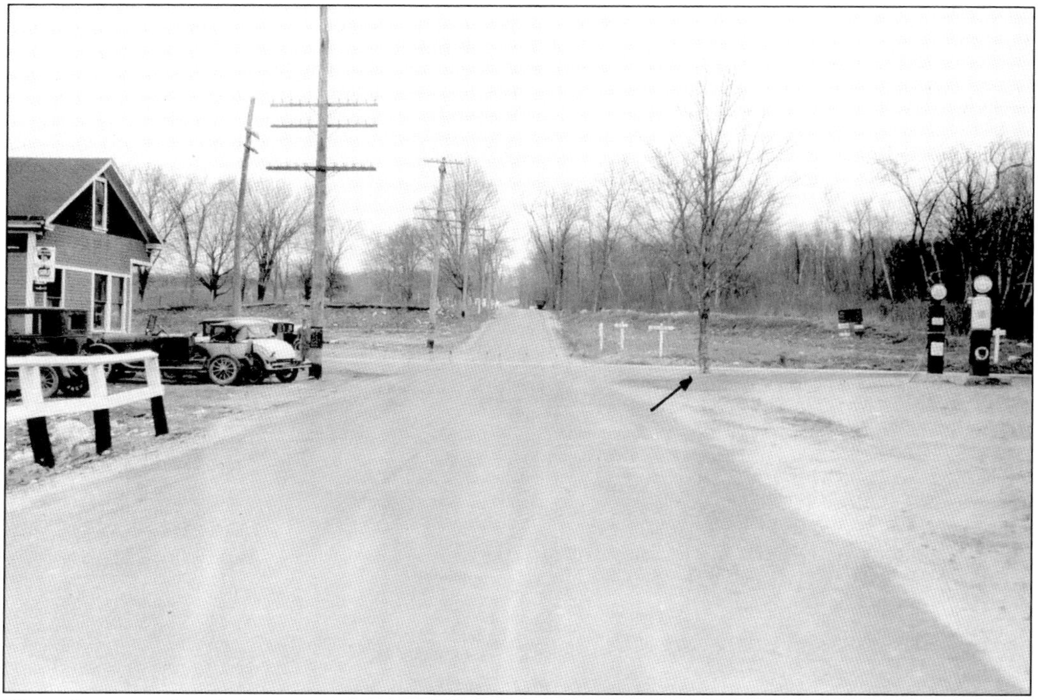

This photograph of the intersection of Route 85 (102) and 82 (153), taken from Route 82 facing Norwich, was a photograph submitted in a proposal to install a rotary due to numerous accidents at Salem Four Corners. Six accidents reported in 1930 resulted in $1,815 worth of damage. It was estimated that a $200 rotary "would be well worth while from an economic as well as safety viewpoint."

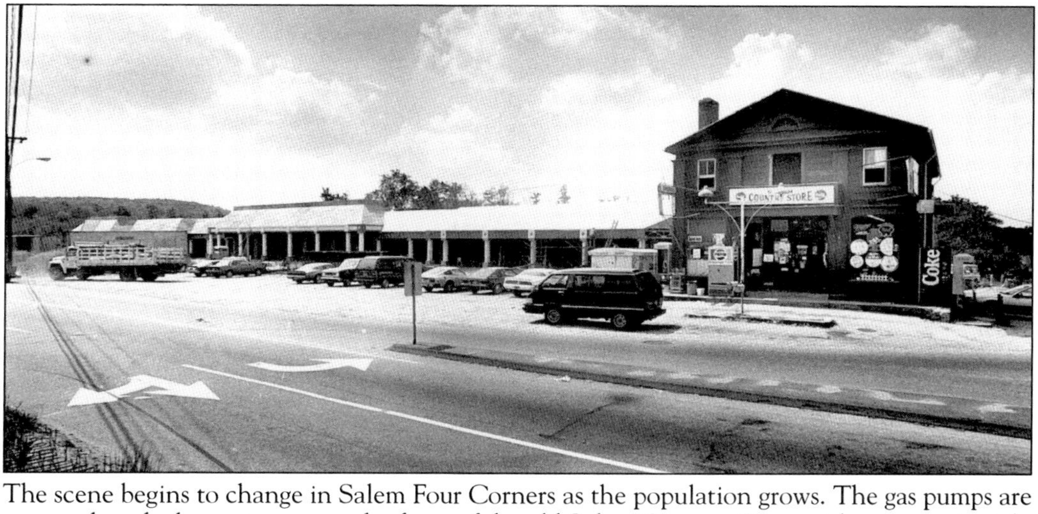

The scene begins to change in Salem Four Corners as the population grows. The gas pumps are removed, and a large sign graces the front of the old Salem Country Store with a new paint job. The convenience store is to the left, while a package store is in the right-hand side. The strip mall is added and is still in progress from the looks of this photograph taken in 1988.

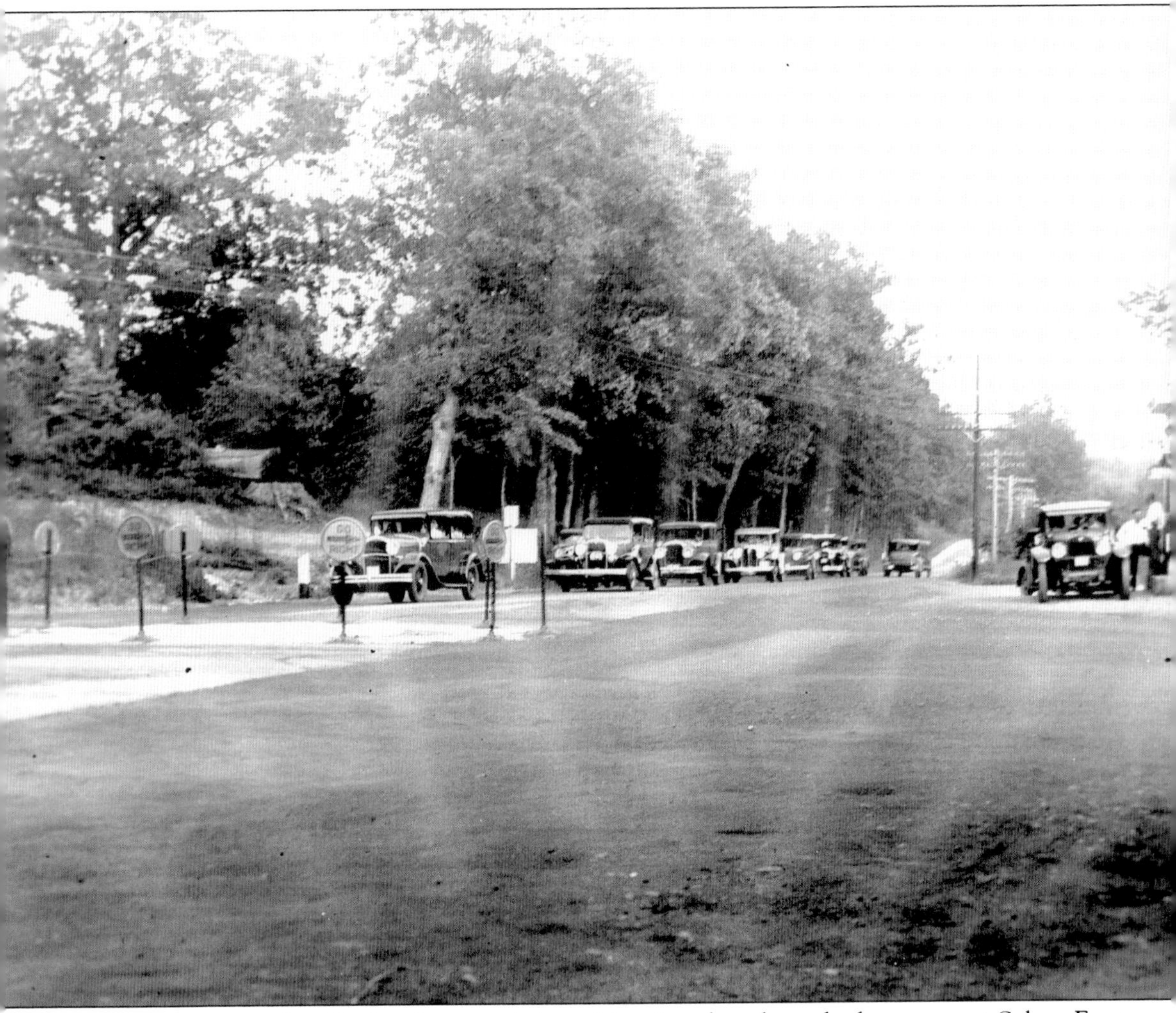

Here is a view of traffic heading north from New London through the rotary at Salem Four Corners. The proposed speed of the rotary was originally 30 miles per hour. Motorists speeding at up to 50 miles per hour around the rotary became a problem. The constable's dirty looks did not seem to slow down the enthusiastic speeders, so a sermon at the Congregational church was given to help curtail the hot rods. At one time, the rotary signs were not chained to one another. On one occasion, an inebriated motorist carried off one of the signs all the way to Colchester. It was decided to chain the signs together to make them more difficult to move. If motorists took one, they had to take them all. In 1938, eight 400-watt mercury vapor lights were installed at Salem Four Corners.

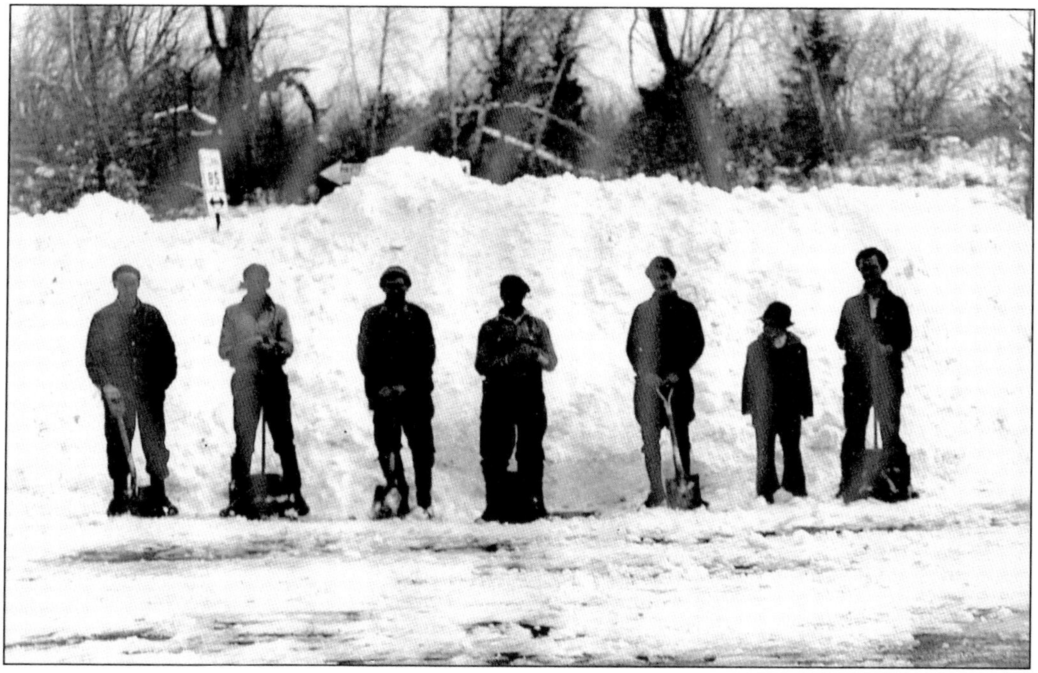

Here is a photograph of Mitchell Flats, Route 82, heading toward East Haddam from Salem Four Corners after a snowstorm in February 1934. Since there were no plows, roads were shoveled by hand by residents of Salem. In this photograph are, from left to right, unidentified, Mike Dembinske, unidentified, Peter Zachcefski, Ken Cornell, Robert McCall, and George Day.

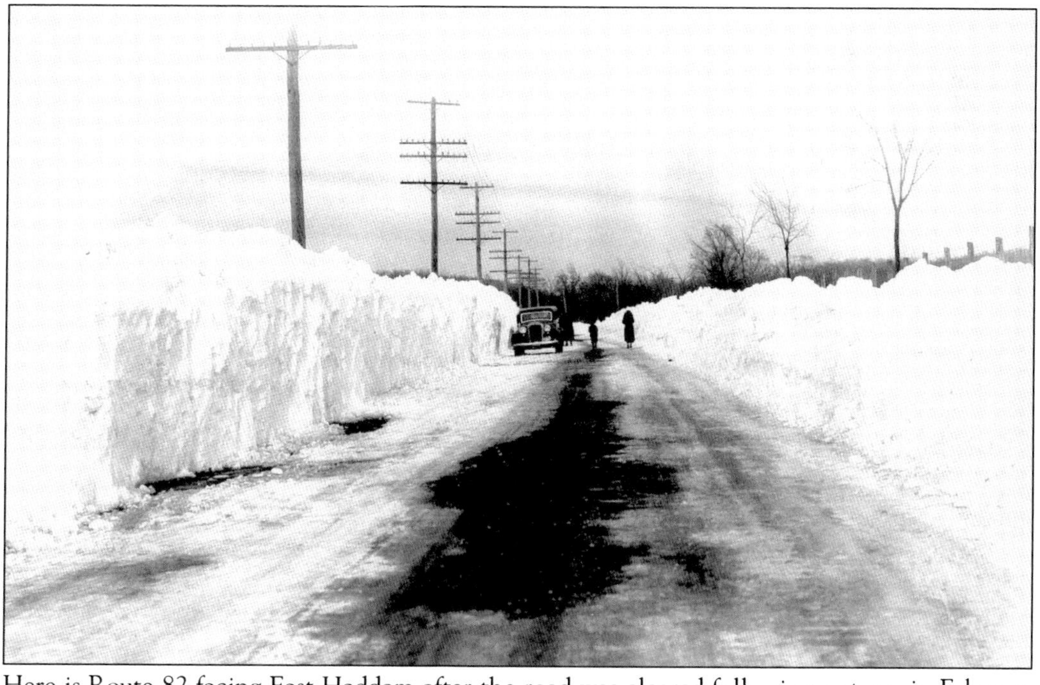

Here is Route 82 facing East Haddam after the road was cleared following a storm in February 1934. Sanding and salting were not common in these days, resulting in treacherous road conditions. These women may have gotten stuck on the icy road.

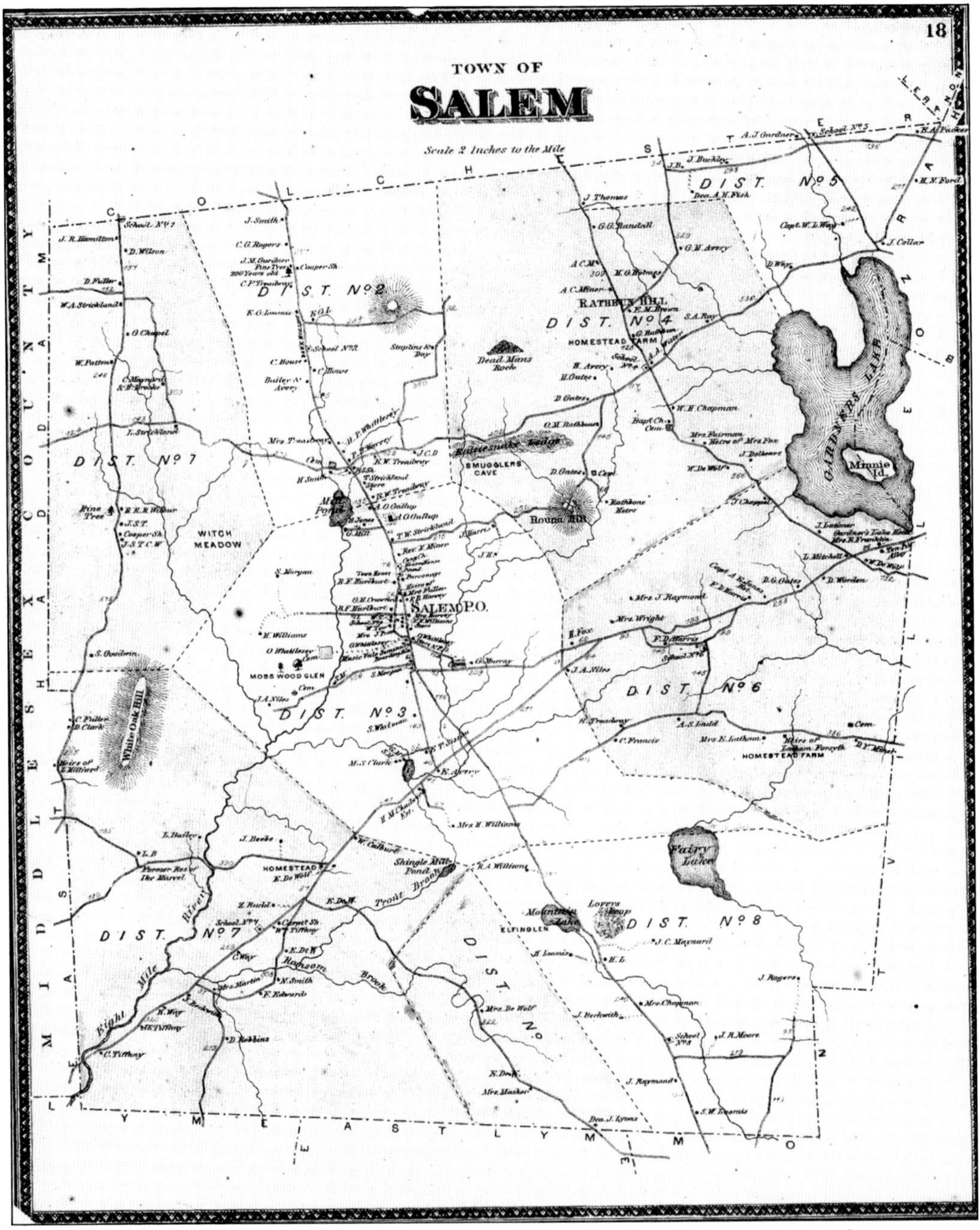

This is the town of Salem, from *Beer's Atlas of New London County*, 1868. This map was specifically marked as school districts; eight in total. One was never numbered, as can be seen toward the bottom of the map.

Two

Schools, Churches, and Public Buildings

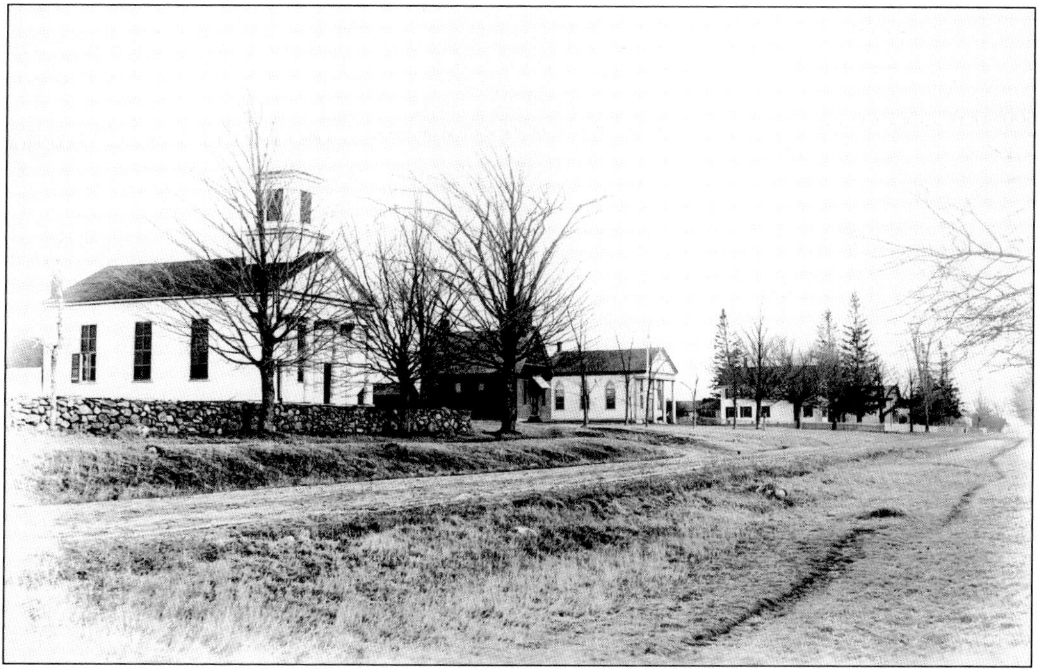

Salem Town Green is located on Route 85 about one mile north of Salem Four Corners. The first building on the green was the Episcopal Church in 1831. The second building added to the green was the Salem Congregational Church, built in 1838, and the Center School was built in 1885. The parsonage just beyond the town green was built in 1856. The house after the parsonage, called the Fuller house, was built in 1851. Religion and education were very important to Salemites even early on in the town's history. At one time there were eight one-room schoolhouses, which was quite a few for a small agricultural town. Pictured from left to right are the Salem Congregational Church, the Center School, the Episcopal Church, and the parsonage. This photograph was taken around 1900.

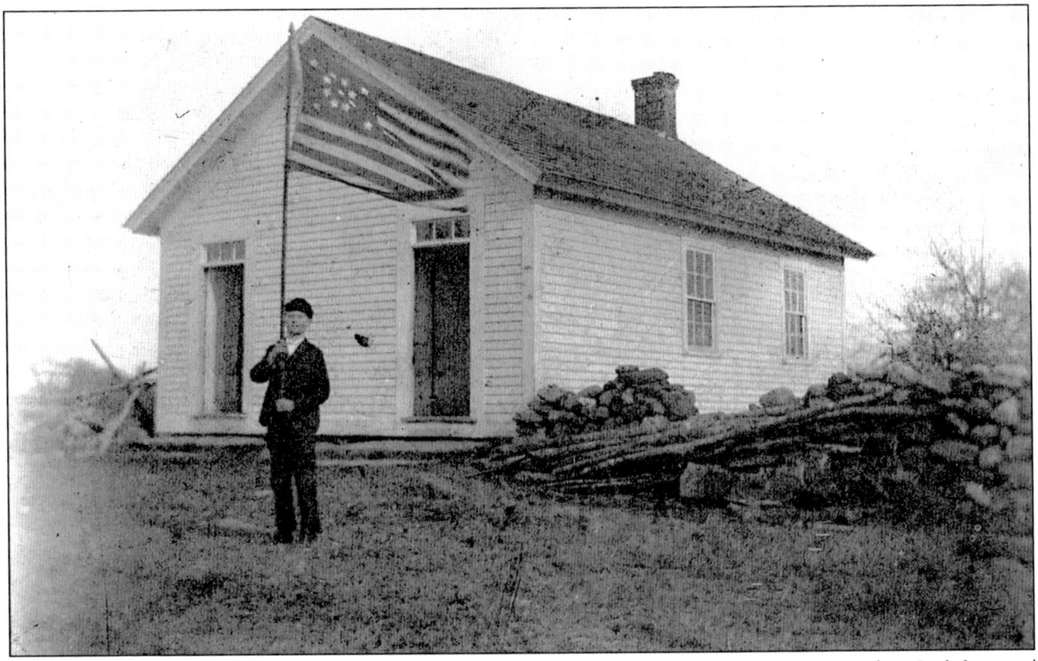

This is a photograph of West Road School located in District No. 1 right on the Colchester/ Salem line across from the Newton Ransom Cemetery. It was taken down in the 1970s. It was still being utilized up until 1940 when Salem Elementary School was opened. Notice the boy holding a flag with what appears to be only 13 stars. This photograph was taken around 1900. West Road School lost a privy during the Hurricane of 1938 and was repaired for $24.87.

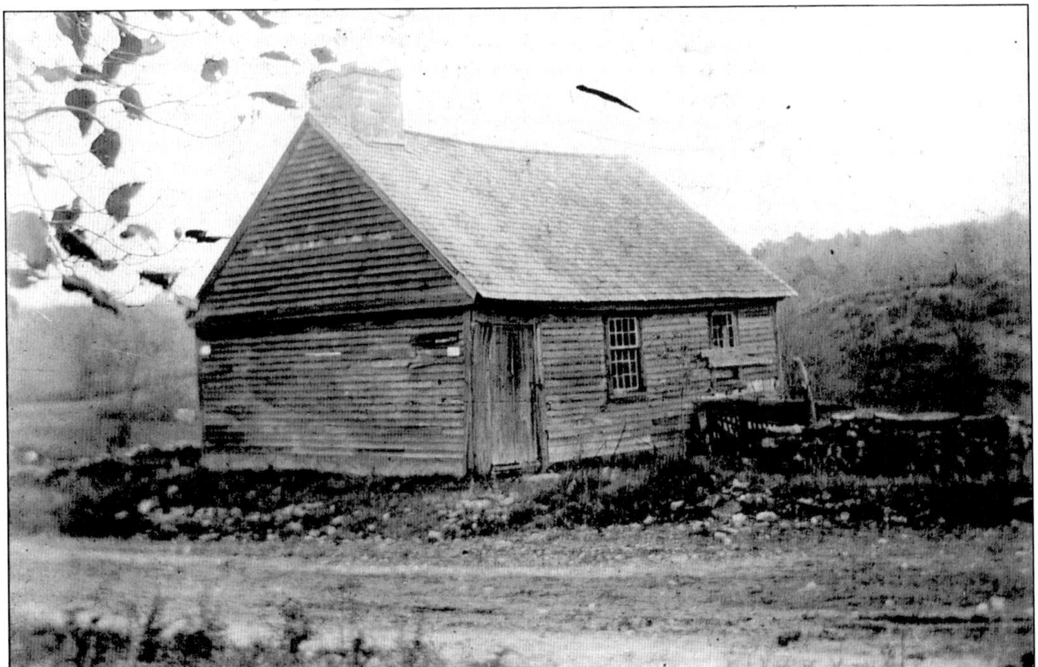

Dark Hollow School was located in District No. 2 on Route 85, also known as the Governor's Road back then. It was located near where Sullivan Road is today.

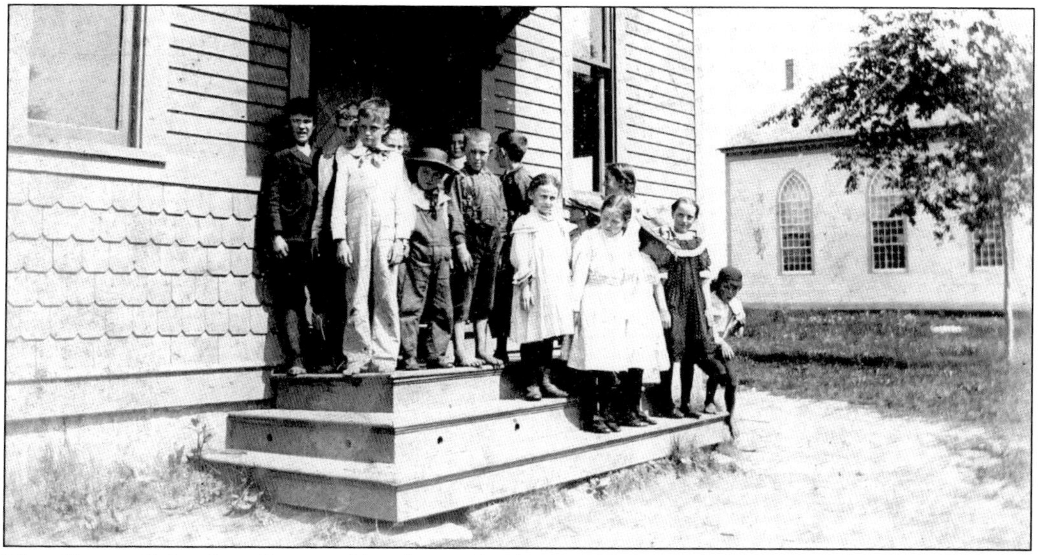

The Center School in District No. 3 was the last one-room schoolhouse to be built and still stands on the Salem Town Green on Route 85. Julia Herrick was the teacher at this time. Apparently shoes were not a requirement to attend school as can by seen by looking at the feet of the children.

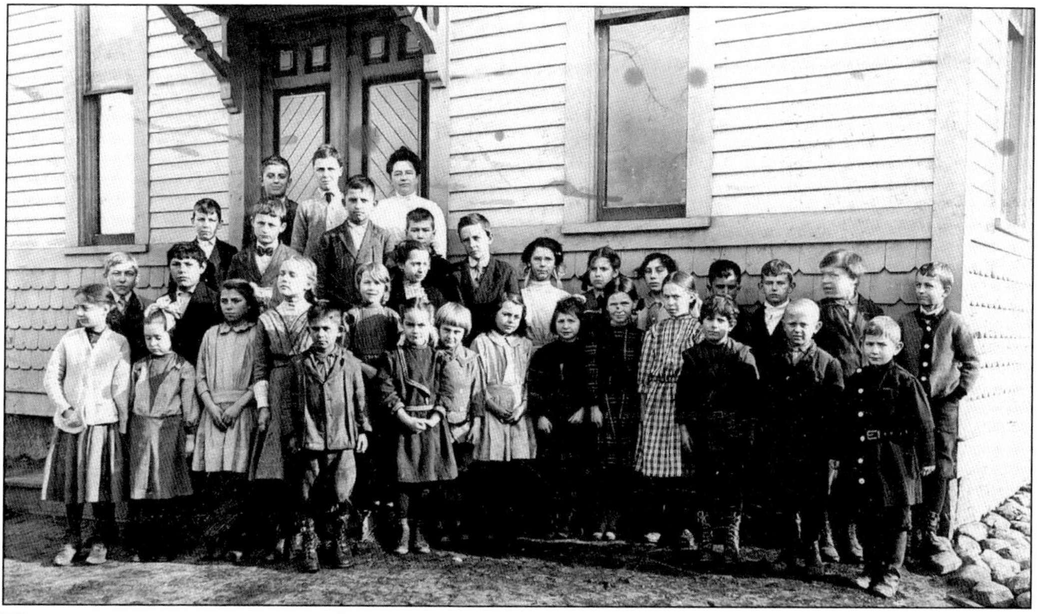

The seating arrangement went by size and grade. First graders sat in the front row in the smallest seats. The number of children varied from year to year. The average number of students was 20. Some of the seats were double, but most were single. The single ones were placed close to conserve space. The desk had an open shelf underneath and a small hole on the top for an inkwell with a flip top to dunk the pen when writing. There were no ballpoint pens and very few fountain pens. The teacher replaced the points from her own supply. The teacher made the ink a quart at a time from a powder. There were eight grades in the same classroom. Busy work created a lot of work for the teachers. There were no workbooks, so the teacher had to develop her own. Every morning and afternoon there was a 15-minute recess.

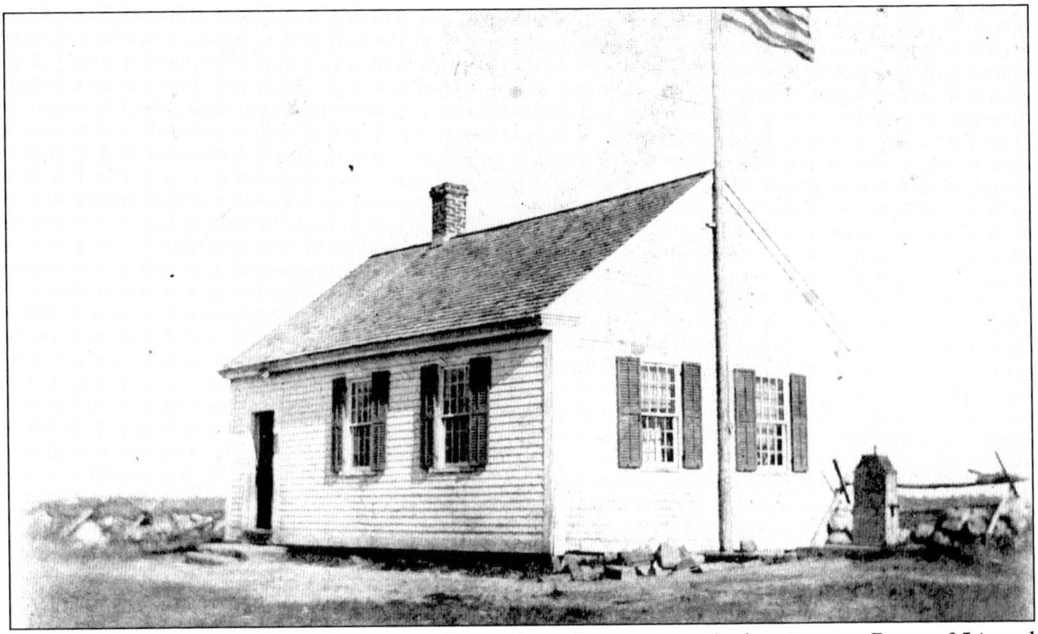

Gates Hill School, District No. 4, was located on the corner of what is now Route 354 and Rattlesnake Ledge diagonal from the old Congdon's Garage. After this school burnt down, classes were held on Rathbun Hill Road. During the 1938 hurricane, children were still in school. Helen Woronik remembers being carried all the way home through the woods by Mr. Heilweil during the storm. The school lost its roof shingles and was repaired for $9.13. A student monitor hoisted the flag due to respect for the flag; it was not flown in inclement weather. It must be a nice day, as the flag waves in this photograph.

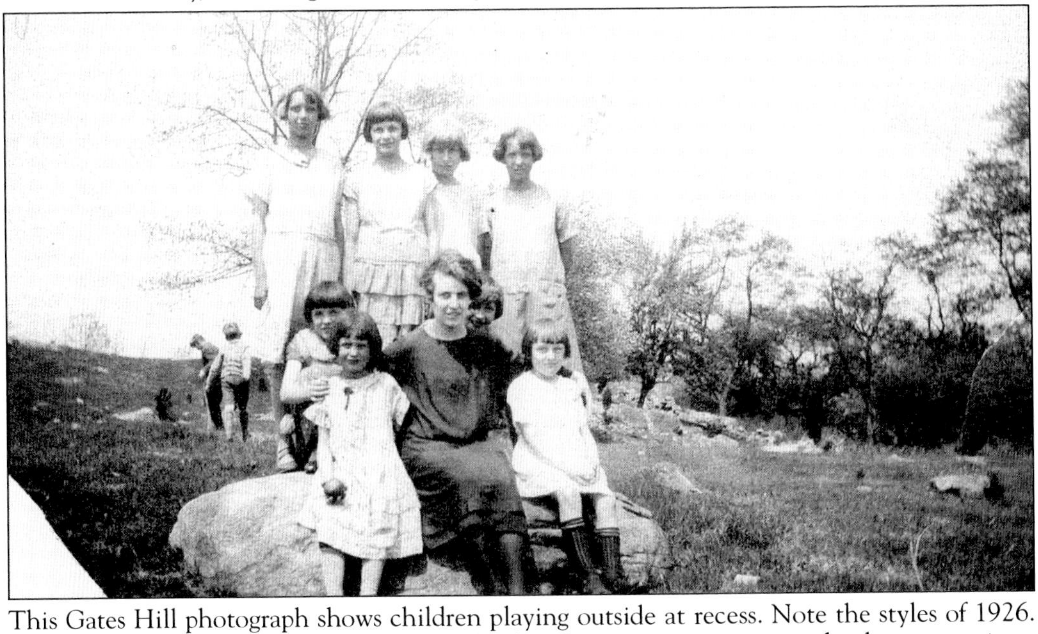

This Gates Hill photograph shows children playing outside at recess. Note the styles of 1926. Although younger and older children usually played in separate areas outside, there were times they chose to intermingle and all play together. On rainy or snowy days when they were all inside, they might all play a game together.

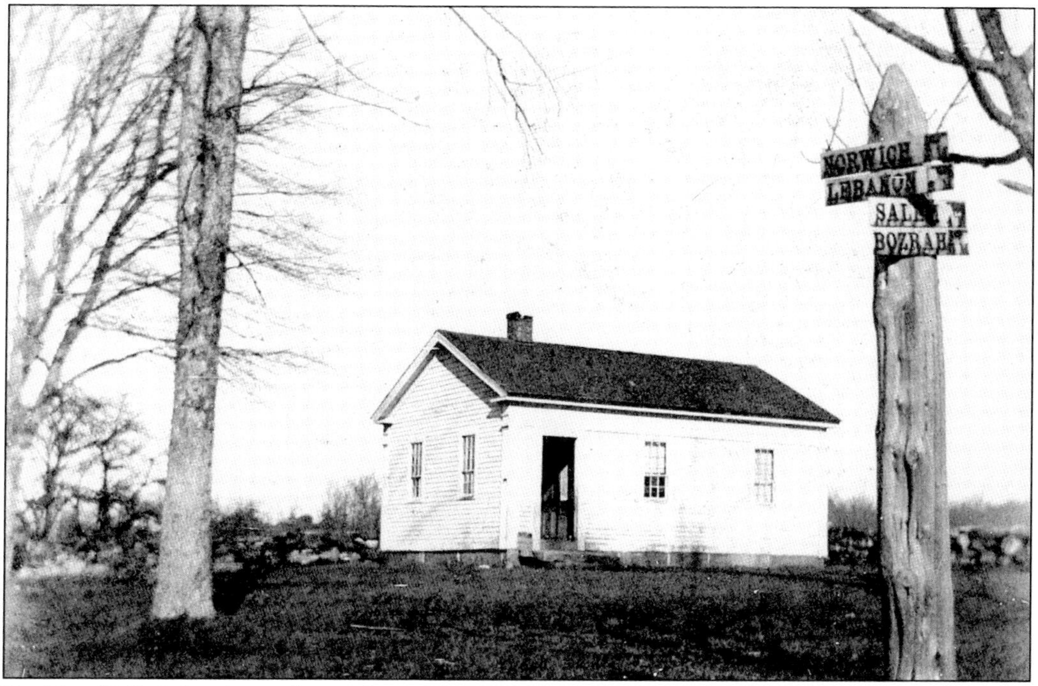

Buckley Hill School was located in District No. 5 on the Salem-Colchester line near the northeast corner of Way and Buckley Roads. Note the sign that says Norwich, Lebanon, Salem, and Bozrah. The mileage appears to be too small to read. This school closed, and the children went to Gates Hill.

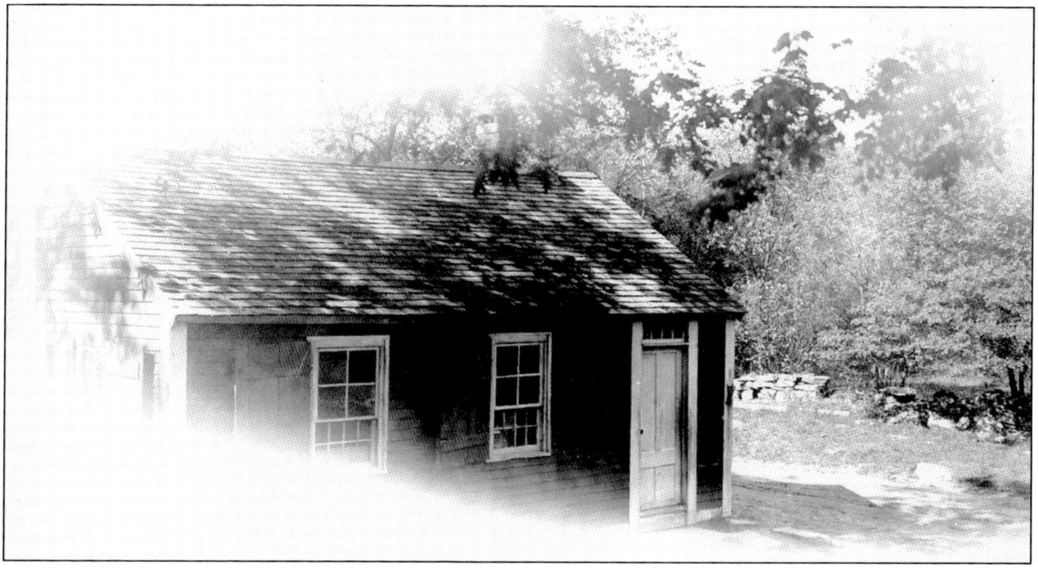

Harris School, District No. 6, was located on Harris Road Extension. This school is now gone. Privies, or bathrooms, were little buildings 40 to 50 feet away. In the back of the class was a small sink and a little shelf to hold a water jug with a spigot at the bottom. Each child had a small folding cup. On the side were paper towels cut in half due to limited supplies. Water was brought fresh twice a day from a neighbor's well. Each morning and noon water was brought in by appointed student monitors.

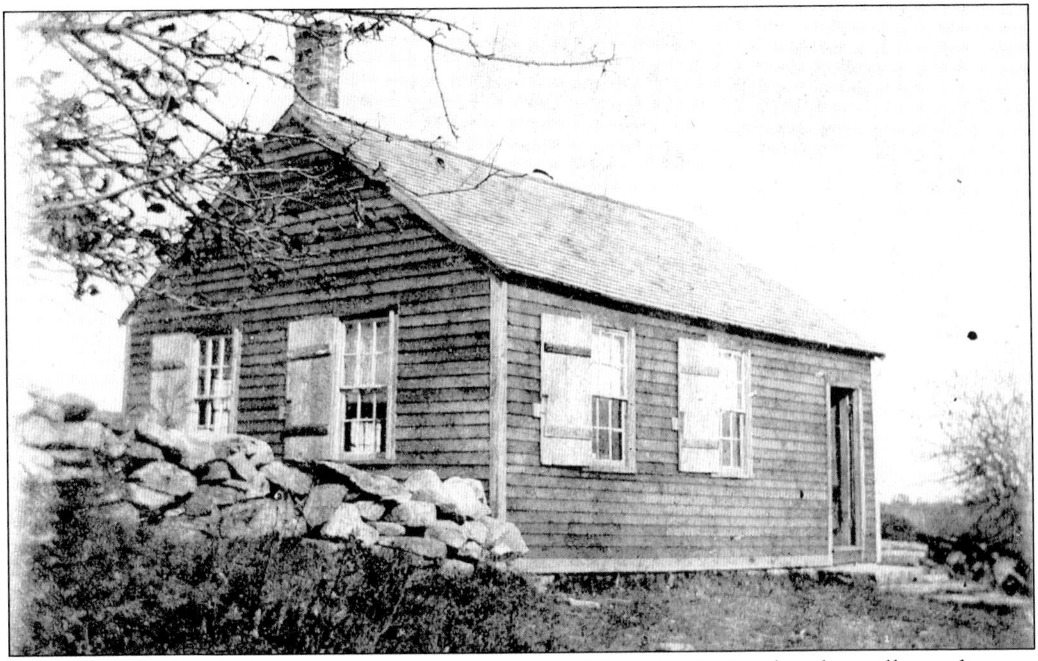

White Birch School, District No. 7, was located on White Birch Road and is still standing on the left-hand side going south on White Birch. White Birch and Center School are the only two one-room schools still standing in Salem today. White Birch is used as a shed now.

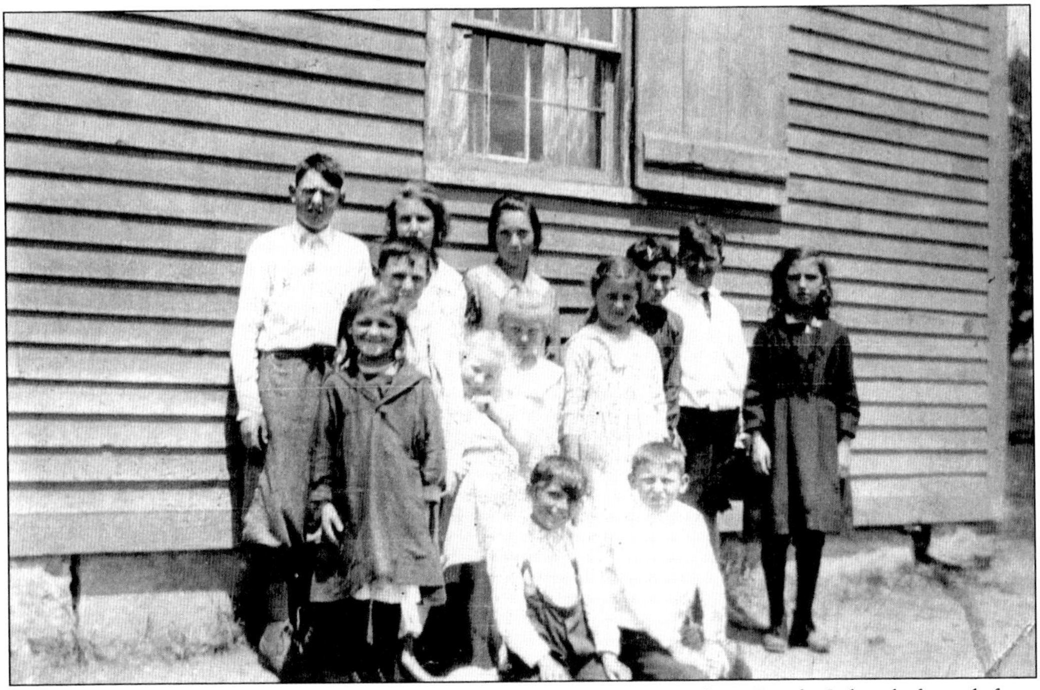

In this photograph taken around 1918–1922, the students at White Birch School, from left to right, are (first row) James Hatt and John Urbani; (second row) Frances Hatt, Michael Urbanik, Musa DeWolfe, Maezie DeWolfe, and Mary Schaeber; (third row) Ray Ames, Maria DeWolfe, Helen Urbanik, Joe Gacafalo, Ralph Hatt, and Erma Hatt.

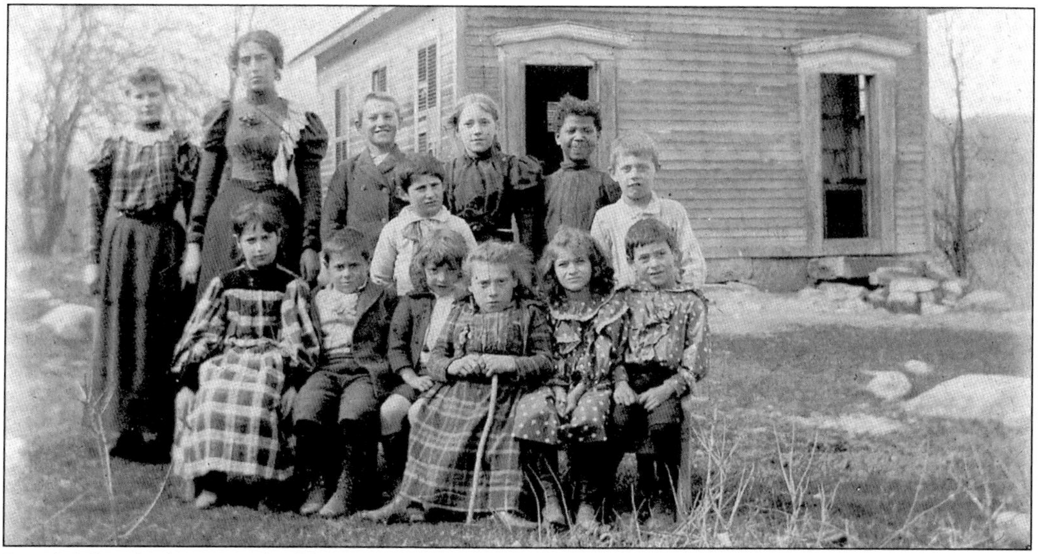

Pond School, photographed here in 1890, was located in District No. 8 just north of Woodchuck Road going north on Route 85 on the right-hand side. In one-room schoolhouses such as this one, there were separate entrances for the girls and the boys. Upon entering, they placed their lunch pails on a shelf and hung up their coats and hats. The privy at this school was also damaged during the 1938 hurricane, costing the town $11.42 to repair.

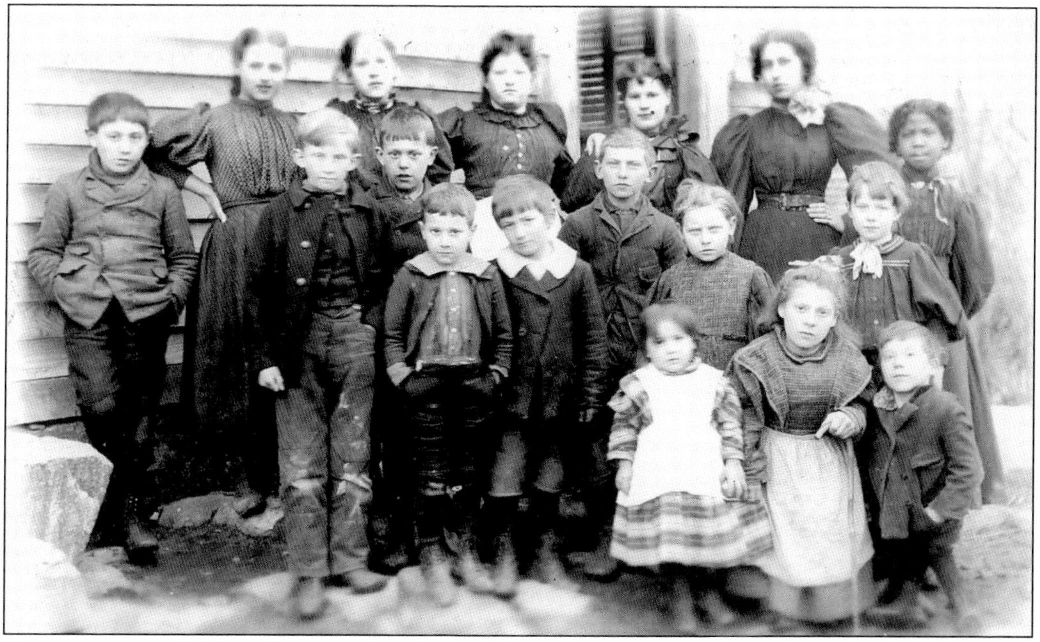

Here again are children shown at Pond School. Inez Spencer, the aunt of Lawrence E. Spencer, was the teacher at this time. In many ways, no large schools could replace that family feeling of a one-room schoolhouse. Tutoring amongst the children was quite common. Christmas was a family affair: they strung popcorn, strung cranberries, and made paper chains. Cornucopias were filled with candy, and plays were very common. Parents made cookies and cake and all enjoyed hot cocoa. The yard was filled with horses and carriages with the sounds of bells jingling from the harnesses.

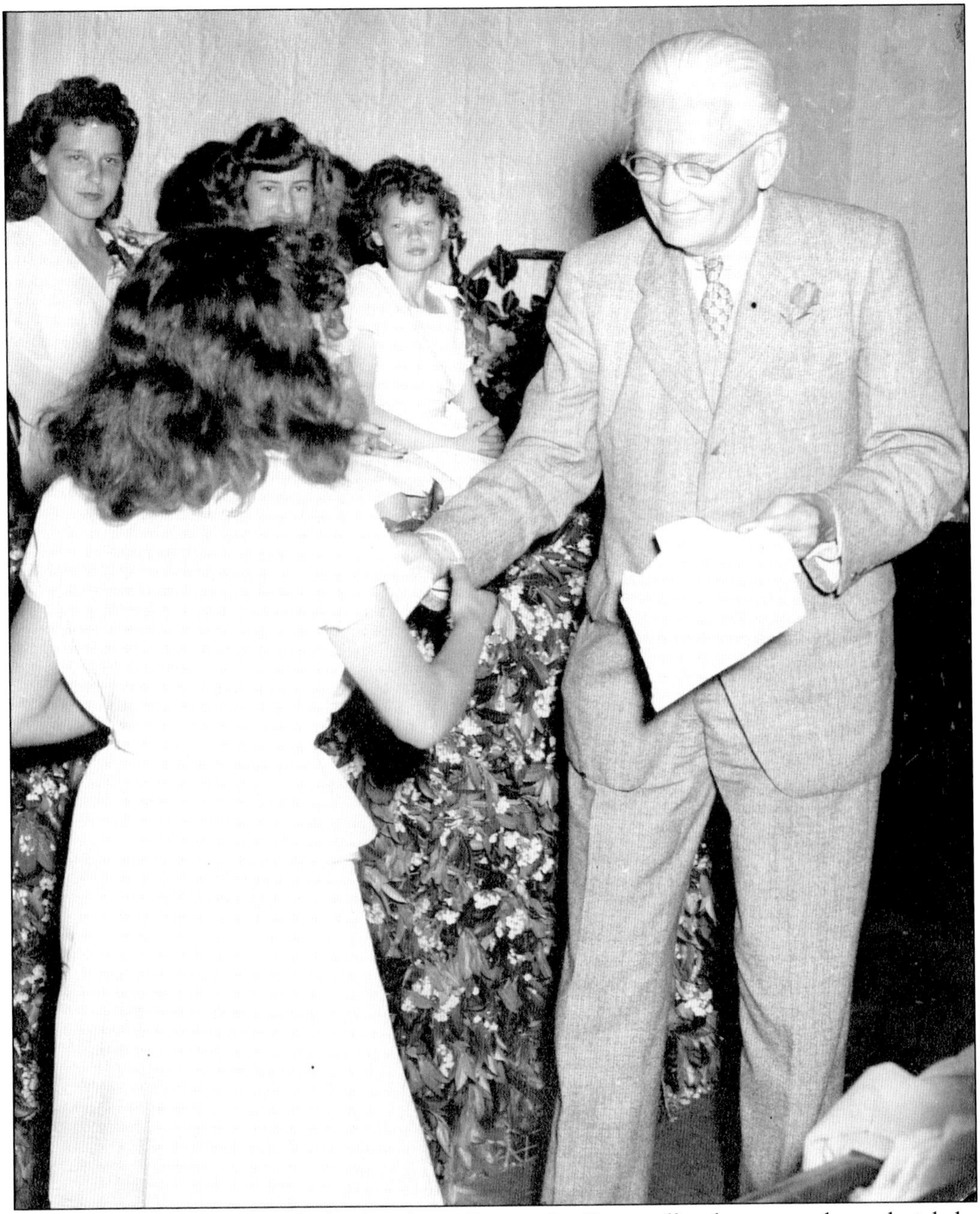

Sen. Hiram Bingham awards the Bingham Geography Prize, offered to seventh- and eighth-grade students, at graduation. The three best essays written about any country were awarded the prize of a book and certificate given out at the eighth-grade graduation. Since Bingham was an explorer, he earnestly promoted geography by giving these awards since at least 1918. This photograph was taken in 1948. In the background, from left to right, are Jackie Pierce, Marilyn DeWolfe, and Shirley LaMagdalaine.

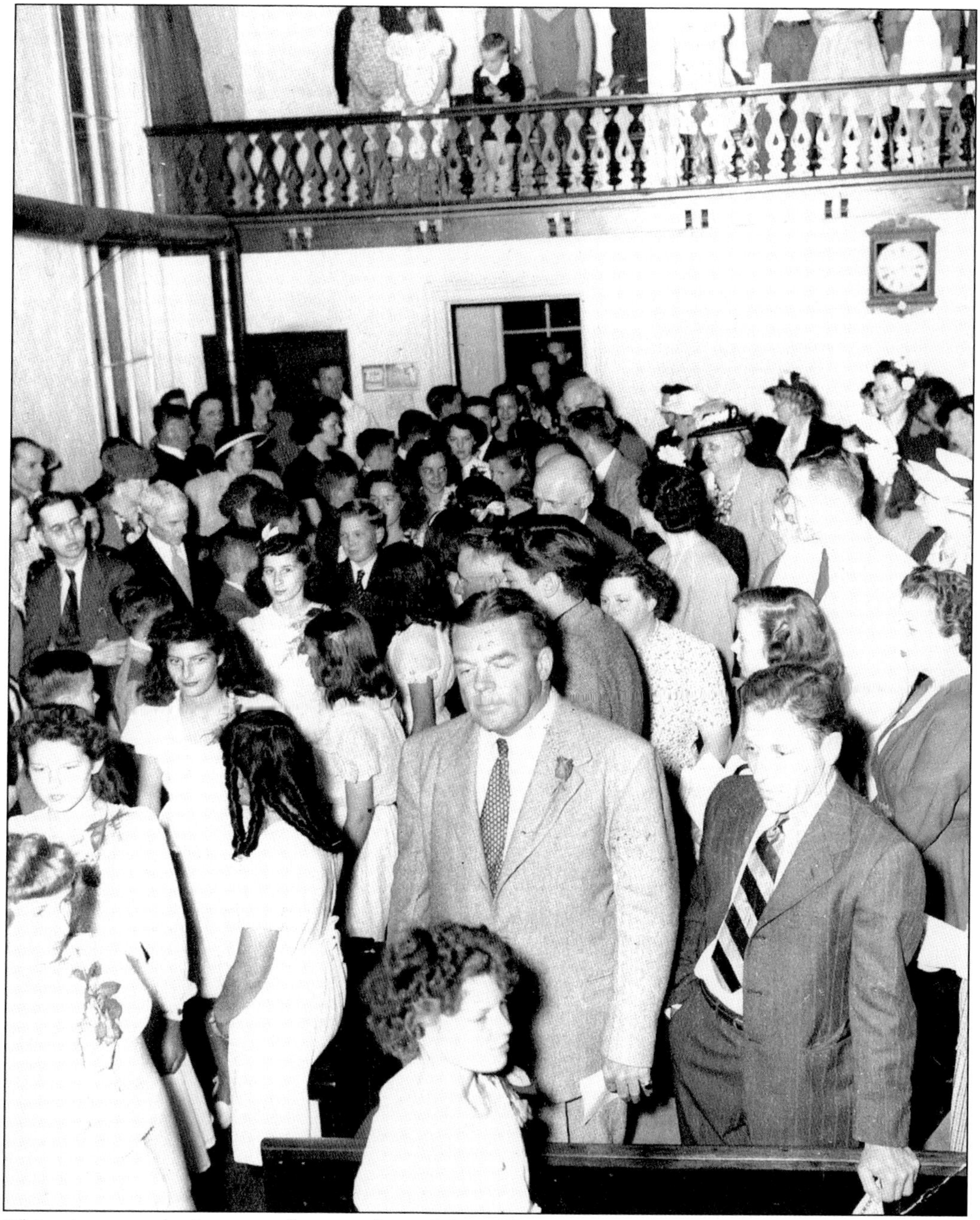

This photograph shows graduation from Salem Elementary School in May 1997. Graduation ceremonies were originally held in the town hall (the Salem Town House). The earliest recorded date of these was in 1913. At some point they were then held at the Congregational church, with records indicating 1921. The year 1956 was the last graduation ceremony in the Congregational church. The graduation of 1957 was held at the Gardner Lake Firehouse Auditorium. The 1958 graduation and all those following were held in Salem School.

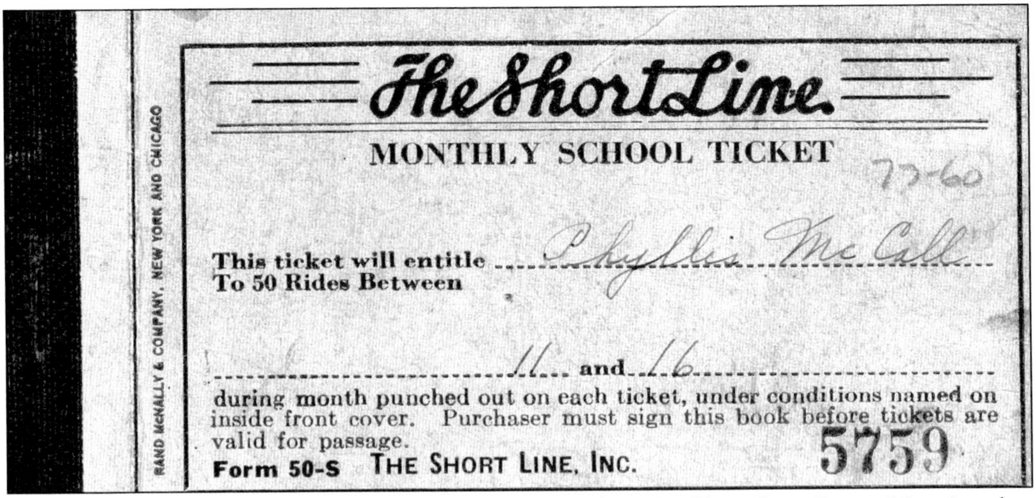

The children on the west side of town were transported on the Shore Line Bus to New London High School. They were provided monthly transportation tickets. The children on east side of town, the Gardner Lake side of town, went to Norwich Free Academy and were provided transportation on a regular school bus. Here are tickets used by a student, Phyllis McCall. If children wanted to go to another school, they needed to provide their own transportation. Some Salem children chose Bacon Academy.

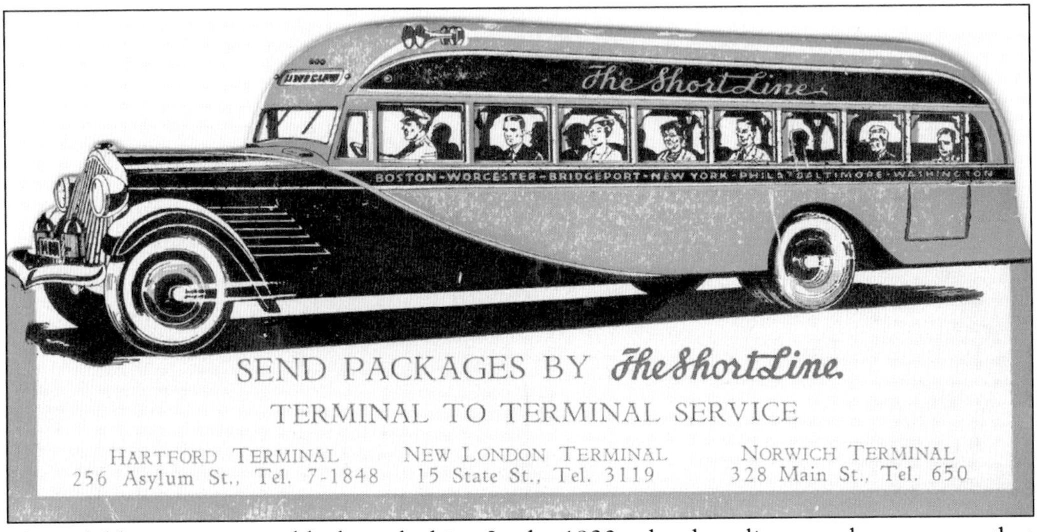

This ink blotter is orange, black, and white. In the 1930s, the short line was the company that ran the buses on Route 85 from Hartford to New London through Salem. A snowplow was attached to the front for snow removal. After eighth grade most children went to New London High School or Norwich Free Academy.

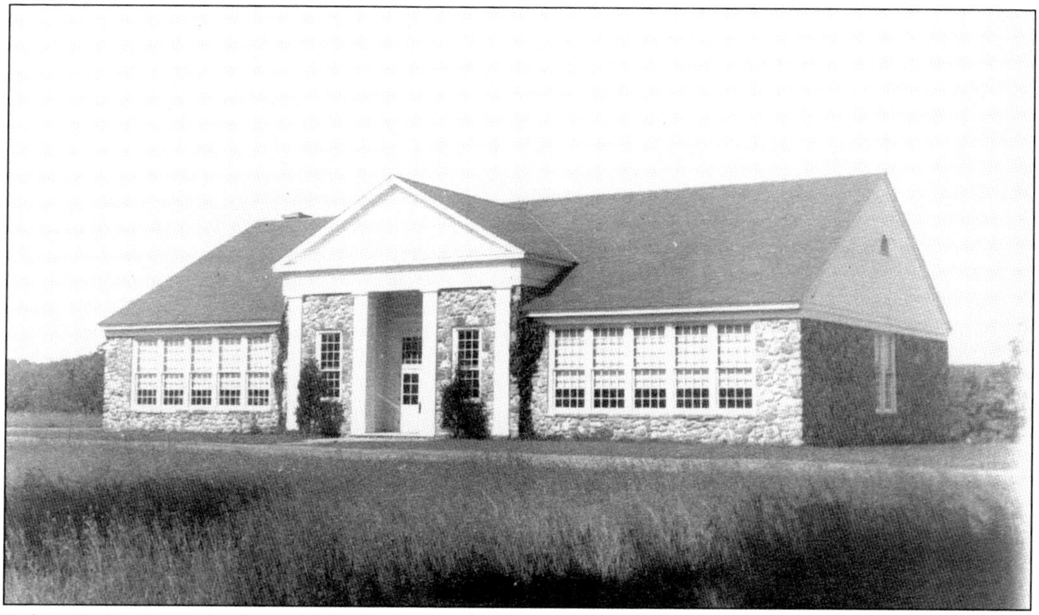

Salem School was built in 1940. In 1938, discussion about consolidating the schools or adding two rooms to the present Center School had begun. It was decided to build a new three-classroom school. The large window to the left was the girls' bathroom. To the left of that was the utility room. The window to the right was the boys' bathroom. To the right of the boy's bathroom was a utility room, teachers' room, and nurses' room. Salem Elementary School started off with two school buses. Routes changed on a yearly basis depending on the population of students.

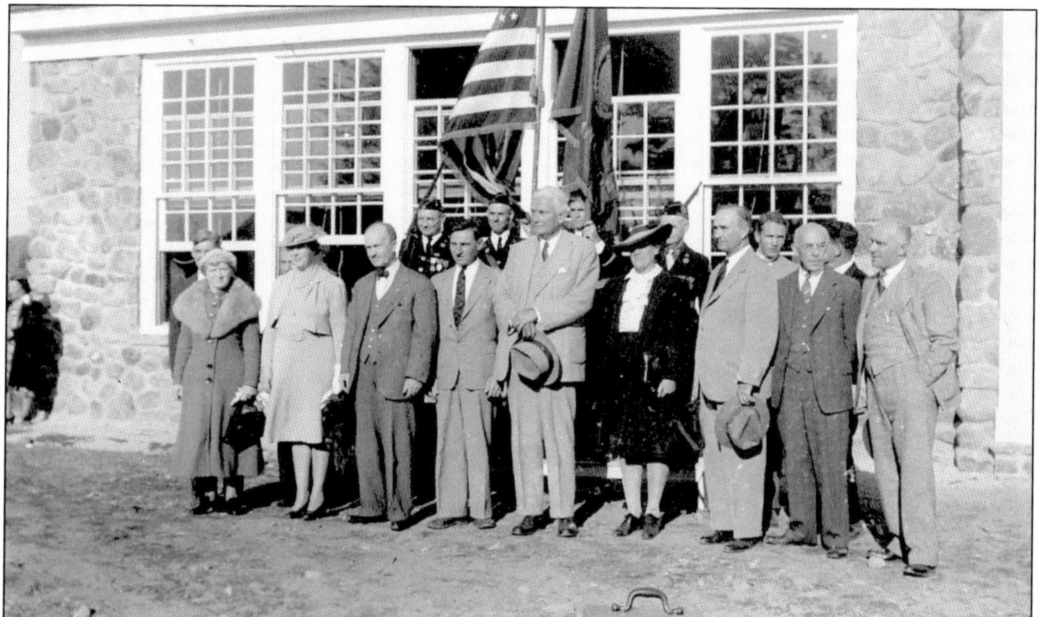

This is a photograph of the dedication of the Salem Elementary School, September 28, 1940. In this photograph is Sen. Hiram Bingham (middle), to the left of Bingham is Michael Urbanik, and to the far right is Donald Fraser Sr. The school site was donated by Bingham. The flagpole was donated by Mr. and Mrs. Nielson.

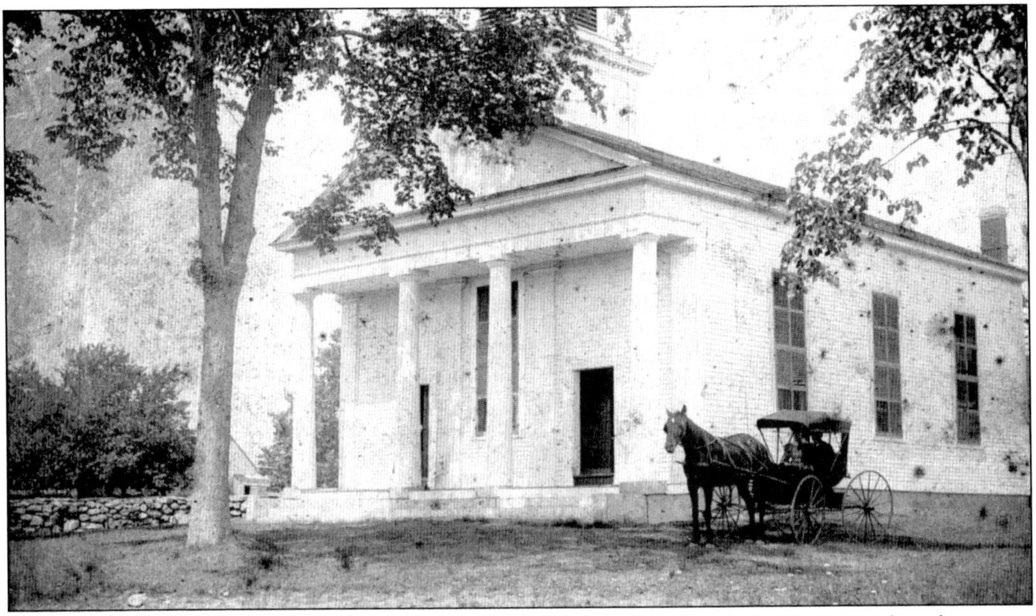

In 1763, Asa Jones deeded 15 rods of land to have a meetinghouse built. Two churches were built in succession over the years on the corner of Witch Meadow Road and the Governor's Road (Route 85). The second church, built on the same location, was taken down in 1836 and erected farther down the road on Route 85, Salem Town Green, where it stands today. In this photograph, the entrances were on either side. This was renovated and now has a central entrance. This photograph, taken around 1900, shows a carriage and passengers Alvah Morgan and her sister.

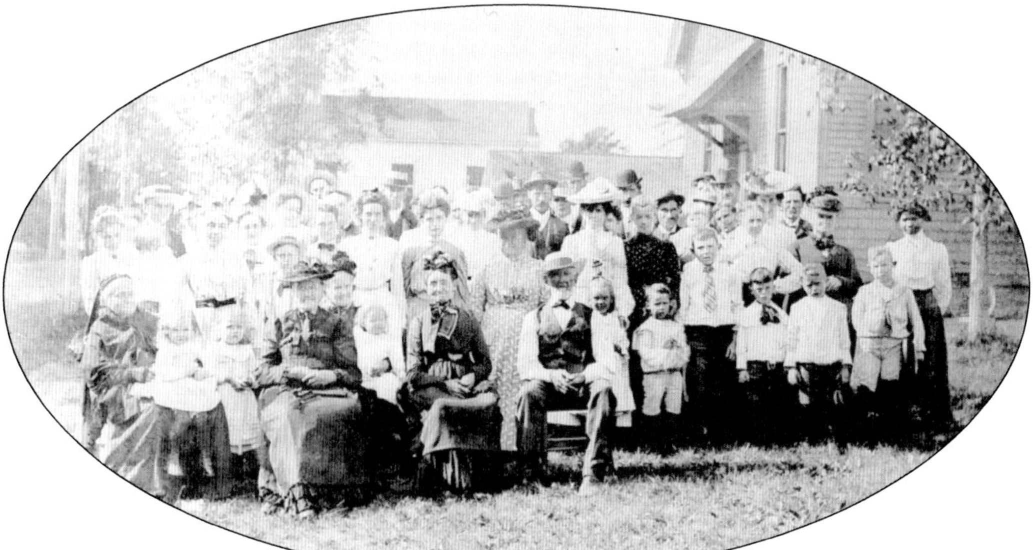

Here is a church picnic photograph dated 1903 on the Salem Town Green. In the back is the church, and to the right is the Center School. Identified here are Grandma Fox, Nellie Tibbetts, Grant Tibbetts, Byron Tibbetts, the Rix twins, Mrs. Ray, Helen Rix Melona, Synthia Webster, the sister of Richard Tibbetts, Ellen Tibbetts, and Sylphia Tibbetts. Martha E. Millen was the first female minister, around 1910.

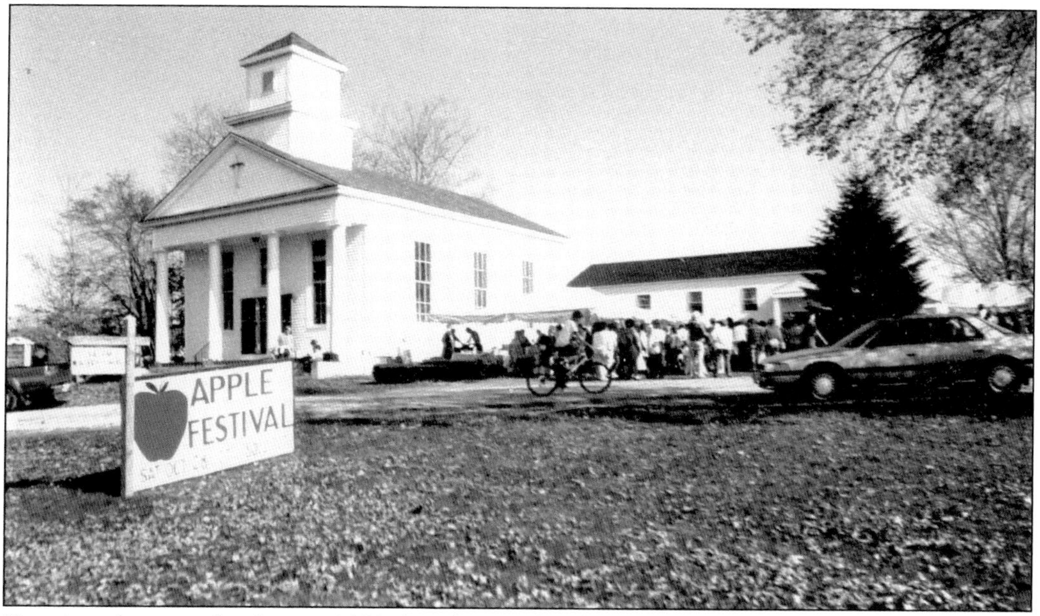

Here is a photograph taken in 1989 that depicts the church today with the Christian education building in the back. The Apple Festival, a fund-raiser started in 1970 to maintain the buildings, is held the last Saturday of October. Apple-related items are sold, and in the past, there have been hayrides, buggy rides, craft and white elephant booths, magic shows, and demonstrations of different kinds, including a cider press. In the parish is a quilt exhibit of old and new quilts. People from all over Connecticut attend this event, and many know from experience to get here early as the pies go quickly.

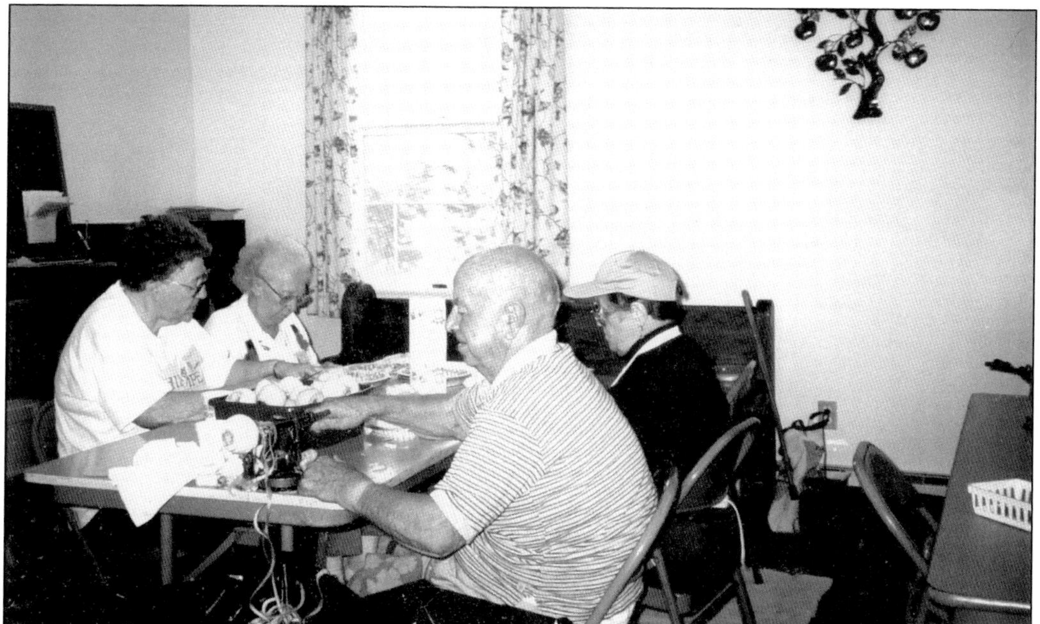

The main attraction of the Apple Festival is the apple pies and apple-related food items. Here folks are gathered to peel apples in 1997. Herman Boldt uses a hand-cranking peeler, while, from left to right, an unidentified woman, Ruth Little, and Gisela Boldt peel with paring knives.

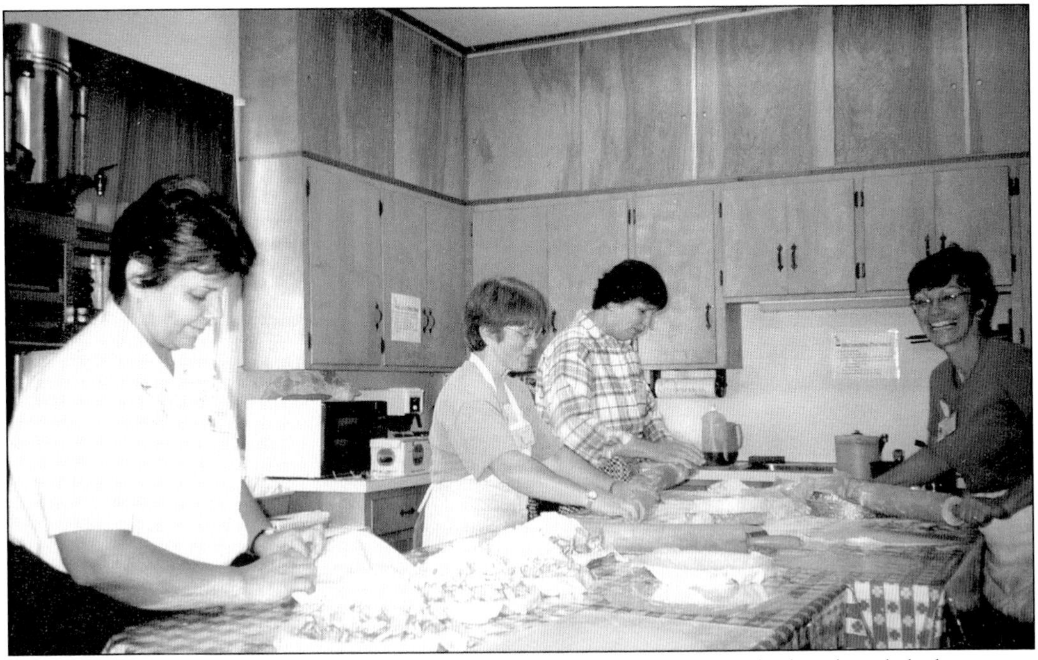

Members of the church and volunteers from town not associated with the church help out, so it has become more of a community event than just a church event. Roberta Bowdler, Nancy Sekinger, Dorothy Wockenfuss, and Shirley Dubeau are seen here in 2000, hand rolling, filling, and covering the homemade pies just as has been done since 1970.

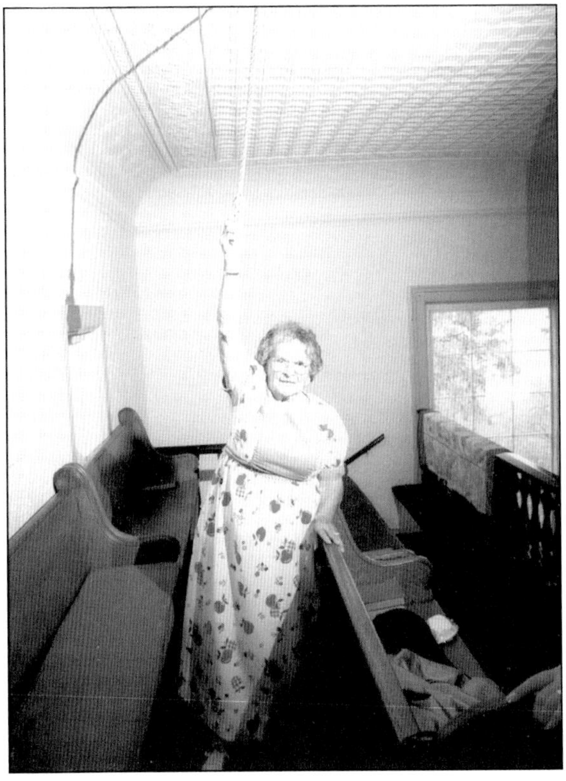

In this photograph, Catherine Dimmock is the bell ringer. The tradition is to ring the church bell after 1,000 pies have been made. Later on this tradition changed. The bell is now rung at the close of apple pie making. Approximately 400 apple crumb pies and 900 two-crusted pies are made each year and can be purchased baked or unbaked. The pies usually sell out within the first few hours the fair is open. Being served at the fair in individual portions are apple betty, apple sundaes (ice cream with apple crunch topping), hot dogs with apple sauerkraut, apple cider, apple coffee cake, apple butter, and the list goes on.

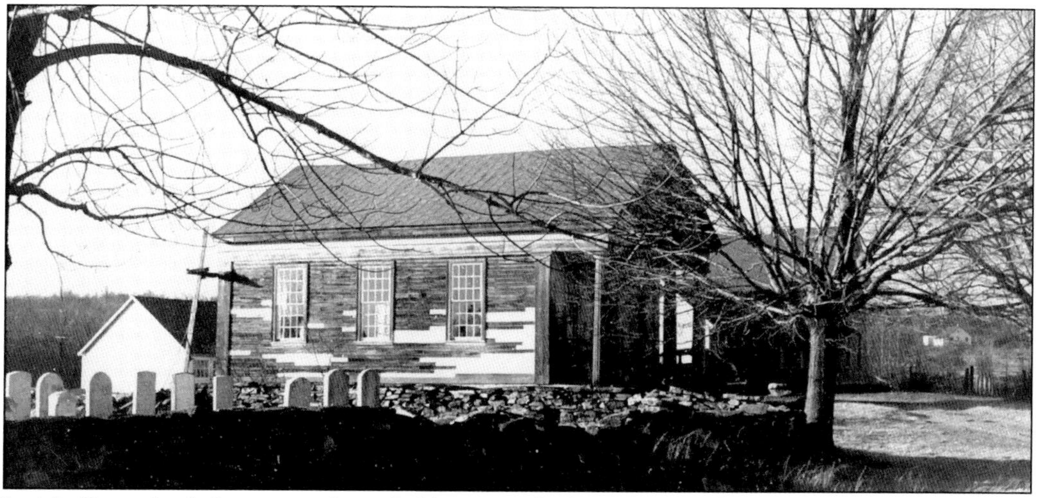

Josiah Gates deeded seven and one half acres and a house to Ichabod Allen of New London to settle as minister of this particular congregation in 1751.This first Baptist church was located on the west side of the Old Colchester Road (now Route 354) near the top of the hill by Paugwonk Cemetery One. In 1846, a new church was erected farther south by the Paugwonk Cemetery Two and still stands today as the Paugwonk Church. It was closed sometime during the mid-1950s and sold to a Mr. Merik, and he used it to store furniture until 2005 when the Baptist Association decided to renovate the church. This photograph was taken on January 2, 1942.

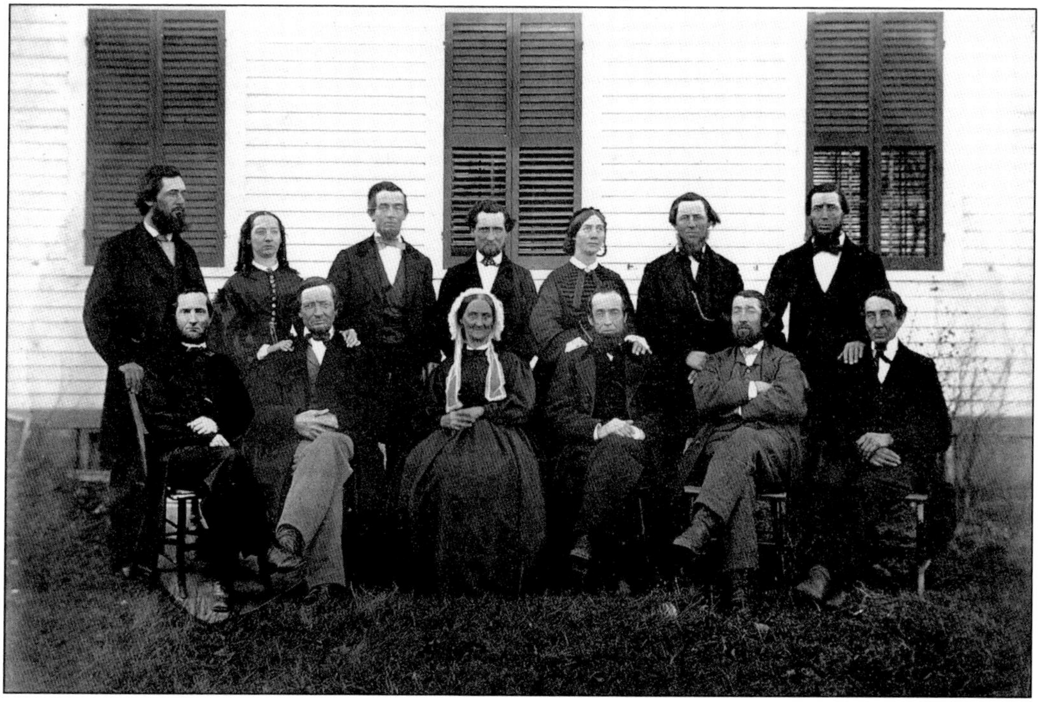

This is the Ulysses S. Gardner family posing on the side of the Paugwonk Baptist Church around 1850. Masons/20 Mile Pond was later renamed Gardner Lake for the Gardner family. Interestingly there was a photographer named Gardner from this family that traveled with Abraham Lincoln to document for him. Also in this photograph, the man on the bottom left-hand side was pasted in after; an example of early editing. He may have been the photographer.

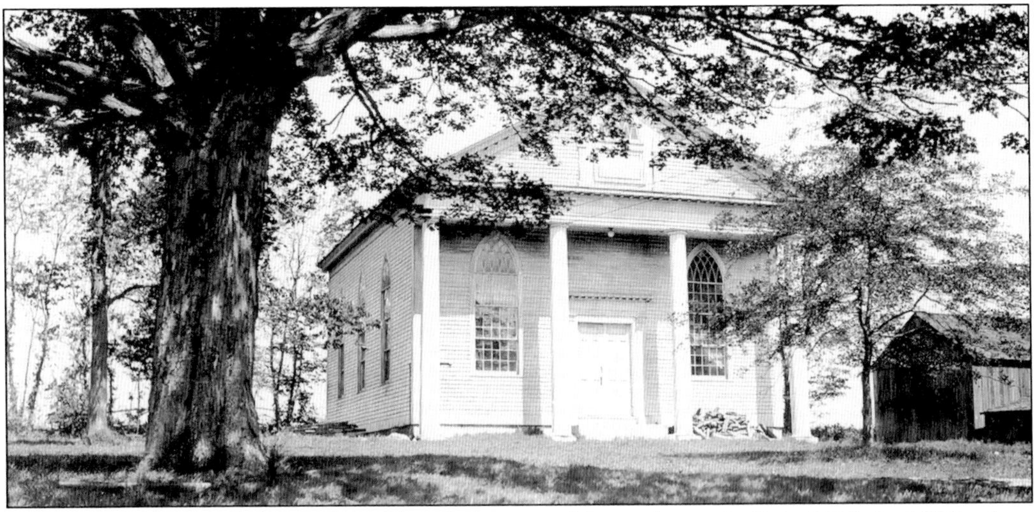

The Episcopal Church, located on Church Street in Norwich, was built in 1749. In 1830, when a new church was built to replace this one, the newly formed Episcopal Society (1829) was interested in acquiring this church. In 1831, the church was moved and rebuilt on the Salem Town Green in Greek Revival style. In 1843, due to low attendance, the building was sold to the town of Salem for $500, communion table and stove included. The spire, tower, and pews were removed. The building was known as the town house, or town hall, where town meetings and business took place until the late 1950s. The town meetings were moved to Gardner Lake Firehouse and then to Salem School auditorium. After years of being used for storage, the Salem Historical Society took a 100-year lease at $1 a year. It was incorporated in 1969.

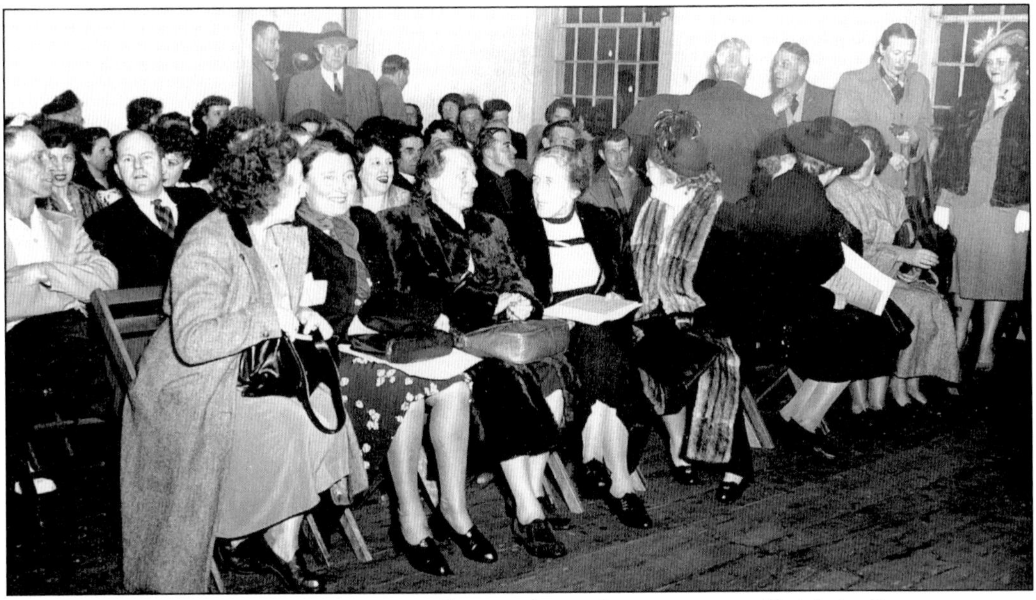

In March 1949, seven German women, all very educated government officials in Germany, came to the United States to study American democracy. They desired to see how city, town, and state affairs were handled. The German women were impressed with how Salem townspeople were able to express their opinions frankly without animosity from others of differing opinions. Mrs. Alfred Bingham entertained the women at her home in Salem. The population of Salem at the time was 504. The German women came to Salem to experience democracy at a grassroots level.

Captain Seaman's Chapel, the second Methodist organization, had 10 members under the Reverend Henry Brown. Built July 17, 1881, it was later used as a Grange hall when the Salem Grange was formed in 1907. It was used by the Salem Grange from 1907 to 1943, when it burned to the ground. The Grange later donated that property to the Town of Salem in 1990s. From 1943 to the late 1990s, the Center School was used for Grange meetings.

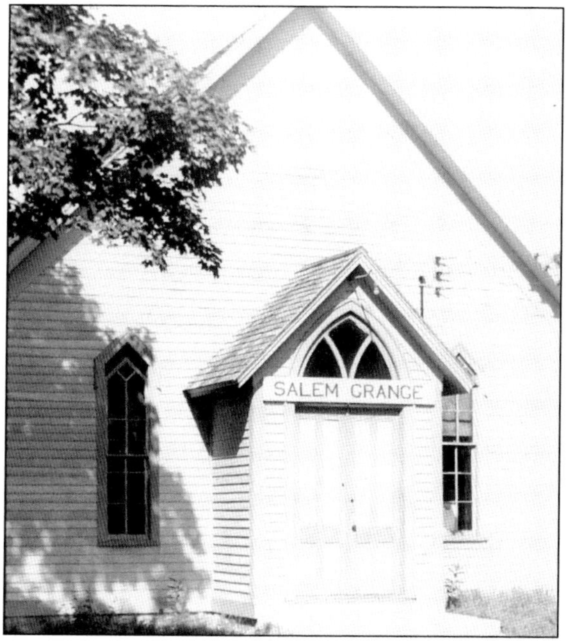

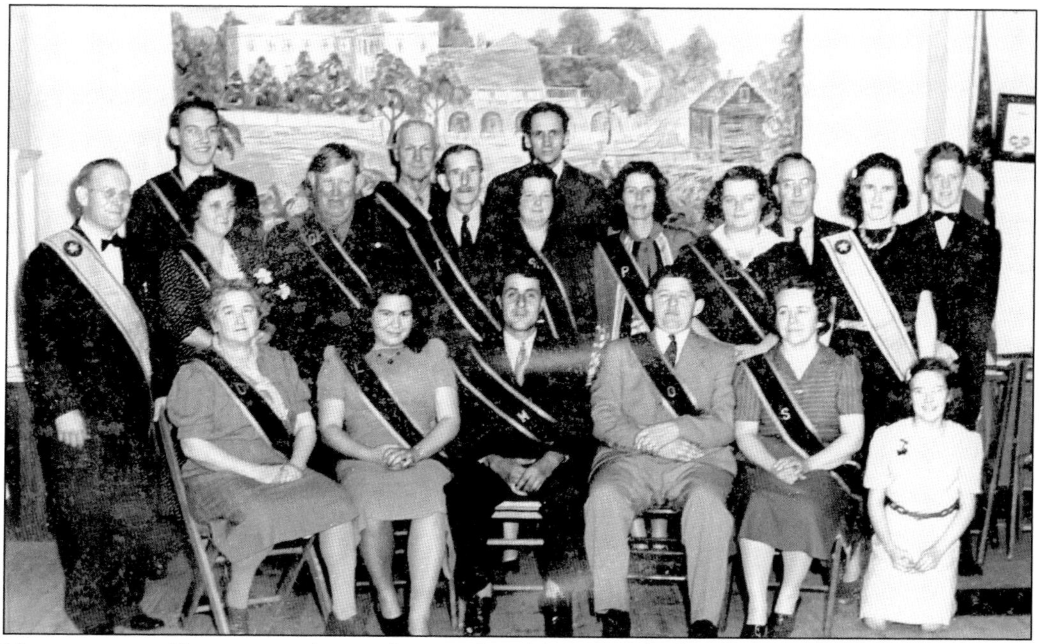

Here are some Grange members, taken at the old Grange hall in 1941 during what may have been an election of officers. A mural painted by Donald Fraser Sr. of Music Vale Seminary can be seen in the background. Note the letters on the sashes; M—master, O—overseer, L—lecturer, GK—gatekeeper, S—steward, T—treasurer, S—secretary, P—pomona (one of three graces), C—chaplain, F—flora, LAS—lady assistant steward, and AS—assistant steward. Pictured from left to right are (first row) Nellie Bliven, Miriam Kurtz, Leo Winakor, Joseph Swider, Mary Clark, and unidentified; (second row) George Higbig, Flora Chapman, Edward DeWolfe, Richard Tibbetts, Gladys Dean, Sylvia Bingham, Clara Day, and unidentified; (third row) Duncan Fraser, Ira Gifford, Alfred Bingham, and two unidentified.

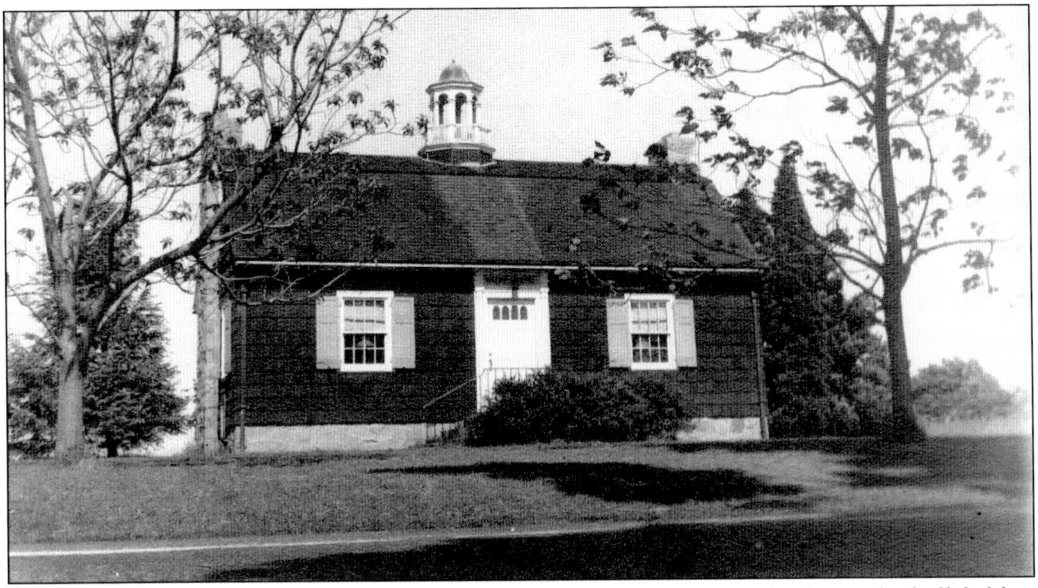

In 1928, Sen. Hiram Bingham contributed four acres of land (part of which was the ball field in back of the library). Mrs. Alfred Mitchell of New London gave a large contribution to enable the physical construction of the new library. Nearly 200 people attended the formal dedication on September 24, 1928. Wooden, life-sized cows were sold as a fund-raiser for a new library. The cows were painted and decorated, and graced many lawns in Salem. Salem then gained the nickname "cow town." The new library opened in 2004.

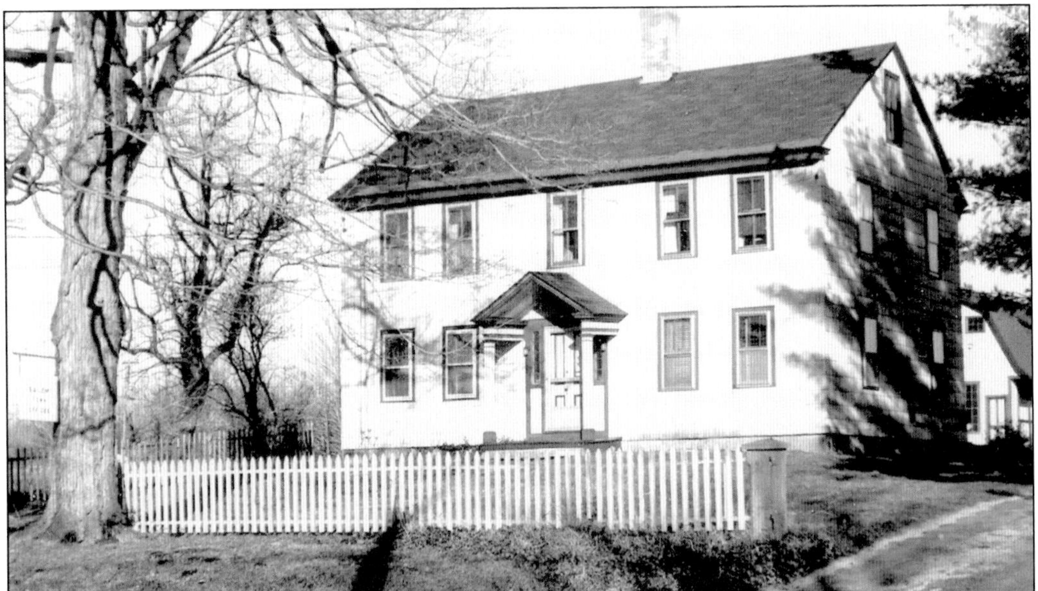

The main house was built in 1818 by John Billings. There have been many owners of this house in succession: Alfred and Elijah Loomis, Rev. Nathaniel Miner, Joseph Rix, Bessie Rix, Alex and Caroline Rovenchuk, Stephen Chop, Jean Chop, and then Alfred Bingham, who sold it to the Town of Salem on July 1, 1976. Before this building was purchased, all town officials provided space in their own homes for business. Town meetings were held in the town house. This building, with additions, still exists as Salem's present town hall.

Three

Music Vale Seminary

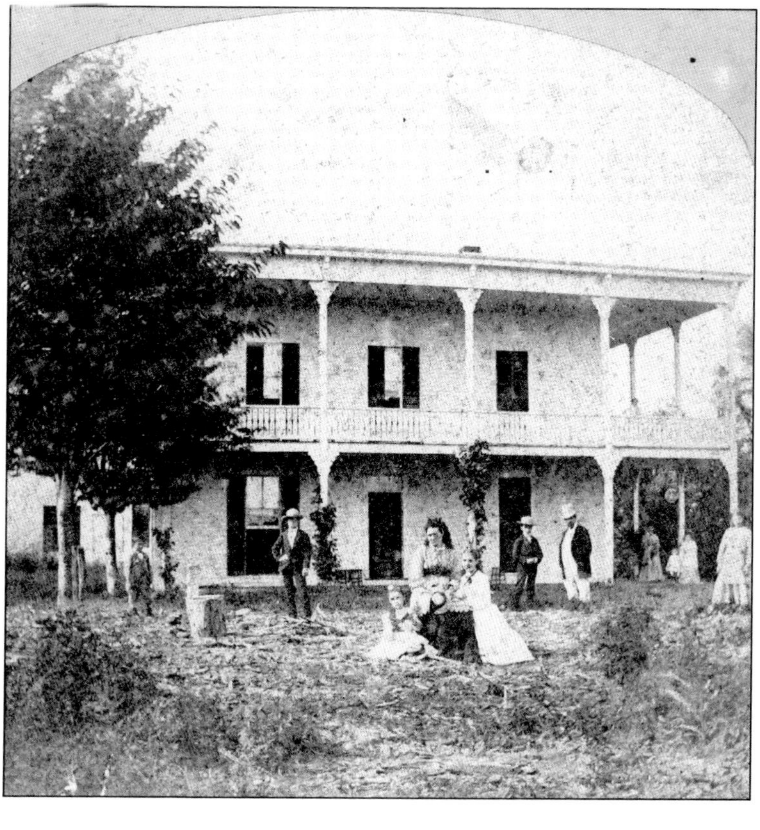

Salem's claim to fame is Music Vale Seminary, the first music school in the United States to confer degrees in music. Music and only music was taught at the school. Oramel Whittlesey adopted the motto by William Pitt: "If I have done so much, it is because I have done one thing at a time." He felt that singleness of purpose was the key to success and successful he and his students were indeed. Here is a view of Music Vale, taken from a double-photograph used in a stereoscope, the forerunner of the modern day "view master."

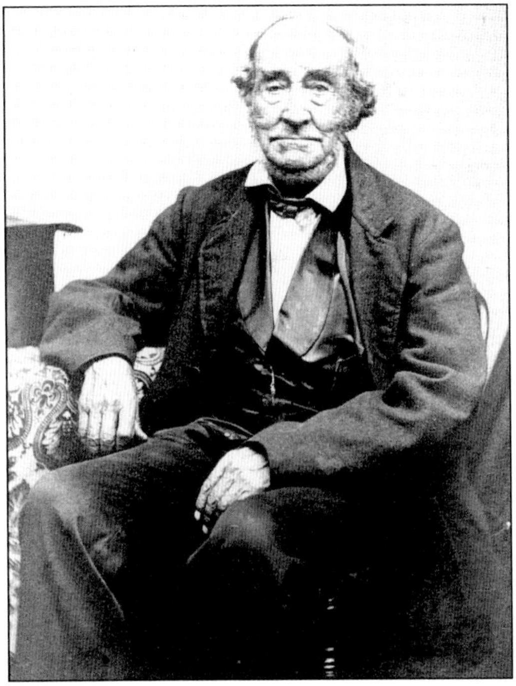

Rev. John Whittlesey, 1780–1864, was a strong-willed Methodist minister of the sect "New Lights." He married his cousin Sally Whittelsey in Westbrook, Connecticut; note the variation on the spelling. They moved to Salem in 1801, the year Oramel was born. Together they had three sons, Oramel, John, and Henry, and two daughters who both died at age two. John ran an ivory factory that made piano keys as his livelihood. At this time, Connecticut had 90 percent of the market on manufacturing ivory. The boys showed a keen interest in music at an early age. Though they purchased a secondhand piano, the elder Whittlesey would not allow them to take time off from their chores to take lessons. On their own time the boys went to New London for piano instruction. They would arrive at 8:00 p.m. and not return until 3:00 a.m.

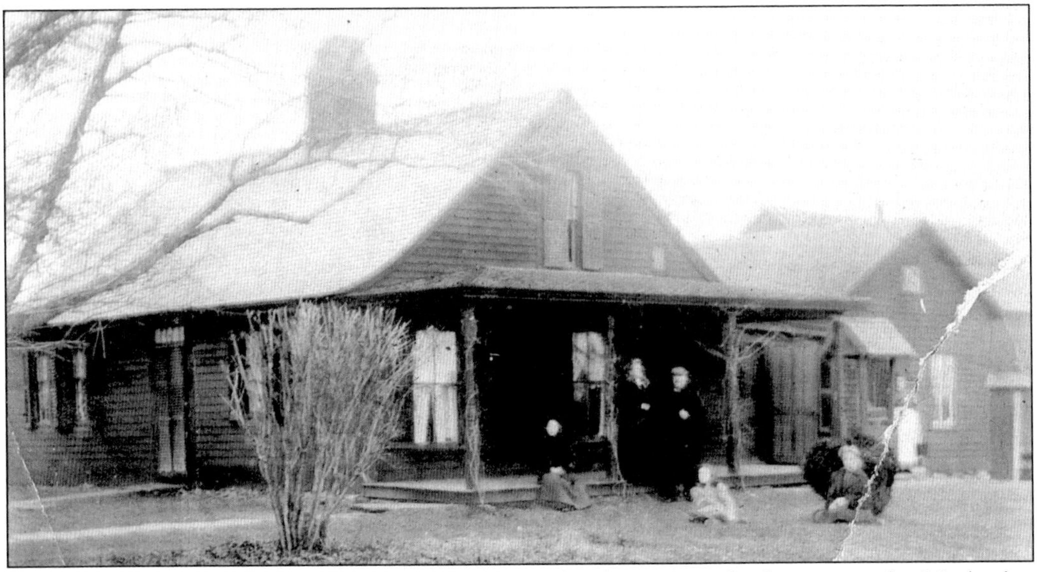

The Little Red Cottage, the home of Rev. John Whittlesey, was also known as the Methodist Tavern because of the great hospitality shown there. This is the oldest house in Salem, and is still standing. On this lot had been another home, the 1706 home of Jonathan Cutler, but there was no mention of this house in the deed to a woman identified only as Sarah, and the former home no longer existed. It is believed that Pelatiah Bliss built the house around 1730. Bliss was the son-in-law of Lieutenant Harris. The land was sold to Jonas Hamilton in 1742 and was then deeded to Jonas's sons. Rev. John Whittlesey bought this house in 1815. One night, Lorenzo Dow showed up to be married. It was late and the reverend was dressed to retire for the evening. Reverend Whittlesey did marry the couple standing below his window in the moonlight. He signed the marriage certificate and tossed it to them.

Oramel Whittlesey was born November 1, 1801. His love of music lead him to take lessons with his brothers despite his father's aversion to the idea. At 21 years of age, he and his brothers took apart and reassembled their first piano, which resulted in a superior instrument. Later with his new wife, Charlotte Maconda Morgan, he left for New York and then Buffalo, where he learned more about building pianos. Upon his return, with the help of his two brothers, he started a piano factory.

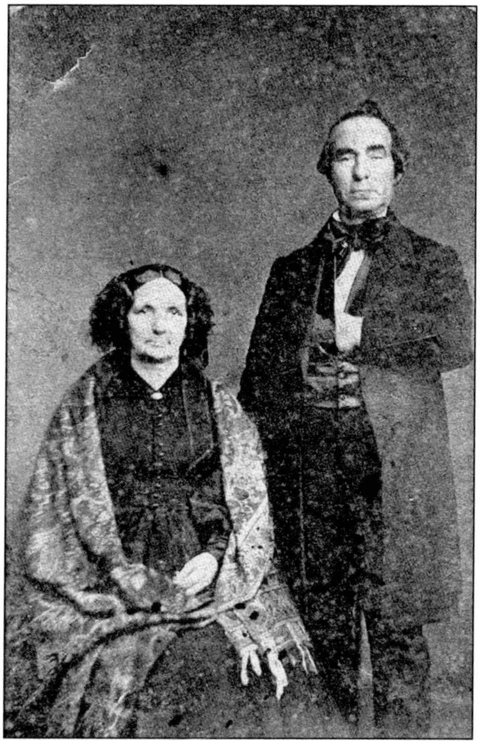

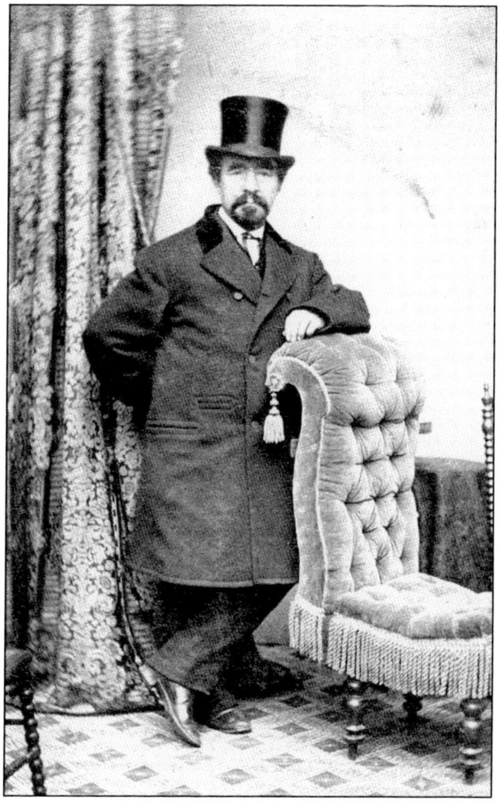

In the early 1830s, Oramel's reputation as a teacher was already growing. In 1835, two young women knocked at the door and invited themselves in, stating they had come to receive instruction, and, hence, Music Vale was born. Oramel was so well liked and respected by his peers in Salem during the operation of Music Vale that he later became postmaster, judge of probate, and was sent for a term of the Connecticut general assembly.

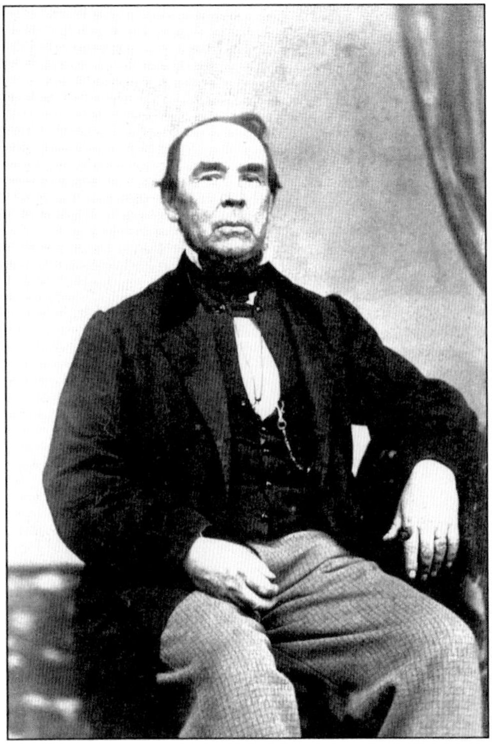

The youngest son of Rev. John and Sally Whittlesey was Henry Packwood Whittlesey, born October 26, 1812. Henry was in partnership of manufacturing pianos with his older brothers; John Whittlesey, born January 27, 1806, and Oramel, who started to drift away from the manufacturing business into the teaching aspect.

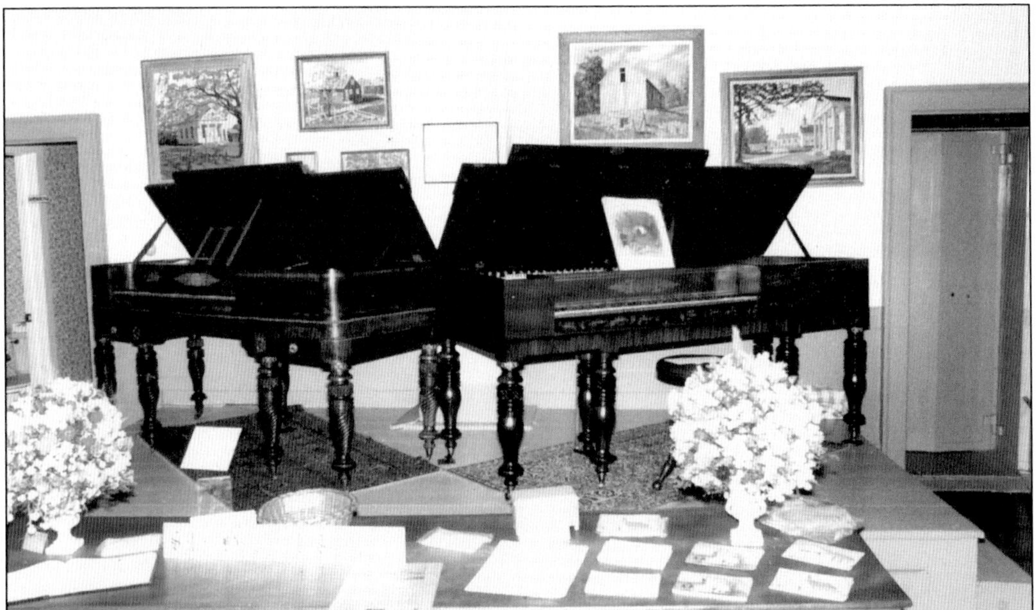

Two pianos made by the Whittlesey brothers are seen here. The pianos were made of rosewood and mahogany with ivory piano keys that had been sawed by hand and mother-of-pearl inlay letters and ornamentation. On the inside of every Whittlesey piano was a brass plate bearing the family name. Henry and John excelled in the mechanics of manufacturing these priceless pianos, while Oramel leaned more to the instruction of music.

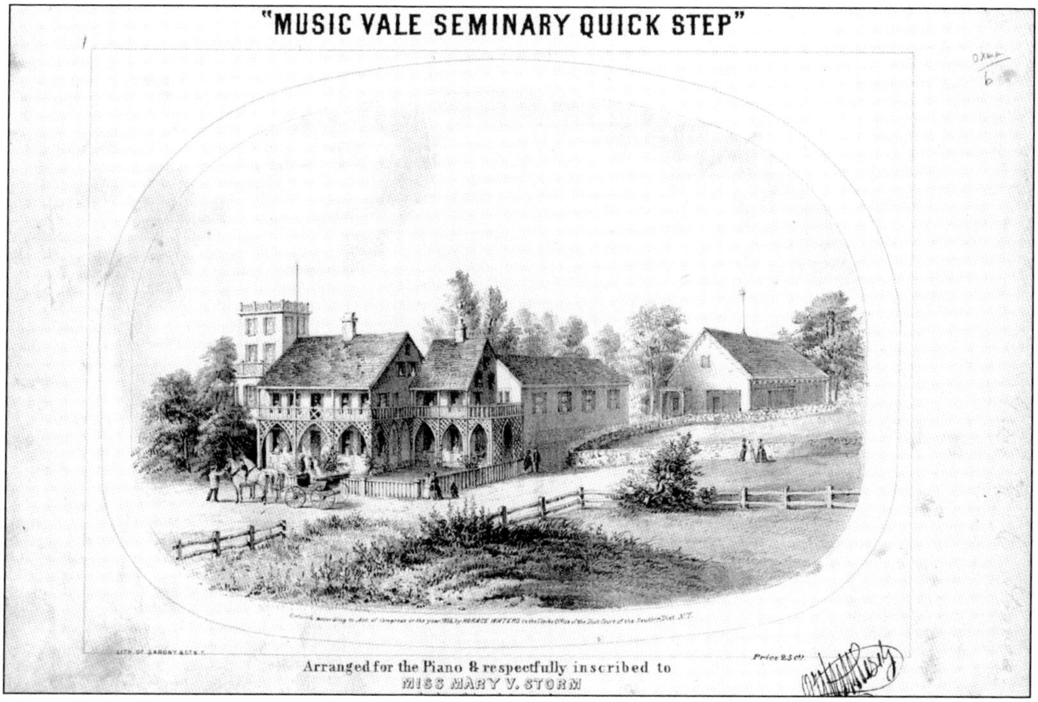

Music Vale Seminary, opened in 1835 by Oramel Whittlesey, was the first normal school of music in the country to confer degrees. Enrollment went to 12 that spring and then jumped to nearly 80 students. Oramel Whittlesey charged $1.50 a day, which included room and board, voice study, and use of musical instruments for practice. The schedule was as follows: rise at 5:00 a.m., practice from 6:00 a.m. to 7:00 a.m., breakfast, dinner at noon, and supper at 5:30 p.m. Students were required to practice four hours each day. The first Music Vale shown here is an artist's rendering and also a signed piece of sheet music.

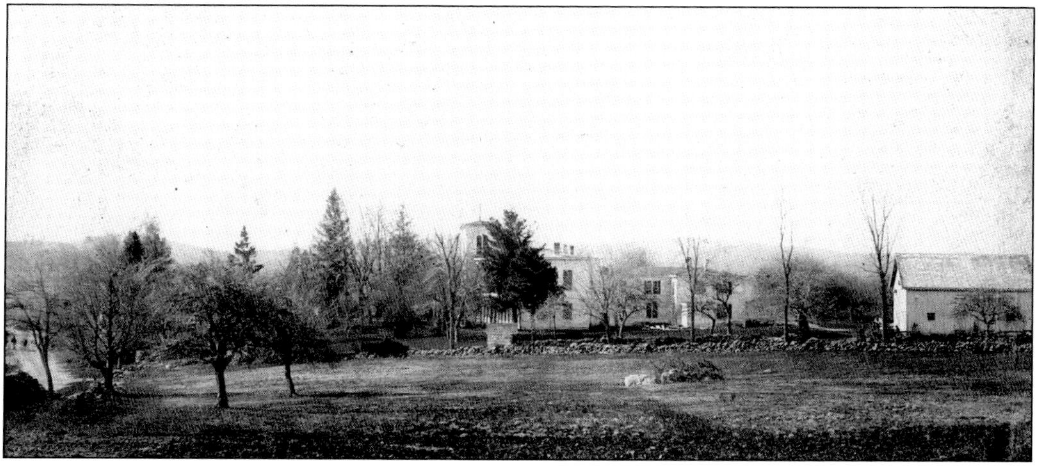

The school flourished for the first 25 years until the Civil War, when Southern attendance dropped. In January 1868, a special-effects display during a performance resulted in a fire. To create thunder, Oramel rolled cannon balls along the back of the stage. To create lightning, he set out pans of gun powder and ignited them. This particular night, the lightning special effects went out of control, and the fire destroyed the school. This is an actual photograph of the second Music Vale.

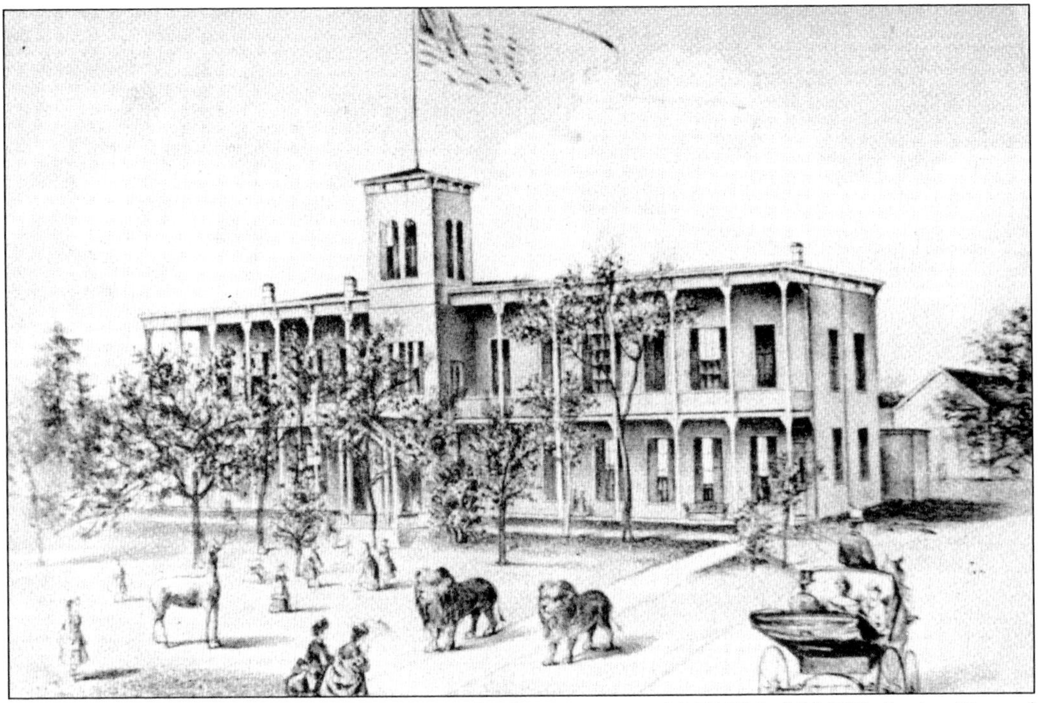

In spring 1868, the second structure was built at a cost of $35,000–$40,000. In it, Oramel built a huge auditorium with dressing rooms at one end with a stage, beautiful curtains, and painted backdrops designed by a New York artist. A gallery in the rear had frescoes adorning the walls and ceiling with lavish recitation rooms and living rooms. Two lions, a stag, and a harp weathervane graced the front of Music Vale. In September 1876, the school closed. Twenty years after Oramel's death, this structure was also destroyed by fire. Another artist's rendition of the second school is seen here.

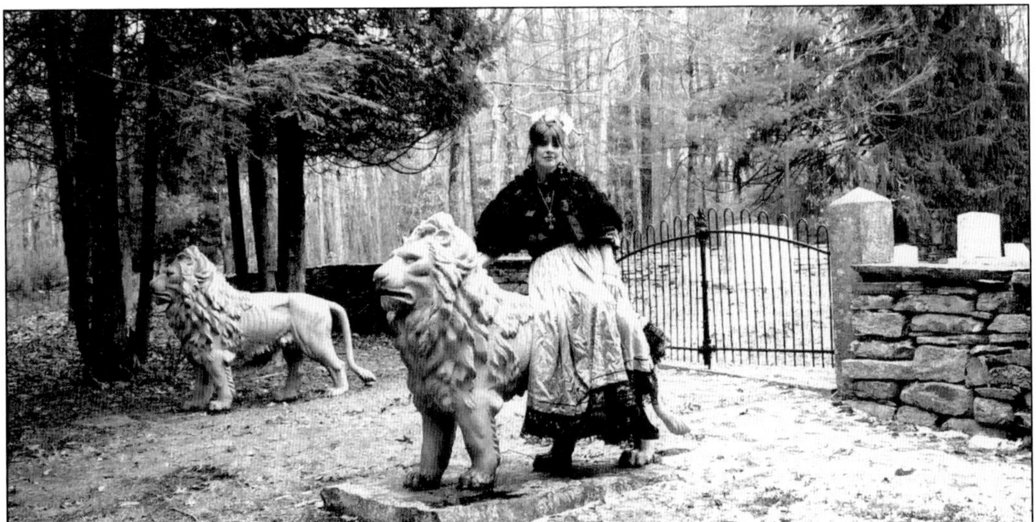

After the school closed, the lions were moved to the entrance of the Whittlesey cemetery, where they stand like sentry guards. The cemetery has a second set of stone walls that surround the lions. The unidentified girl shows how the lions appear life-size in comparison to herself.

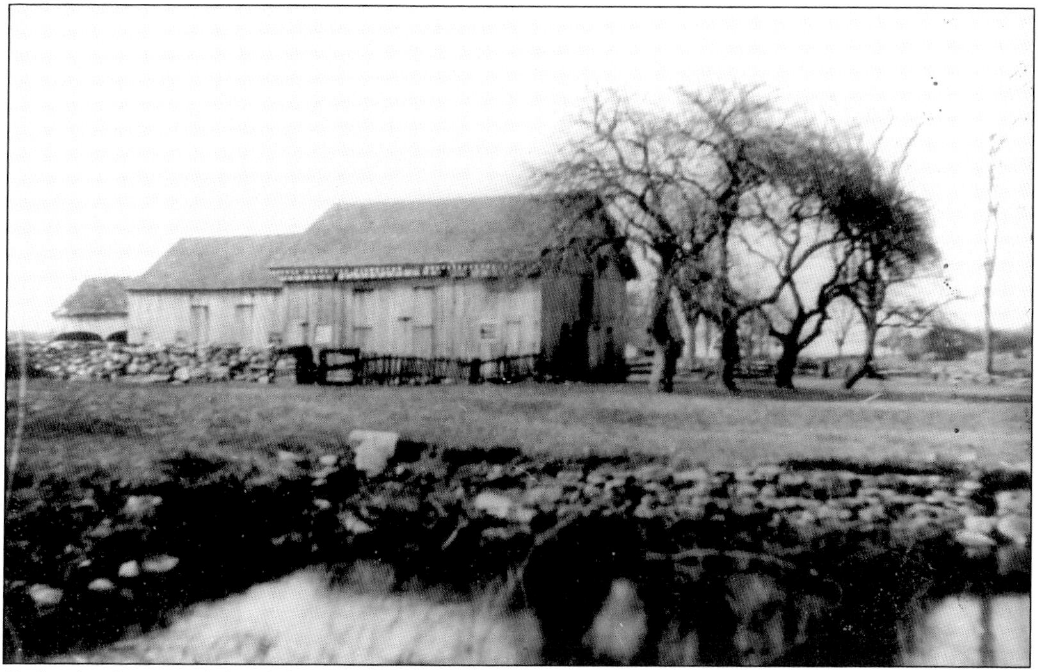

Only the barn is left of the once thriving music school. A sign near Route 85 states rather unobtrusively: Music Vale Seminary. In the foreground is the cellar of Music Vale filled with water.

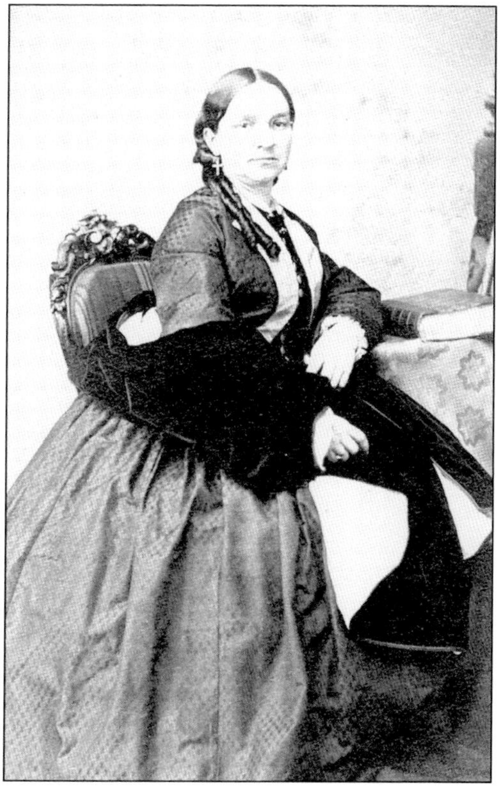

The eldest daughter of Oramel and Charlotte, Elizabeth (Eliza) Maginnis (née Whittlesey), born October 5, 1826, was a teacher and later vice principal at Music Vale. After her husband John's death in 1864, she started a school of music called Maginnis Institute of Music in New London. It is now a rectory of St. James Church. John and Eliza had two daughters.

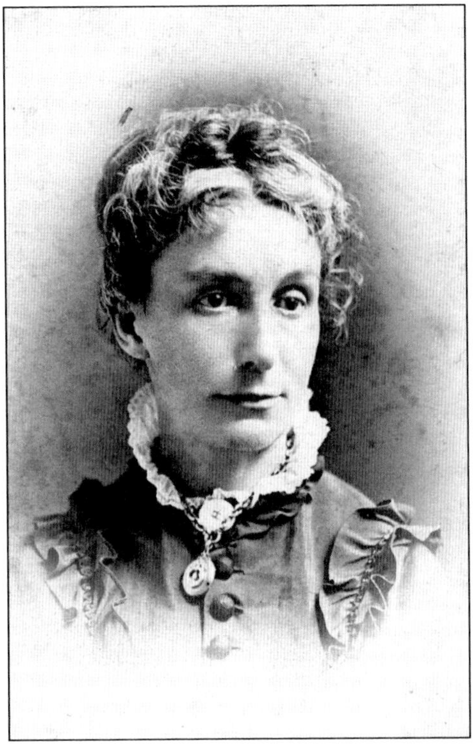

The second daughter, Sarah Victoria Whittlesey, born May 23, 1831, also taught at the Music Vale Seminary. On July 31, 1858, she married lawyer George Pratt of Norwich, where they lived for many years before moving to Kansas City, Missouri. Sarah and George Pratt had six children.

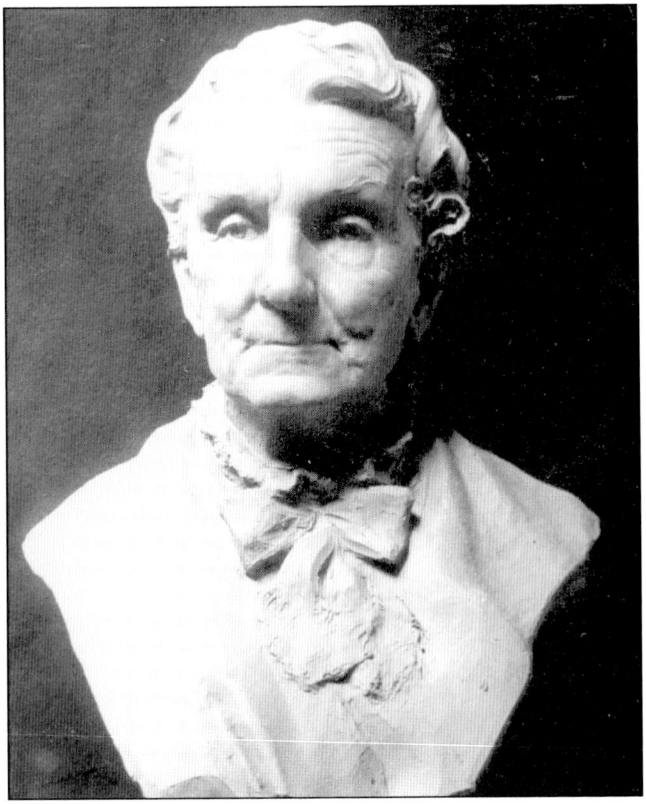

Bela Lyon Pratt, one of Sarah's sons, was born December 11, 1867, in Norwich. At 16, he attended Yale School of Fine Arts and later became a teacher at the school of the Boston Museum of Fine Arts. He is credited with 175 impressive sculptures, including the *Nathan Hale* at Yale and the *Andersonville Prisoner Boy* in the state capitol building in Connecticut. His graduate degree was from Harvard. He also designed coins for the United States Mint. He designed a reverse-relief coin. Music Vale property was sold out of the family, and in 1910, Bela Pratt purchased 100 acres of his grandfather Oramel's original land. Here is a bust Bela did of his mother at 82.

Jeanette Morgan Whittlesey, the third daughter, was born March 29, 1836, and married William Henry Maginnis, the brother of Elizabeth's husband, John. She was a talented singer, teaching voice lessons to the young women of Music Vale. Jeanette and William had seven children.

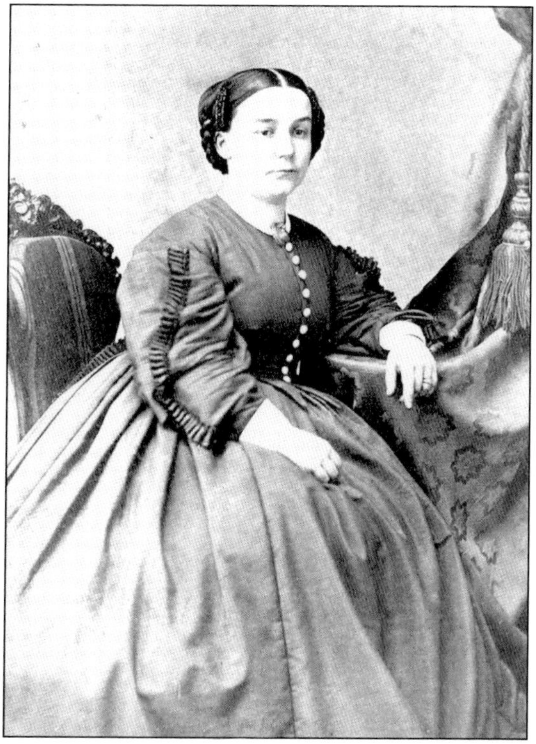

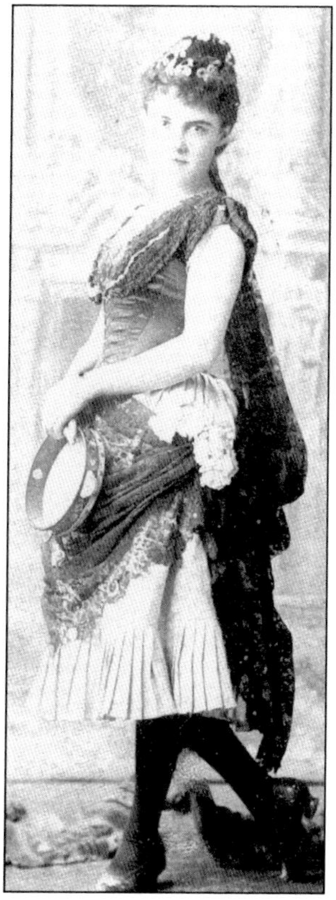

Charlotte Maconda Maginnis, daughter of Jeanette, was born March 12, 1863. She became known as the prima donna in New York, where she studied and performed in famous operas until she married William Wellington Walters of New York City. Pictured is Madame Maconda dressed in costume for a concert at Music Vale.

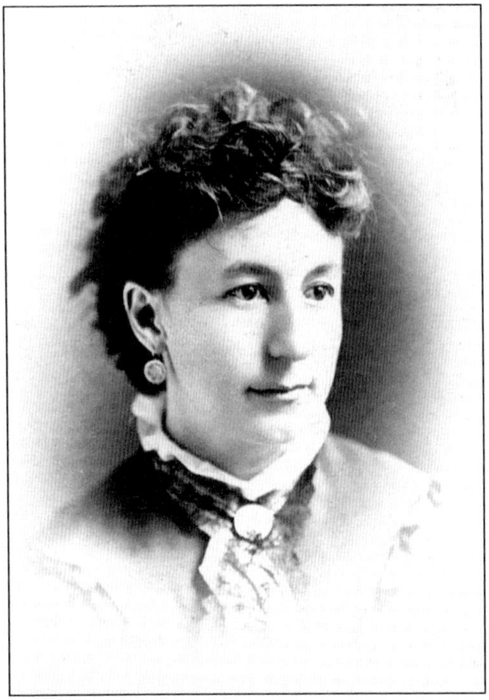

The youngest daughter of Oramel and Charlotte was Karolyn (Kate) Bradford Whittlesey, born April 2, 1843. She taught harp, piano, and guitar at Music Vale. Kate, never married. She moved to Topeka, Kansas, to teach music. She became head of the music department at Bethany College in Topeka.

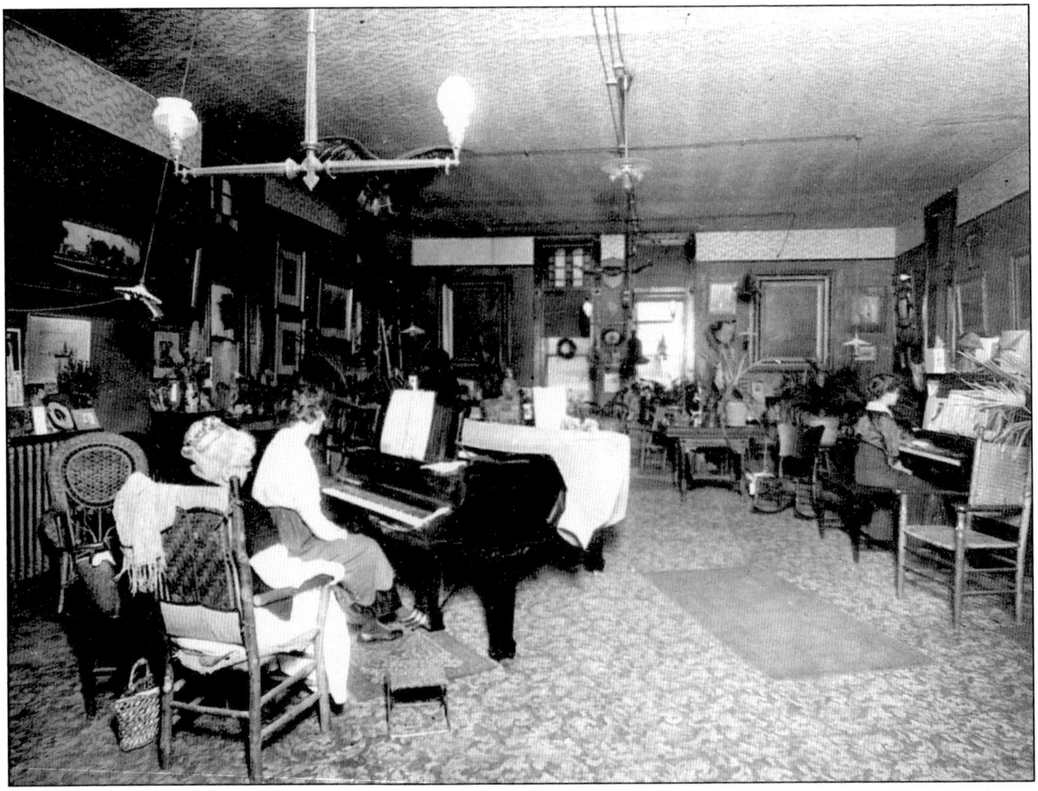

Kate is seated with her back toward the photographer. It looks as though she has two students practicing at the same time in her studio in Topeka.

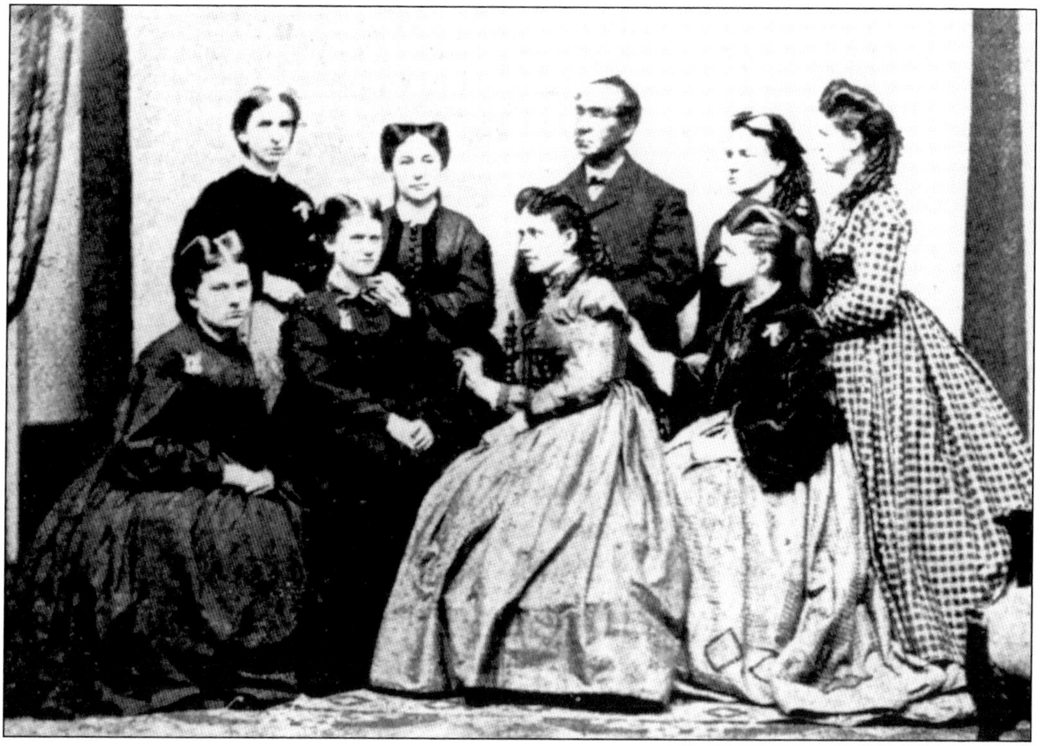

Oramel Whittlesey is flanked by his two daughters and the rest of the faculty of Music Vale Seminary in 1865. Two noted lecturers came to the school to visit, Dr. Lowell Mason and Dr. George F. Root, stopping at the Dolbeare Tavern on their way through Norwich.

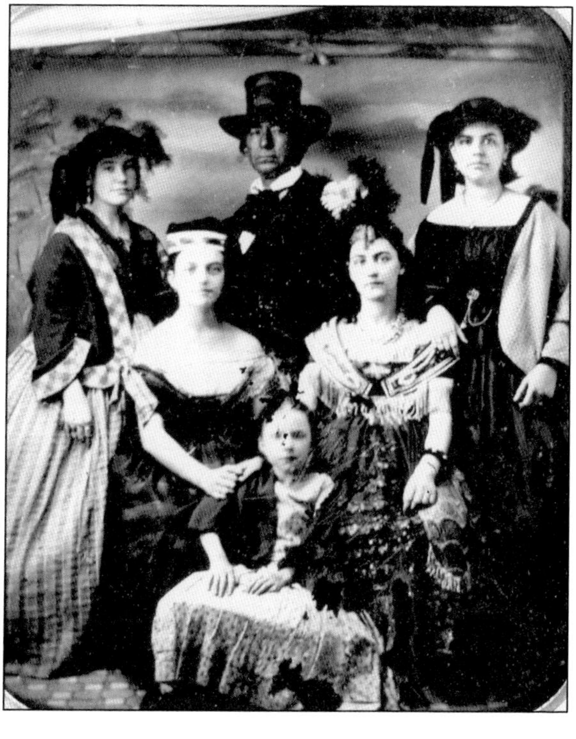

On rare occasions Professor Whittlesey joined the young women in one of their productions. Here the girls are seen dressed in costume for an opera.

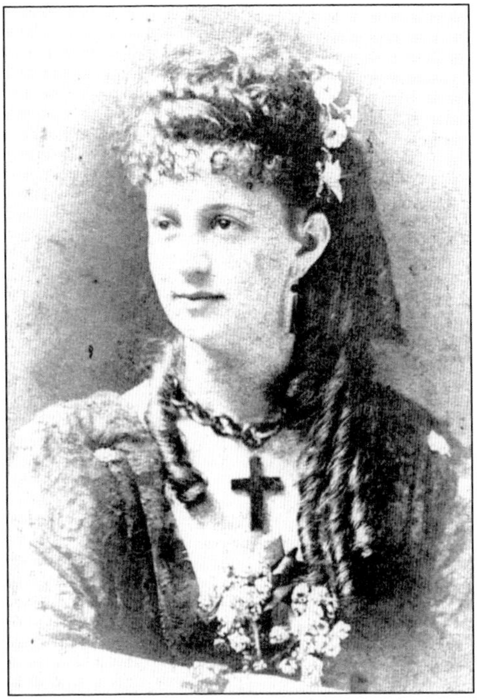

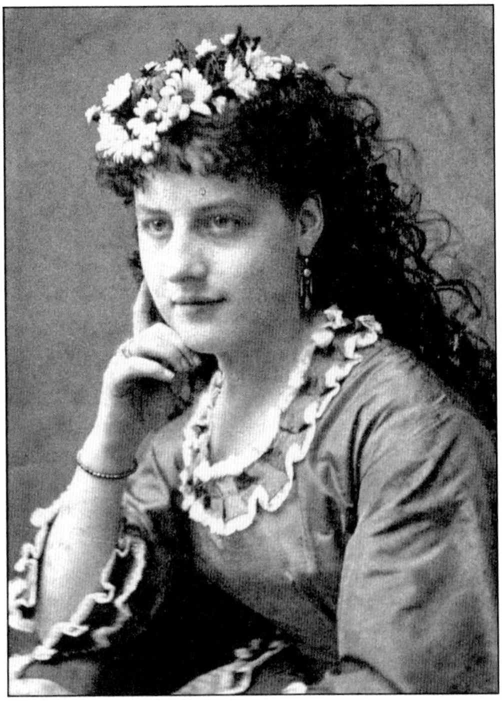

Young women came from the Carolinas, Kentucky, Kansas, Nova Scotia, and some as far as the West Indies. They rode in from Norwich, Connecticut, in the brightly colored carriages of Music Vale called the Bluebird and the Robin. The *Gleaner of the Vale* was the school newspaper, written entirely by the student body of young women. The women spent their limited free time in writing poetry and stories and fanciful excursions into the hills, dales, and vales of Salem. They described with youthful imagination locations where faries and witches danced throughout Salem. Note the flowers in their hair and the big chain-link crosses, almost Gothic in appearance.

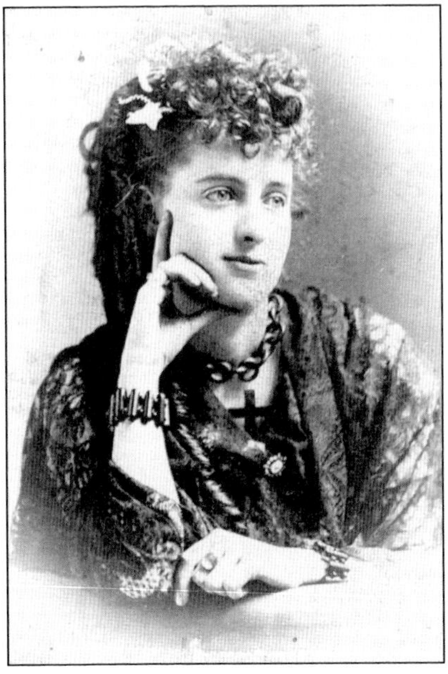

Some of the Southern gals' parents were astounded when they were told that Oramel's intense loyalty to the Union cause made all the students make a declaration to the North. This may have resulted in some attendance drop. The Ladies Loyal Union League, with a strong book lock and key, held the names of members and their resolutions; however, most of the pages were blank. Oramel enthusiastically shot a cannon on the front grounds of the school every time the Union North had a victory.

Four

MILITARY

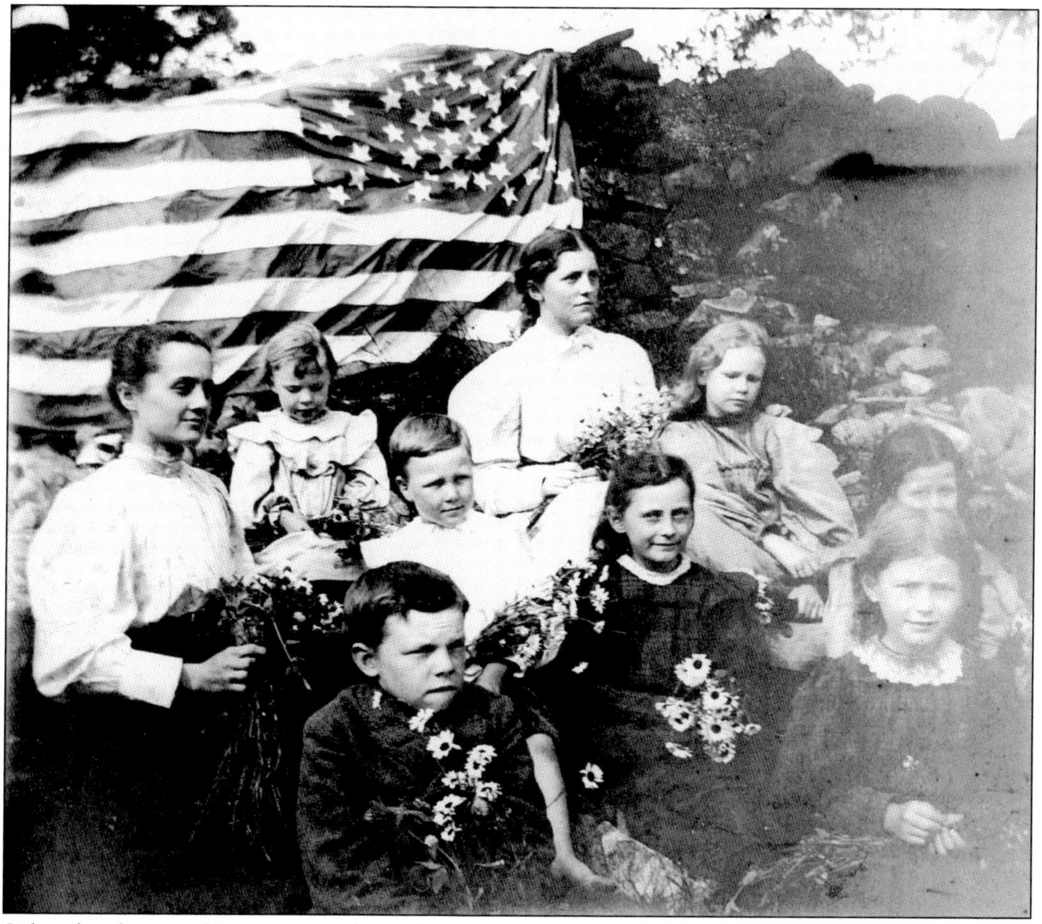

Salem has honored its veterans throughout generations with Memorial Day celebrations on the Salem Town Green, and parades on the Governor's Road (Route 85). Harriet Goldie, daughter of Charles Williams, views one such parade around 1900 with an unidentified young woman and children. Note the daisies and also note that the flag appears to be draped backwards against a stone wall. Salem has sent many soldiers off to war. Buried in Salem are 1 from Queen Anne's War, 21 from the Revolutionary War, 3 from the War of 1812, and 12 from the Civil War. Twenty-three men served in World War I, 60 men and one woman served in World War II. It is not known where all are buried from these two wars. The number that served in the Korean and Vietnam Wars is unknown.

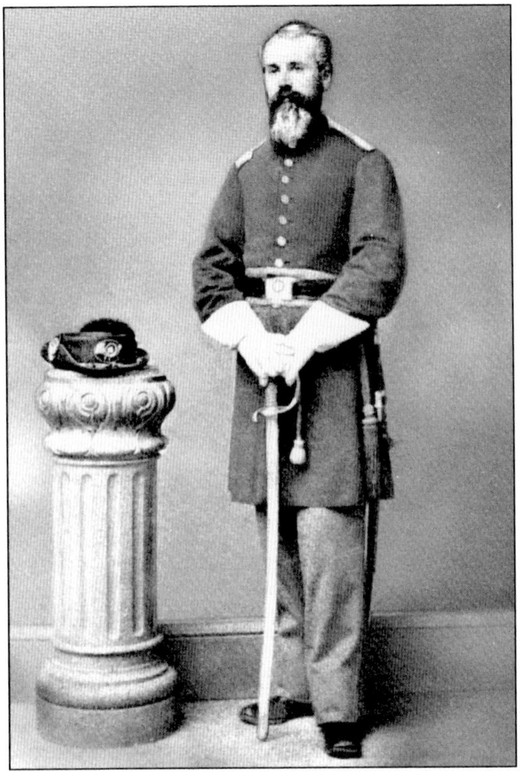

Lt. John Thomas Maginnis was born April 5, 1825, in Stamford. On December 18, 1851, he married Elizabeth Tully Whittlesey of Salem, daughter of Oramel Whittlesey, founder of Music Vale Seminary. When the Civil War broke out, Maginnis was one of the first to volunteer and enlisted in 1862 in Company E, 18th Regiment, Connecticut Volunteers. Promoted to lieutenant August 18, 1862, he later fought in the Battle of Winchester, June 12–13, 1863, and was captured. He spent nine months in Libby prison, where he contracted a cough at which time he was released on furlough. After returning home, his restlessness lead him back to the front at the skirmish at Piedmonts, where he took a small musket ball to the temple and died in the arms of a comrade on June 5, 1864. Initially buried on the battlefield, he was later exhumed and reinterred in Mosswood Glen Cemetery at Music Vale in Salem. Between skirmishes, he had found time to send beautiful letters addressed in envelopes in various styles of calligraphy in different colored inks to his wife, Elizabeth.

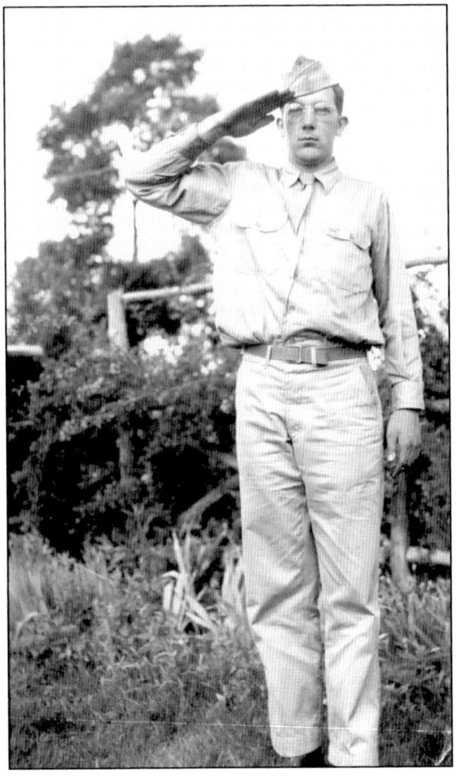

In 1944, Robert Hale McCall, 18, foreseeing enlistment as inevitable, voluntarily signed up in Old Lyme. On January 26, 1944, he left for army training at Fort Devens, Massachusetts. By November 1944, McCall was paralyzed by an eight-millimeter slug that had ripped through his spine in the Huertgen Forest, Germany. At age 21, after a two-year stay in an army hospital, where he received walking classes, driving lessons, and photography and radio work, he returned to civilian life. Despite incessant hospital visits and the challenges of crutches, McCall managed to learn to drive a 1946 Ford, racking up 90,000 miles in about four years. He spent a great deal of time building and restoring furniture in what was then a plane-spotting post erected behind his father's house. One room was used by McCall as a darkroom for his photography. In 1954, he met Verna Watrous, whom he married on Valentine's Day 1958. Together they had three children, Jeffrey Hale and twins Robin Hazel and Robert Jonathan.

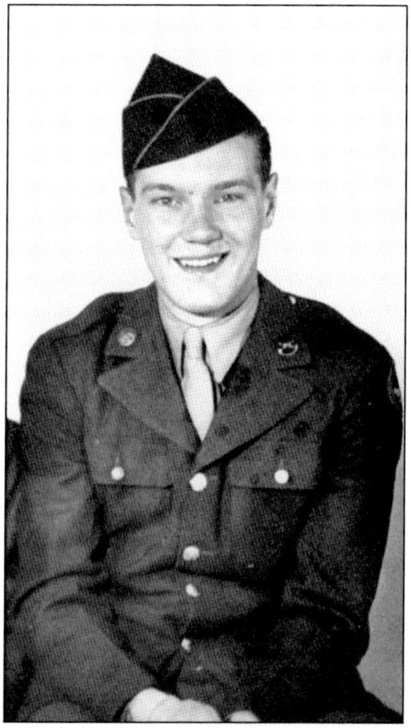

Duncan Fraser, age 19 in this photograph, had joined the army in August 1943. He received his basic training at Fort Benning, Georgia, and attended Princeton University in the Army Specialized Training Program for three months and then joined the 104th Division at Camp Carson, Colorado. He was wounded after his battalion had advanced too far and was cut off for more than two days, being hammered by enemy fire until reinforcements came.

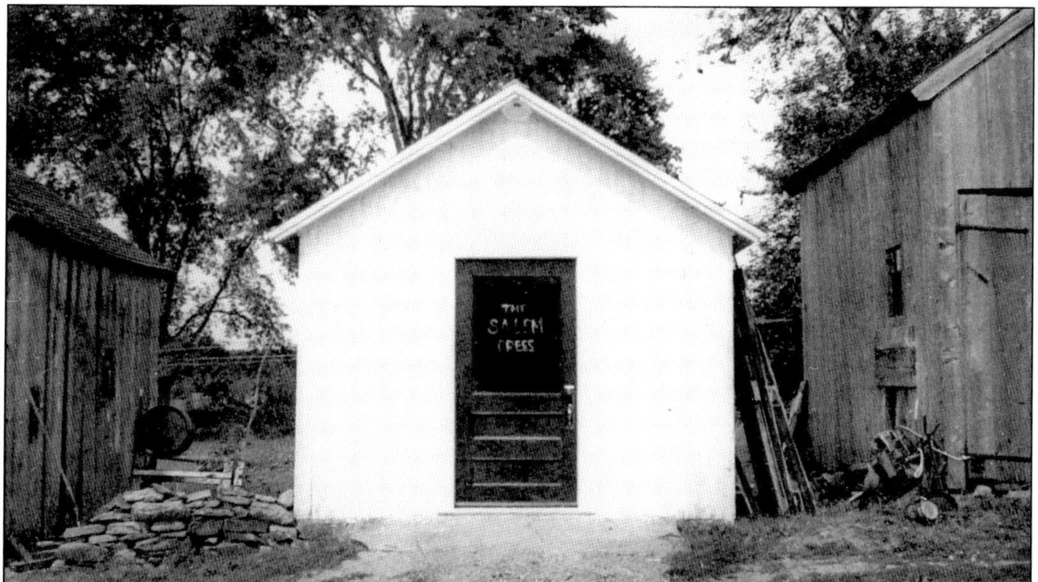

Duncan Fraser, reporter, editor, typesetter, pressman, advertising agent, and circulation manager, was only 12 when he started the first newspaper in Salem: the *Salem Press*. Fraser started with printing jobs, which he edited and typeset by hand. The *Salem Flash* was the first attempt to publish a newspaper in 1937, which lead to the successful *Salem Press*. It started as a one page paper, and grew to a two-sided, two-column paper with headline news, classified advertising, and cartoons. Customers often helped themselves to the newspapers, priced at 1¢, that were placed in Duncan's father's store at Salem Four Corners. This is the photograph of the young boy's print shop.

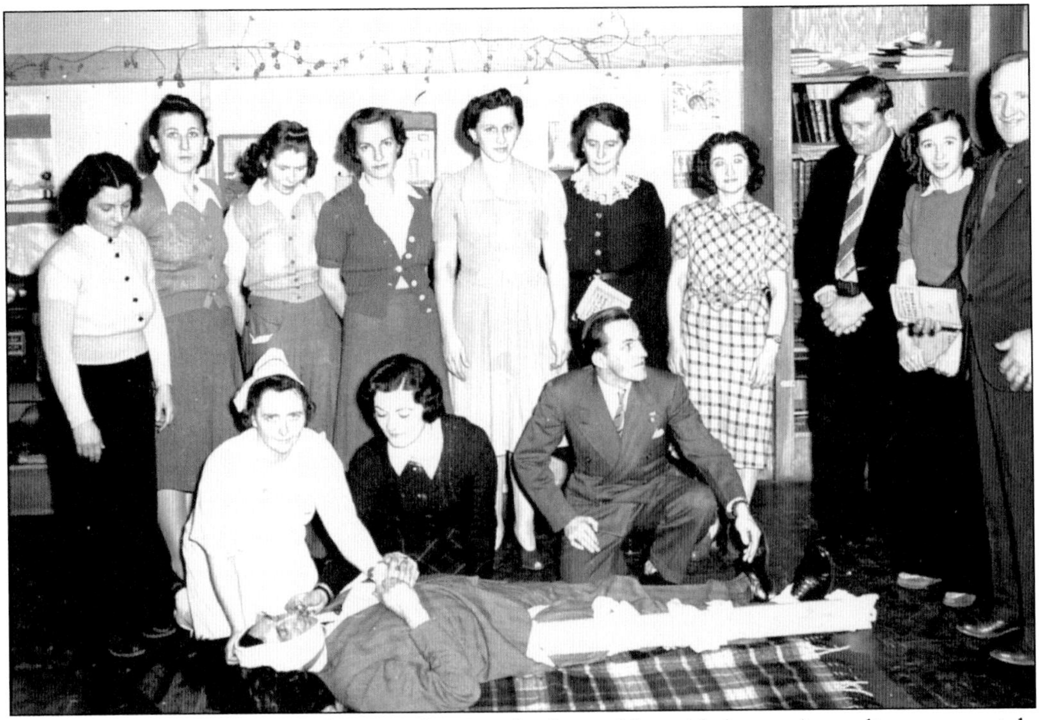

The Town of Salem set up civil preparedness in the form of first aid classes. According to an article in a New London paper, *The Day*, dated February 11, 1942, it was the high incidence of automobile accidents that prompted the first aid classes. This class, supervised by Kenneth F. Skinner of the New London County division of the Red Cross, gets a practical demonstration on handling a patient with a broken leg. Pictured from left to right are (standing) Elsie Maynard; Mary Senkow; Edith Hill; Mrs., J. Burton Byron; Stella Chapman; Mrs. Charles B. Tinker; Florence Heilweil; John DeWolfe; Iola Sellew; and Ralph Mudgett; (kneeling) class instructor Marion Sullivan, R.N.; Fay Bloom; and Kenneth F. Skinner of Norwich. The patient is Albert Hampton Sr.

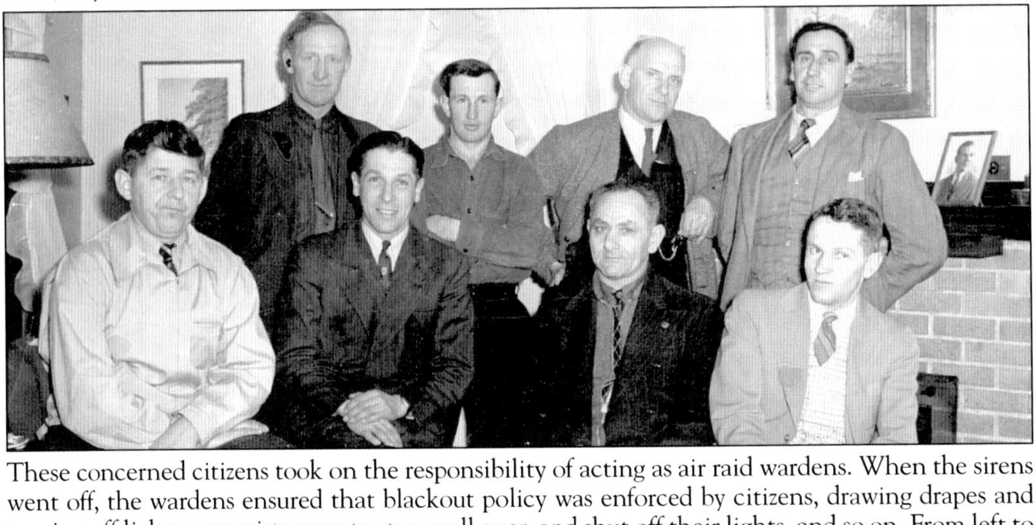

These concerned citizens took on the responsibility of acting as air raid wardens. When the sirens went off, the wardens ensured that blackout policy was enforced by citizens, drawing drapes and turning off lights; motorists were to stop, pull over, and shut off their lights, and so on. From left to right are (front row) Joseph Swider, Edgar Bordeau, Isaac Heilweil, and Mitchell Bingham; (back row) Ralph Mudgett, Charles Dimmock, Donald Fraser, and Albert Hampton Sr.

During an air raid, Alfred Bingham is photographed shutting off lights at Salem Four Corners during World War II.

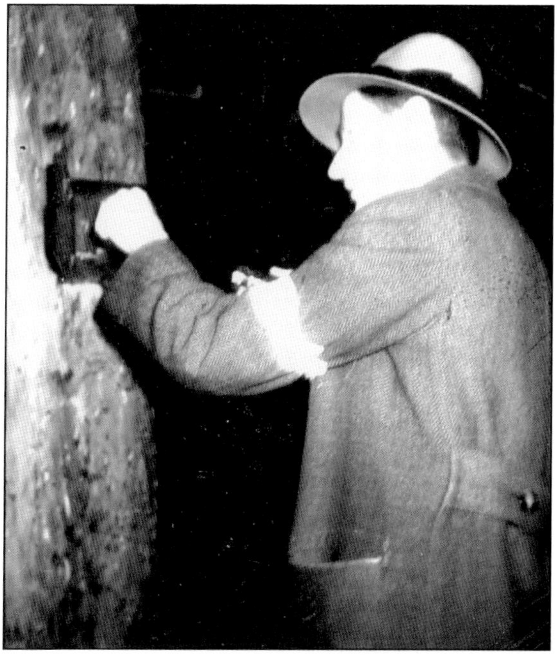

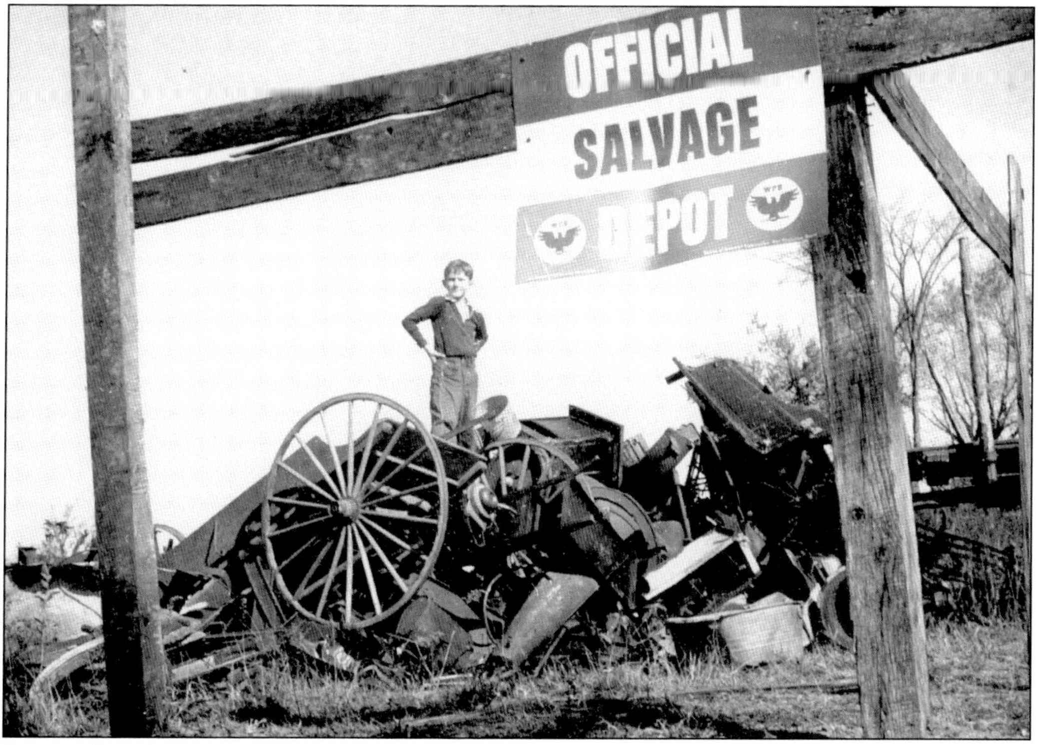

Diagonal to the Country Store and across from the Willows Garage (McCall's), now Bad Boy Toyz, was an empty lot. During the war, it became an official salvage depot for scrap metal. Scrap metal was used for bullets, planes, and so forth. Even tin cans and cast-iron pots and pans were used for the war effort. Donald Fraser Jr. standing on top of this pile of metal would make any mother cringe.

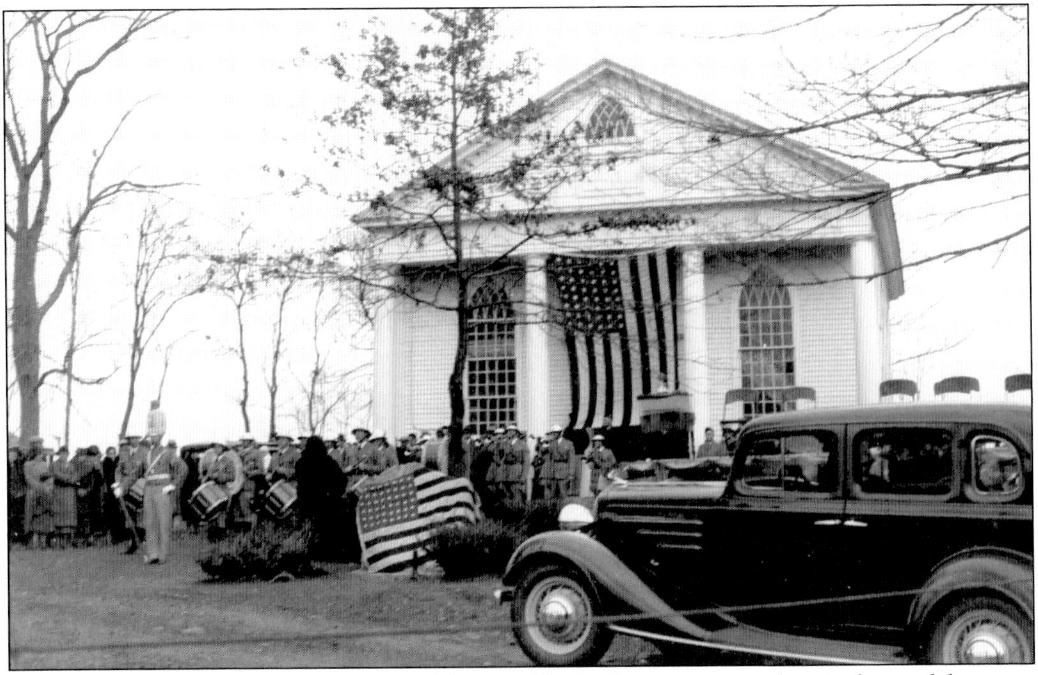

Here is a photograph of the unveiling of the World War I monument, taken in front of the town house on the Salem Town Green. The American flag hanging from the town house gives a very patriotic air to the event. A marching band and speakers graced the ceremony.

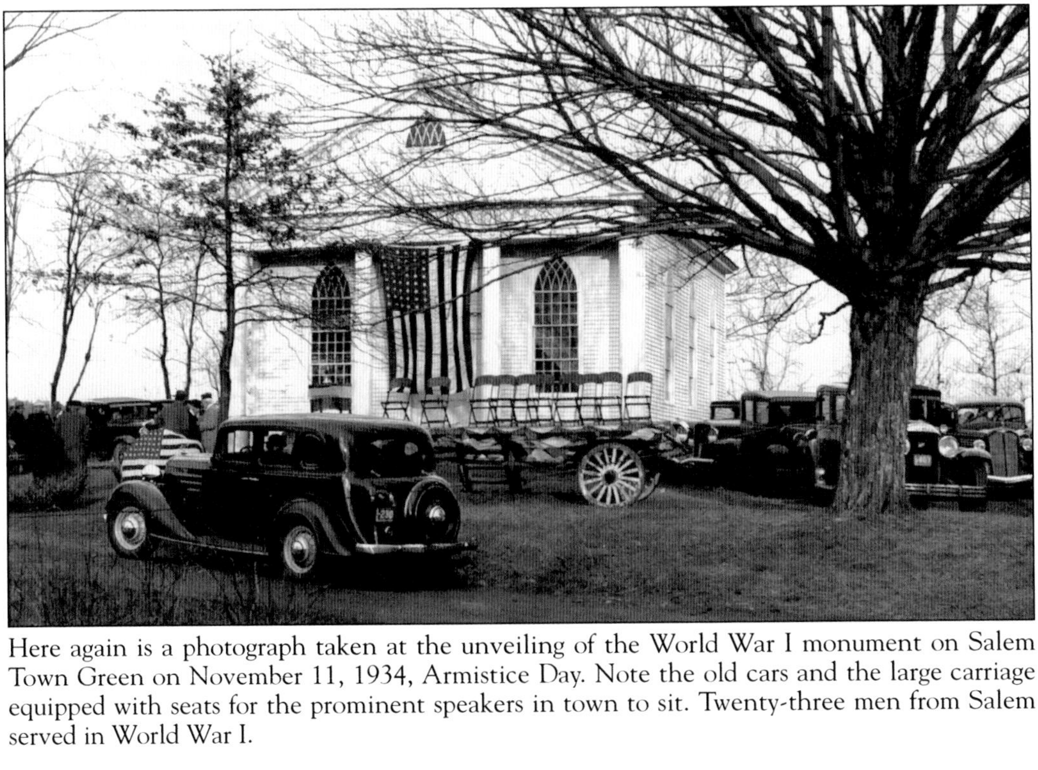

Here again is a photograph taken at the unveiling of the World War I monument on Salem Town Green on November 11, 1934, Armistice Day. Note the old cars and the large carriage equipped with seats for the prominent speakers in town to sit. Twenty-three men from Salem served in World War I.

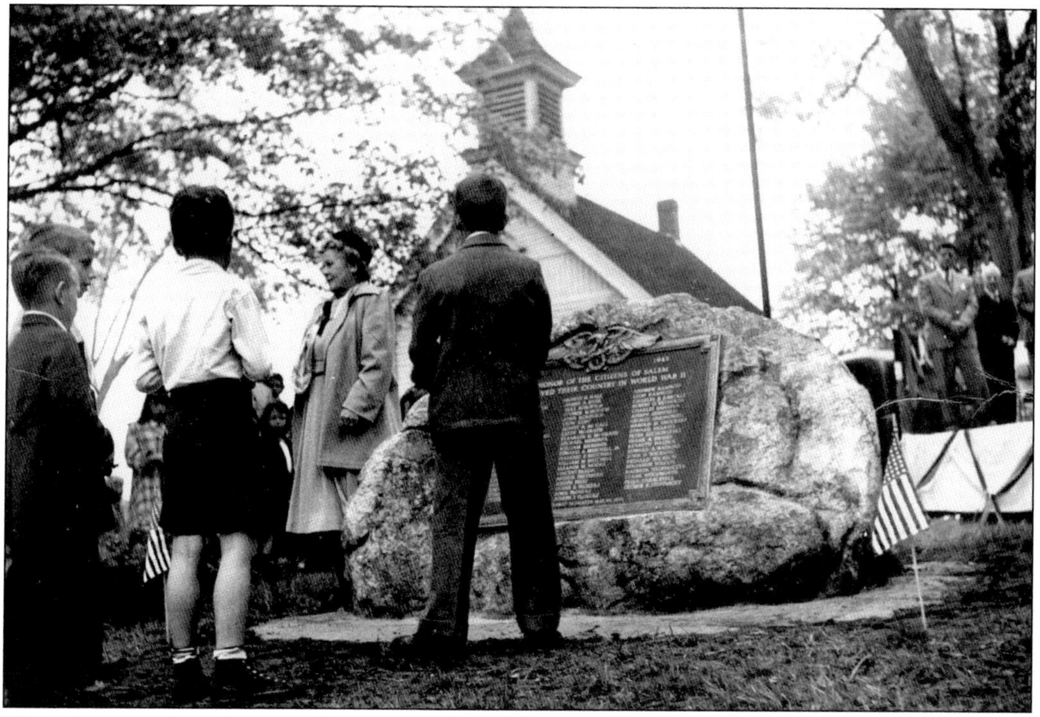

This photograph is the unveiling ceremony for the World War II monument on May 30, 1950, Memorial Day. Sixty men and one woman served in World War II from Salem. Standing in the background is Mrs. Hale, a gold-star mother. Her son is the only one from Salem who was lost in battle.

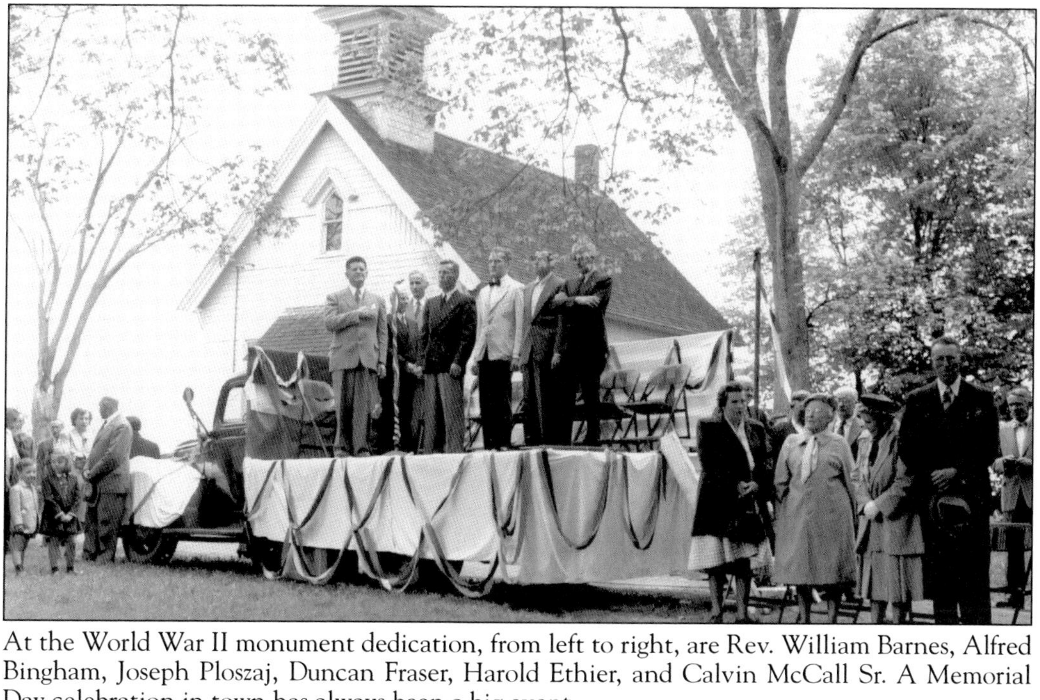

At the World War II monument dedication, from left to right, are Rev. William Barnes, Alfred Bingham, Joseph Ploszaj, Duncan Fraser, Harold Ethier, and Calvin McCall Sr. A Memorial Day celebration in town has always been a big event.

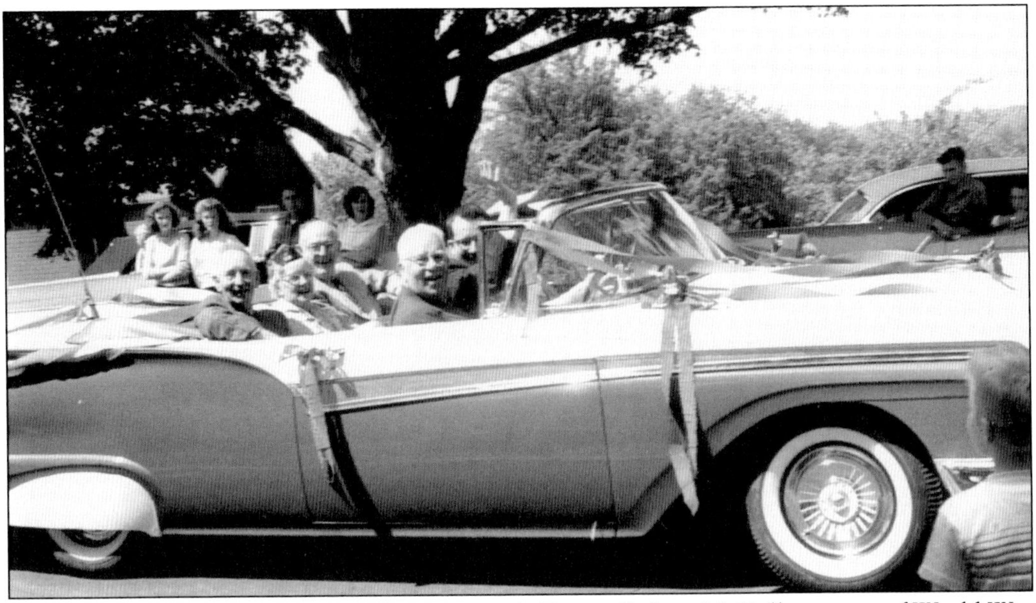

A Memorial Day celebration in 1958 is pictured. Here is Robert McCall, veteran of World War II, driving with veterans of World War I Robert Kogrt (passenger), and from left to right in the backseat are George Day, Francis Keenan, and Charles Keenan.

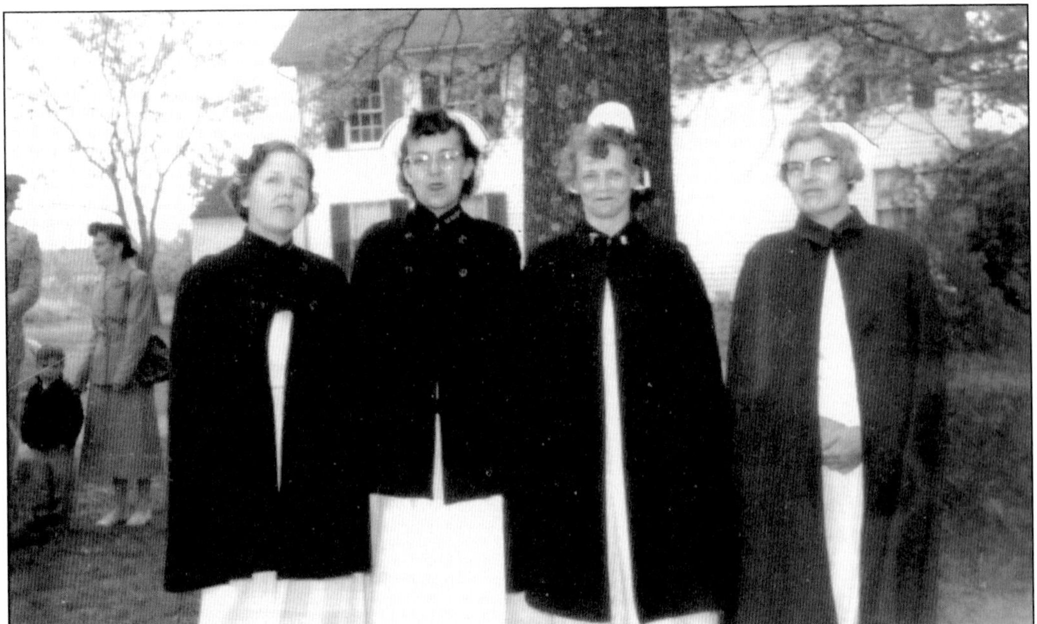

Pictured from left to right in this 1962 Memorial Day parade photograph are nurses Magel Coffey, Phyllis McCall, Shirley Blackman, and Eleanor Moore. Eleanor Moore was the only woman from Salem to serve in World War II.

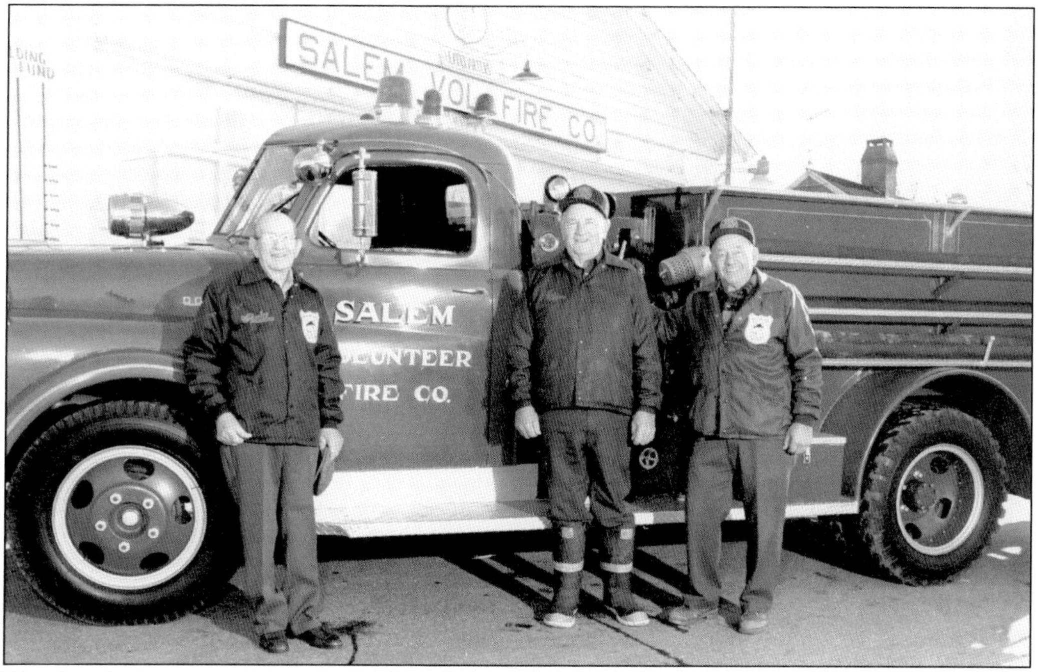

The first firehouse in Salem, located on Route 85 just north of Witch Meadow Road, was built in 1942. Some land was donated by Louis Smuckler. In 1990, the old firehouse was taken down and rebuilt to accommodate the needs of a growing town and to support the dedicated 150 volunteer firefighters in town. This is the first "real" fire truck that was purchased. The other trucks were ones the firemen put together themselves. In this photograph, from left to right, are Charles Dimmock, Kashmir Wlodarczyk, and Andrew Wlodarczyk.

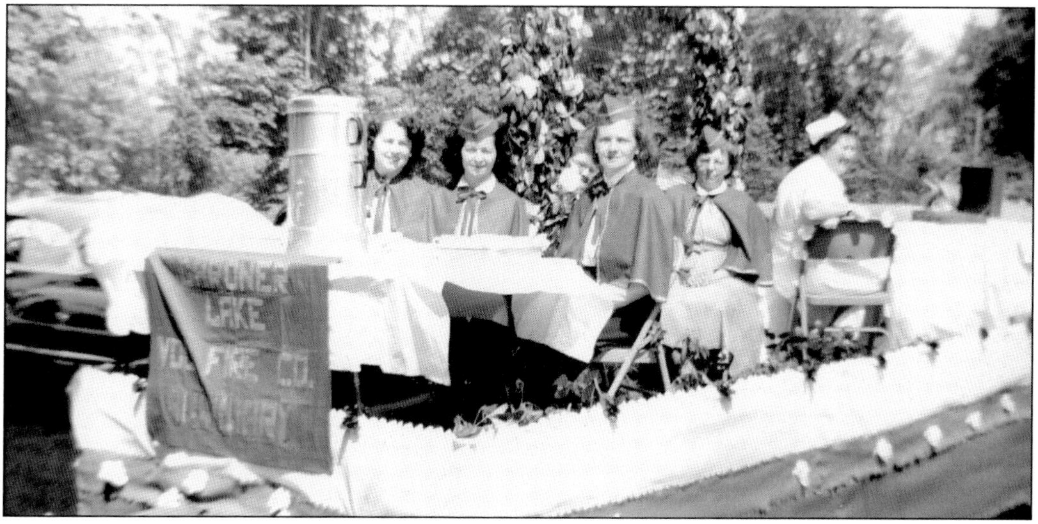

The Ladies Auxiliary was started in 1957 to help raise money for the firehouse with bake sales, bingo, serving refreshments at dances, summer fairs, and so on. At that time, the women were not allowed to be firefighters, so this gave many wives and family members a way to show support. From left to right, Jenny Snarski, Helen Zeleski, Luella Moore, Mrs. Burgess, and registered nurse Edith Congdon are pictured here on a float in this parade. The capes and hats were specifically made to be worn in parades.

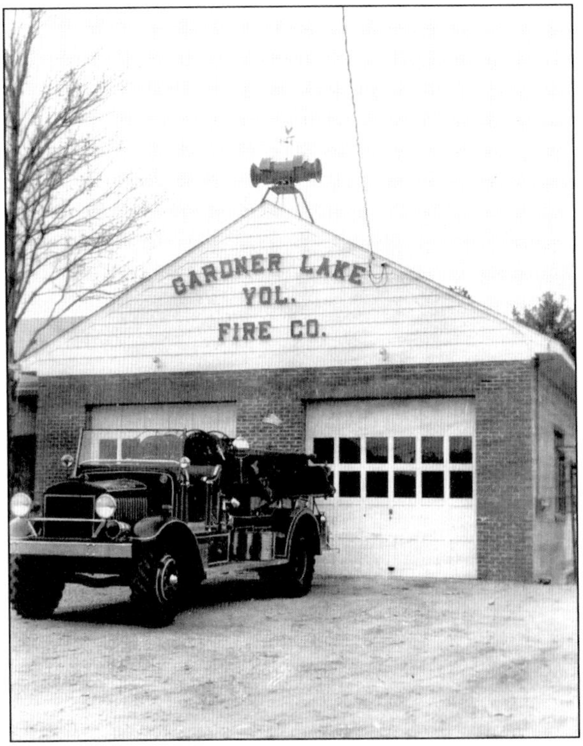

Gardner Lake Firehouse was built in 1956. Because they could not hear the siren at the Salem Volunteer Firehouse from their side of town and there was some disagreement about installing an additional siren, the firemen from the Gardner Lake area decided to build their own firehouse. Here is the first fire truck. The first pumper truck they had was built at Congdon's Garage.

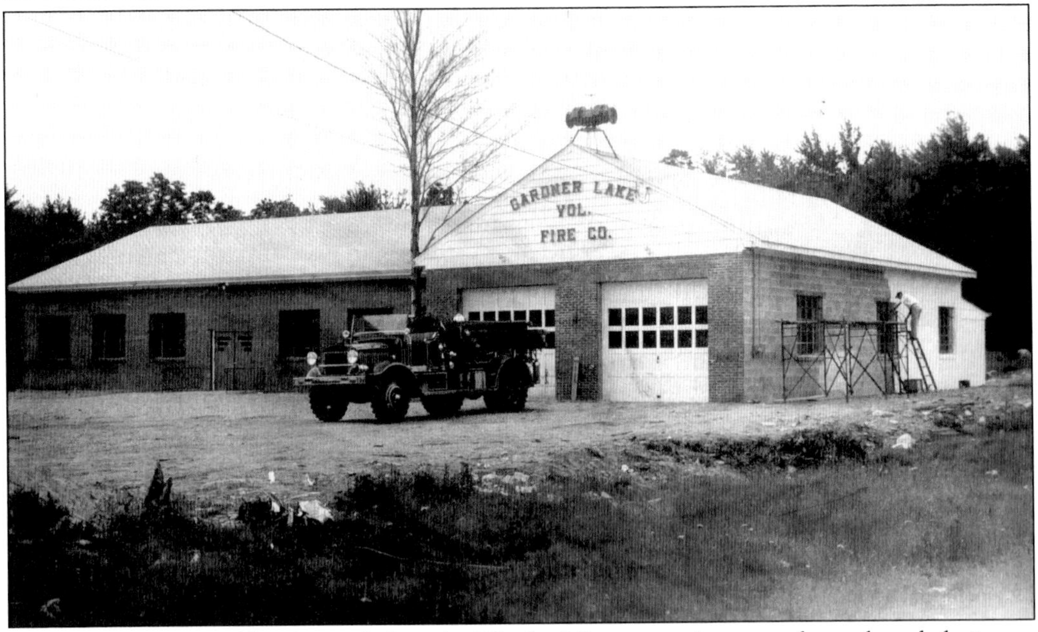

The land was donated by Kenneth Snarski. The building committee was formed, and chairman Joseph Moore designed the building. While on a job, two orders were placed for a gym floor for Fitch High School. When the orders came in, Moore, a plumber and steam fitter by trade, saw an opportunity to get the flooring for the firehouse at an outrageous price, which resulted in the large dance hall included in the plans. Starting in 1957, the firehouse had dances for teenagers with live bands and bingo to help pay off the mortgage.

Five

COMMERCE

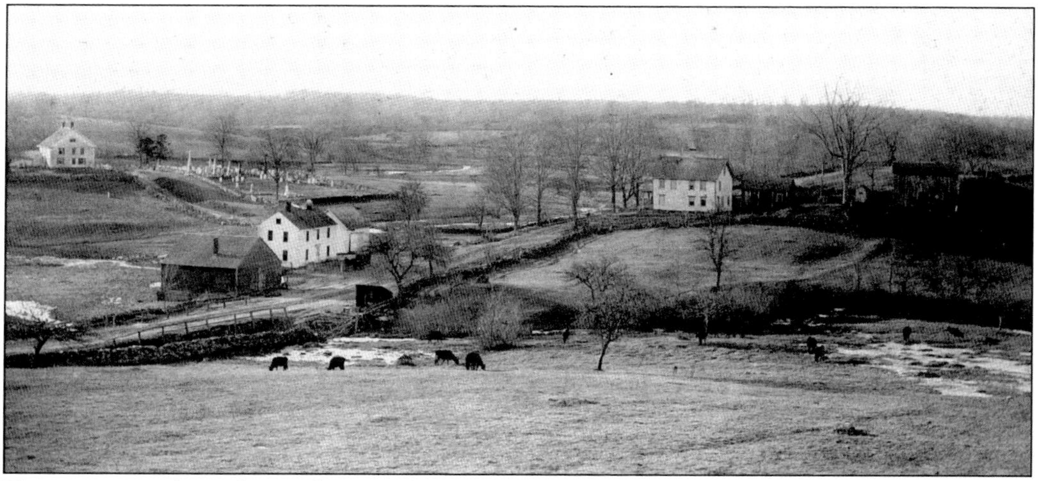

This is a view of Witch Meadow Road and Route 85. The home to the far left, set back, was the Smith house on Witch Meadow. It is no longer there; however, a smaller house is now in that vicinity. The darker barnlike structure on Route 85 is the Herrick Blacksmith Shop and the home of Elijah Herrick. The barn is gone, but the house still stands and is behind a tall fence. The Wesley Brown Cemetery can be seen in this photograph. To the far right on the corner of Route 85 and Rattlesnake Ledge lies what was known as the PB Harvey house on the 1868 map and later became the Spencer house. This house also is still there. In this photograph notice the barrenness as all land was used in farming.

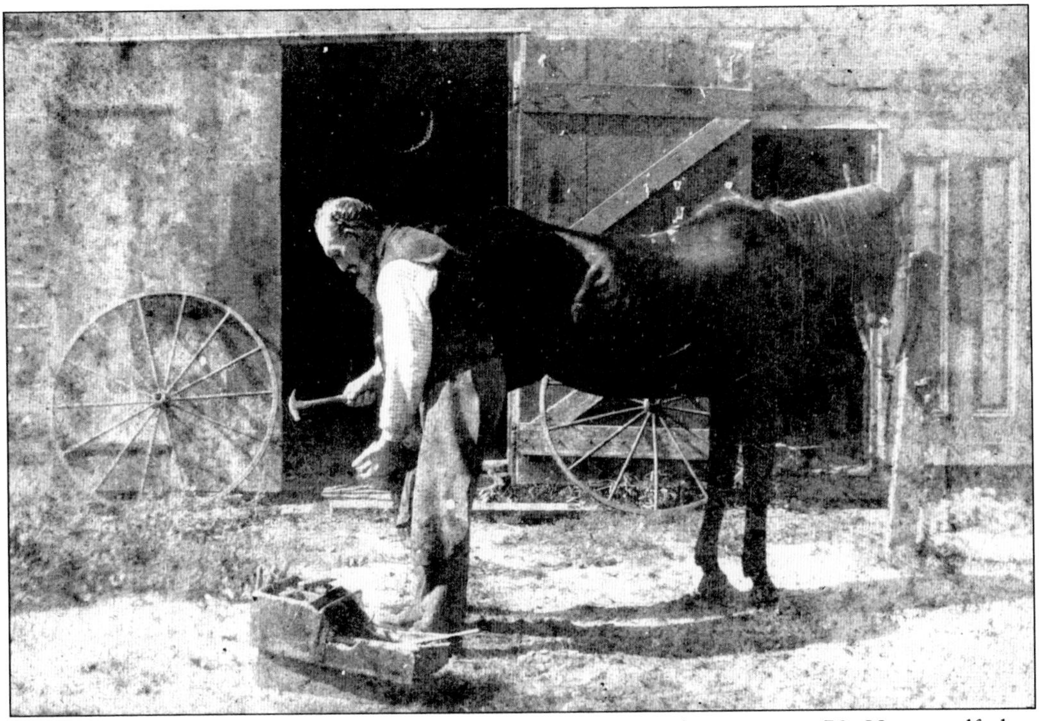

This is a photograph of blacksmith Elijah Herrick shoeing a horse at age 70. His grandfather and father of the same name, Elijah, were also blacksmiths. Marquis de Lafayette had stopped at his father's shop in Norwich around 1824 to get a larger pair of stirrups, in turn leaving his old pair behind and becoming a Herrick family heirloom. Elijah III died here in 1910.

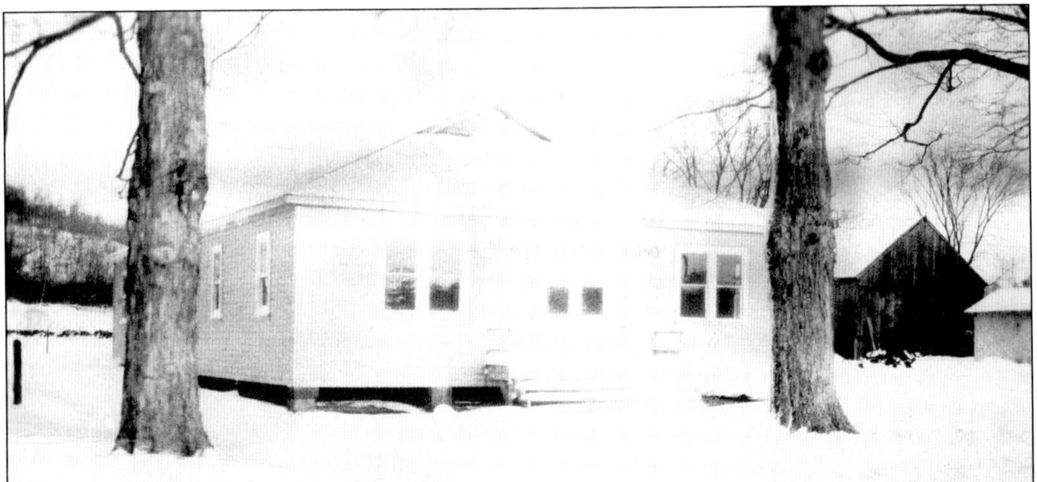

Here is a photograph of Maple Shade Casino as it looked around 1920. It was located next to Smuckler's Garage. The casino was another place for folks to gather for dances and special occasions. It is a far cry from the casinos of today, and not much is known about this small casino. It may have been a hot spot during the time of Prohibition. It could have been a speakeasy for some homemade hooch. The White Eagle orchestra of Montvillle used to play there.

The Day family goes back seven generations. They settled in Cockle Hill. Here is a photograph of George Day while serving in World War I. Day was born in 1889 and died in 1980. A horseshoer, jobber, and wagon maker, he lived until the ripe old age of 91, repairing clocks through his golden years.

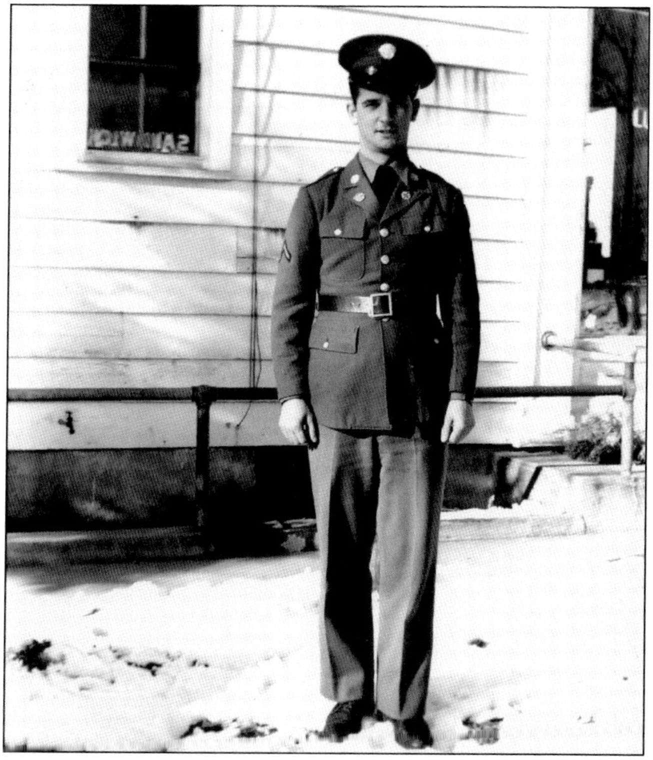

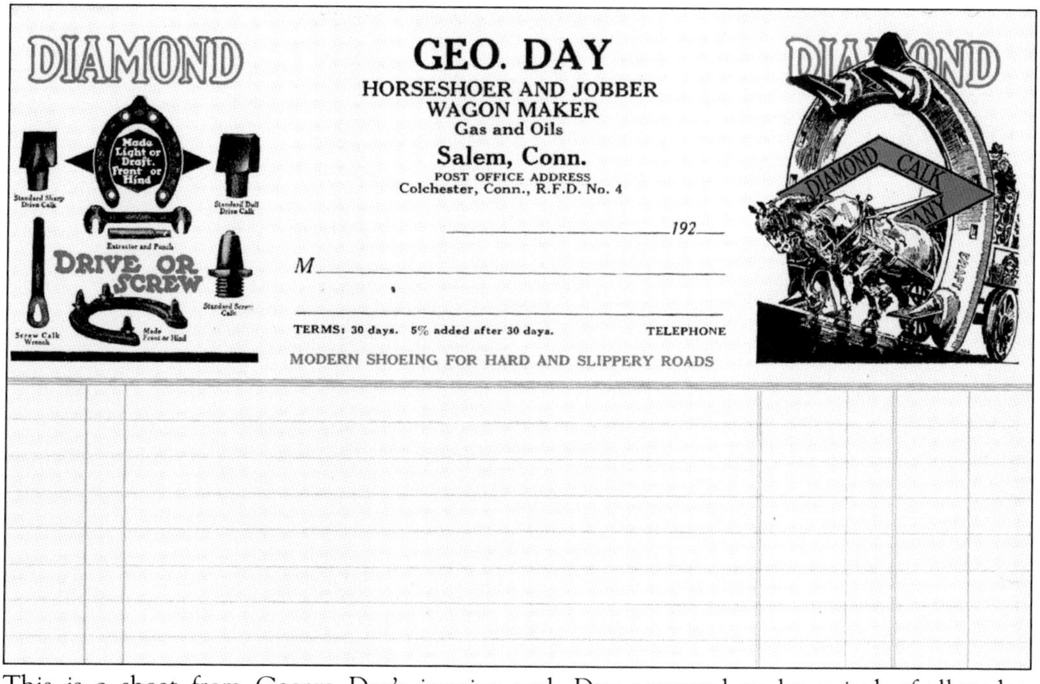

DIAMOND

Made Light or Draft. Front or Hind

Standard Sharp Drive Calk

Standard Dull Drive Calk

Extractor and Punch

DRIVE OR SCREW

Standard Screw Calk

Screw Calk Wrench

Made Front or Hind

GEO. DAY

HORSESHOER AND JOBBER
WAGON MAKER
Gas and Oils

Salem, Conn.

POST OFFICE ADDRESS
Colchester, Conn., R.F.D. No. 4

____________________192___

M________________________________

TERMS: 30 days. 5% added after 30 days. TELEPHONE

MODERN SHOEING FOR HARD AND SLIPPERY ROADS

DIAMOND

DIAMOND CALK

This is a sheet from George Day's invoice pad. Day appeared to be a jack-of-all-trades, blacksmithing, shoeing, wagon making, and he also sold gas and oil. Farmers needed to be able to do a little bit of everything to survive, and in the early days, they were self-reliant. They shared and traded goods and services with other townspeople when needed.

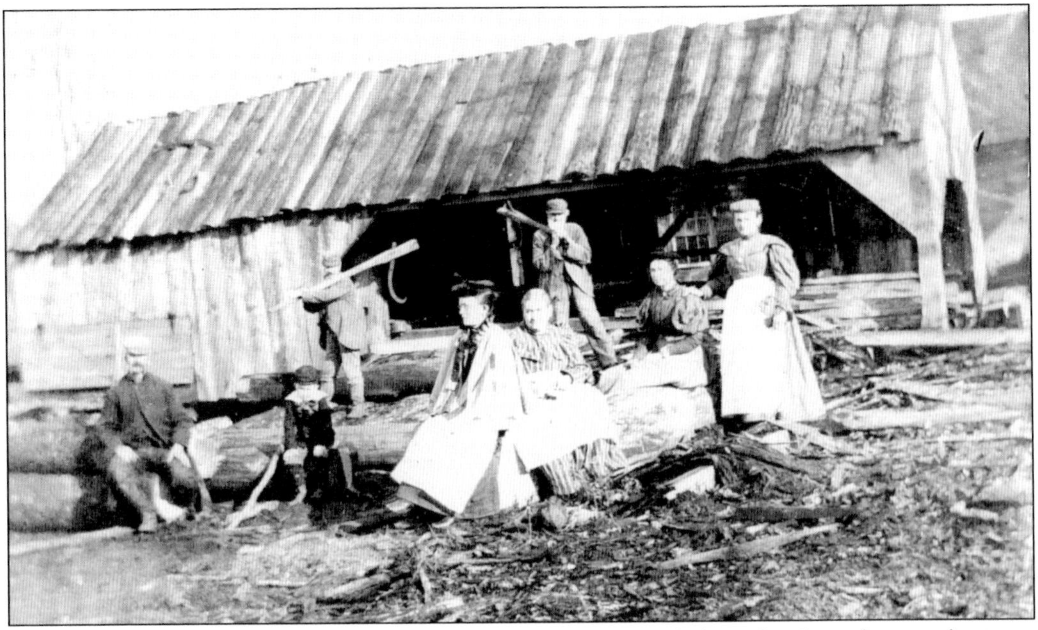

It is not clear exactly when this sawmill started; however, it is believed to have been in business before the town was incorporated in 1819. On a 1854 map, it was owned by T. Fish, and on the 1868 map, it was E. T. Sisson. An old 1869 diary mentions that it was owned by Sisson. Later it became Stillman Clark's sawmill. This photograph shows the Clark family in front of the mill.

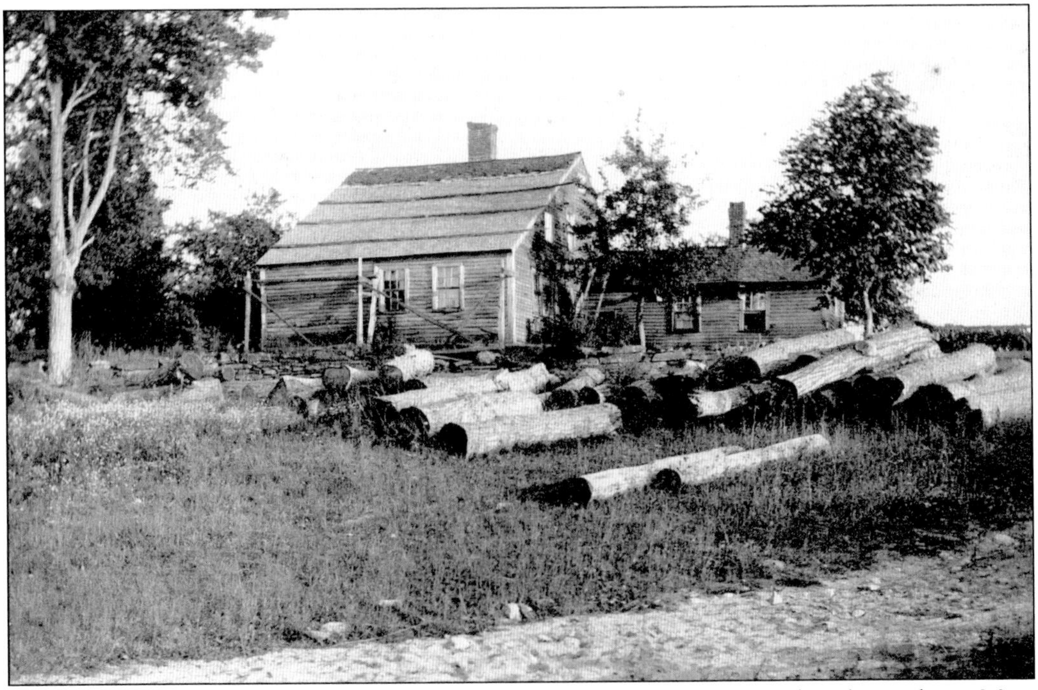

Here is a photograph of the Stillman Clark home with a view of large timbers lying about. Most sawmills were close to a running brook or stream as there was no electricity. Mills were run by waterpower/hydropower. The wood was hewn for building lumber.

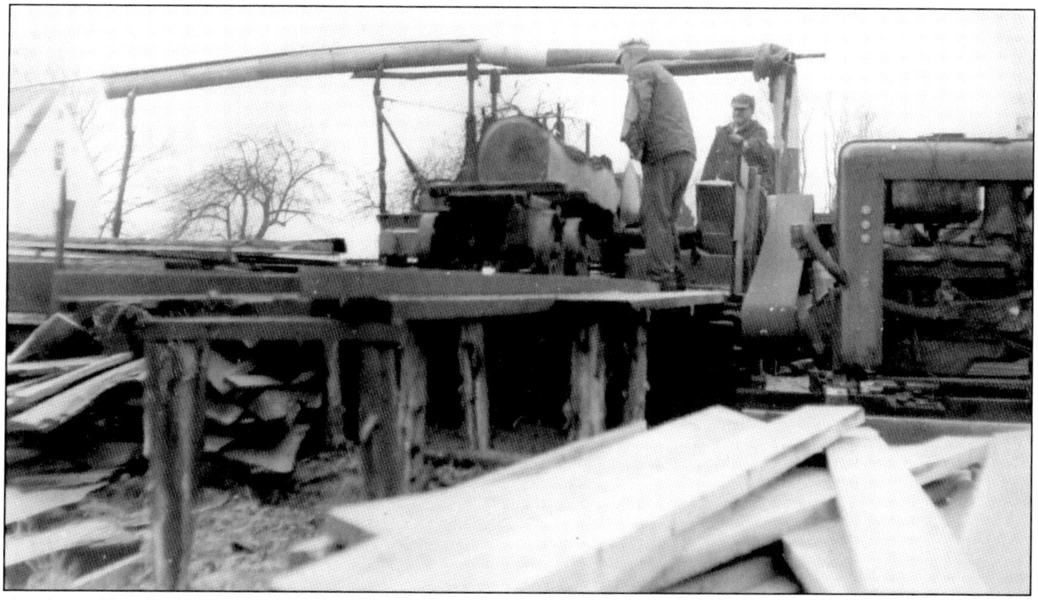

Andrew Zemko's family has been in the lumbering business starting as far back as the 1500s in Siberia. His father began hiring on with companies across the United States and Canada, making railroad ties in the early 1900s. By 1912, Andrew Zemko Sr. was in Connecticut. By 1916, he had moved to Salem and started the family business. The sons, Felix and Andrew, grew up in the business and moved here later from East Haddam. In the 1930s, some of their quality white oaks were used to build navy minesweepers. Competitive chains came in with great prices but at the expense of lower quality lumber. As the small-town dairy farmers feel the strain so do the small family-owned lumberyards.

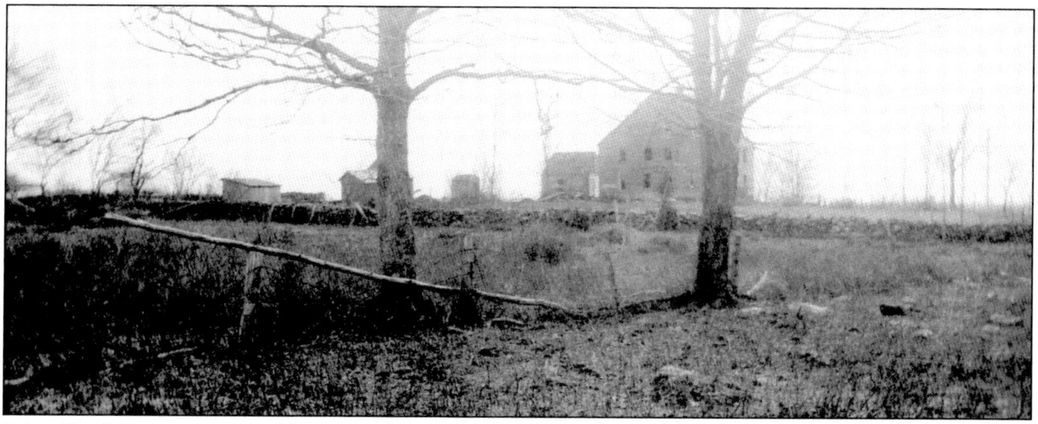

John Dolbeare was a wealthy man from Boston who owned more than 500 acres in Salem and about 2,000 in New London North parish since 1769. He had 24 children and a large estate, which was handed down to his heirs. Samuel and Hannah, a daughter of John Mumford Sr., ran this tavern. There is a small cemetery plot somewhere southeast of the house where Samuel and Hannah are buried. The gravestones and the exact location of the plots have been lost to time. The stones were still there in 1934. This photograph was taken around 1939 facing southwest on Route 82, looking toward Salem Four Corners before it was taken down. There was a pig lot on the Dolbeare property just south of the house on Route 82. Most farmers raised their own pigs for smoking hams and bacon. Sometimes they had a spot right in the chimney of the main house to smoke hams or a smokehouse specifically for smoking and curing meat for the winter.

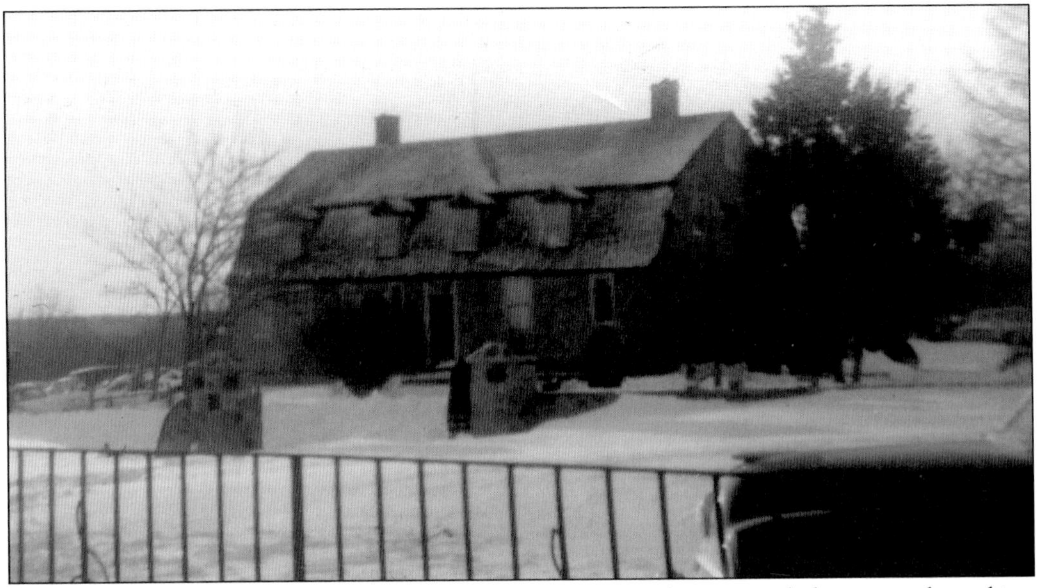

Because of the location of Salem, being between cities, it was always traveled extensively, making taverns a lucrative business. This is Billings Tavern, a gambrel saltbox with gabled dormers and twin chimneys, built around 1783. It was in the Winakor family from 1897 until the mid-1950s, at which time it was abandoned, sold, and moved from Salem in 1990. It was rebuilt in Lyme with an asking price of $1 million. It was located on Forsythe Road. Leo Winakor and Son Used Automobile Parts, a junkyard, operating since 1940, is where the house was located.

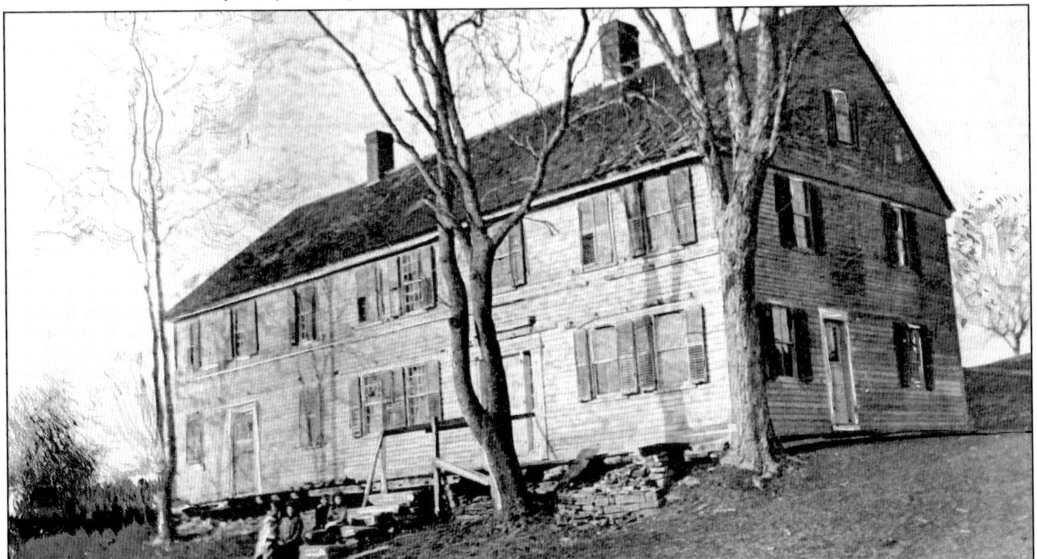

The Strickland Tavern was built by Erasmus Washington in 1795, and some accounts say this is the earliest tollhouse. It was a popular stopping place on the New London Hartford Stage later the New London Hartford Turnpike, or route 85. At one time, it was a hat factory and, another, a tin shop. A Mr. Hall, who owned the house at one time, manufactured tin utensils and peddled them in his wagon around the countryside. Half of the house was taken down and is still standing just south of Rattlesnake Ledge, on the right-hand side looking north toward Colchester, now painted red. The tavern part is the portion that was saved.

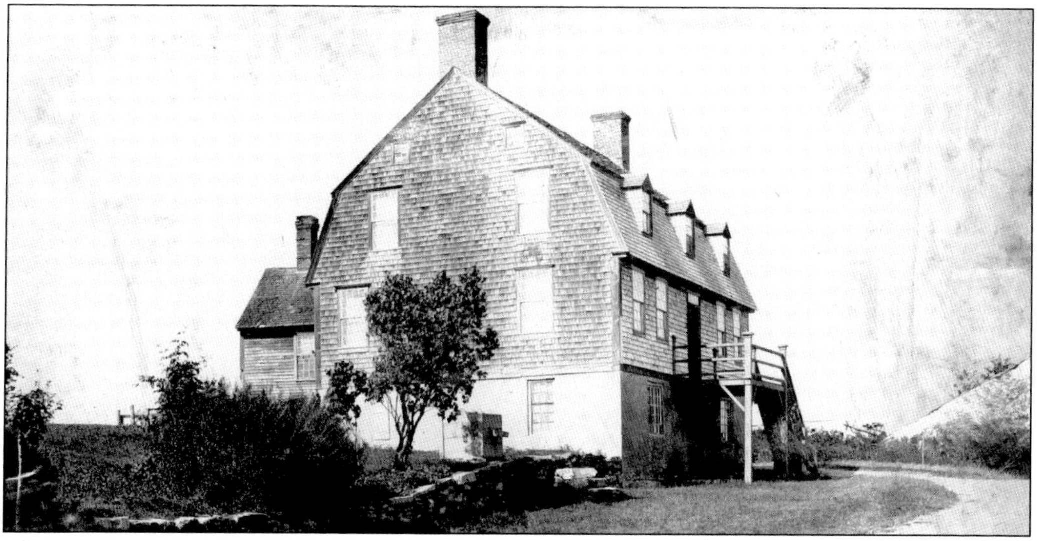

Bland Tavern, built around 1810 at the corner of Routes 82 and 354, was the first stop for changing horses on the stagecoach stop from New London to Hartford. In 1833, Pres. Andrew Jackson (1829–1837) stayed the night, which drew much attention. The president gave a speech from the porch to folks in the field. The field then became known as Jackson's Field, located across from the Bland Tavern on Route 82, which is used presently as a cornfield.

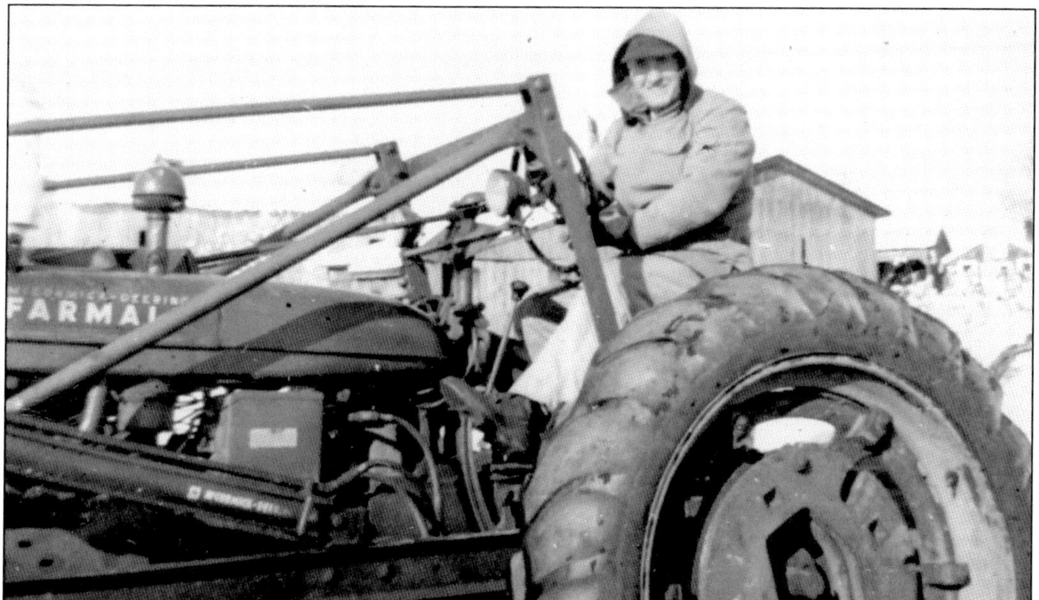

The Gadbois family purchased the Bland Tavern property in 1934 and created a thriving dairy farm known as Maegog (a combination of the names Marion and George) from an original 10-cow operation. It was a working farm for over 60 years and recently has become the last dairy farm in the town of Salem. Stuart, a son of George Gadbois, took over the business in 1973 when his father retired. John, another son of George, joined his father in 1975 after graduation from Norwich Free Academy. At the peak of the business, 236 heifers were utilized. In March 2004, 180 Holsteins were sold to a Vermont farmer as the farm got ready to fully stop operations as a dairy farm.

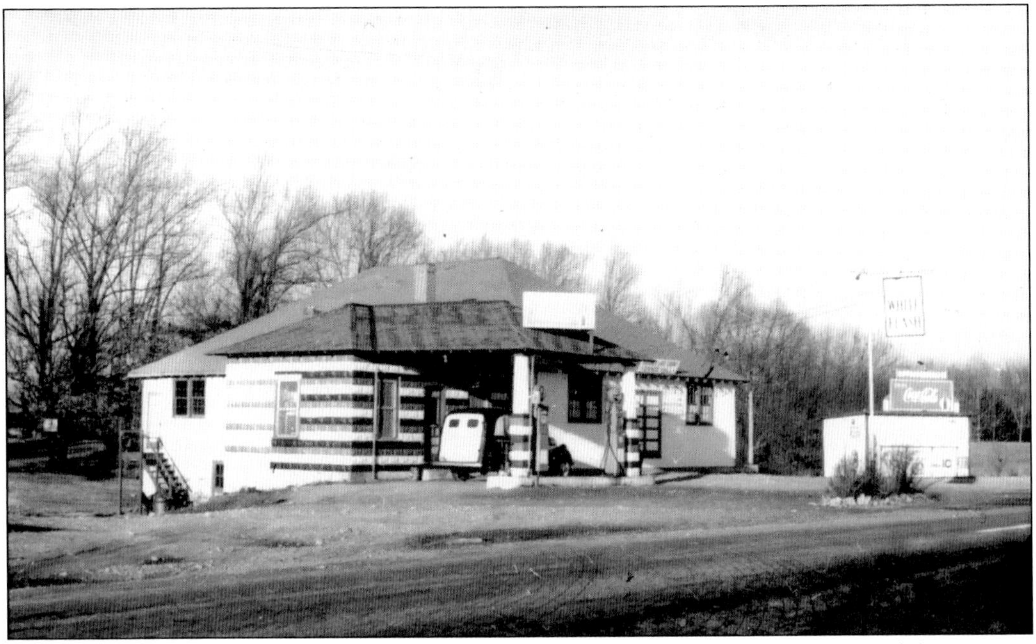

Pulsifer's Store across from Salem Feed and Grain is now an antiques shop. Mr. Puslifer ran it as an auction hall and store. Prior to that it was a dance hall during the 1930s.

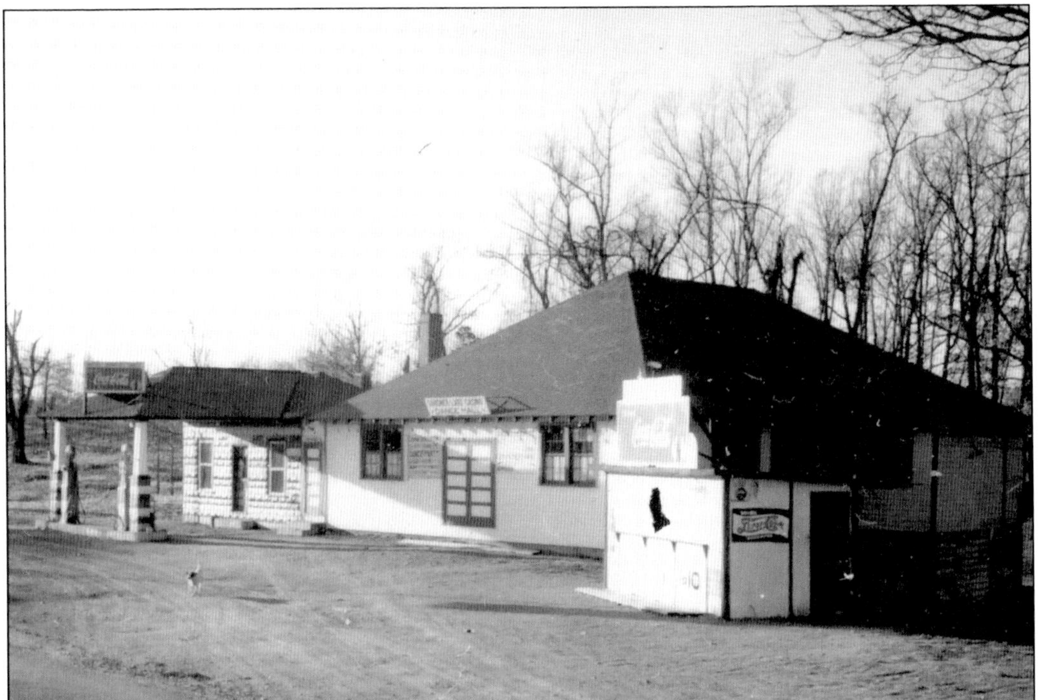

A variety of dances were probably enjoyed at what was once the dance hall. Square dances, waltzes, and polka parties probably highlighted the lives of rural Salemites. Perhaps the dances inspired courting, as many young men would ask a young lady for a dance. This is Pulsifer's from a slightly different angle.

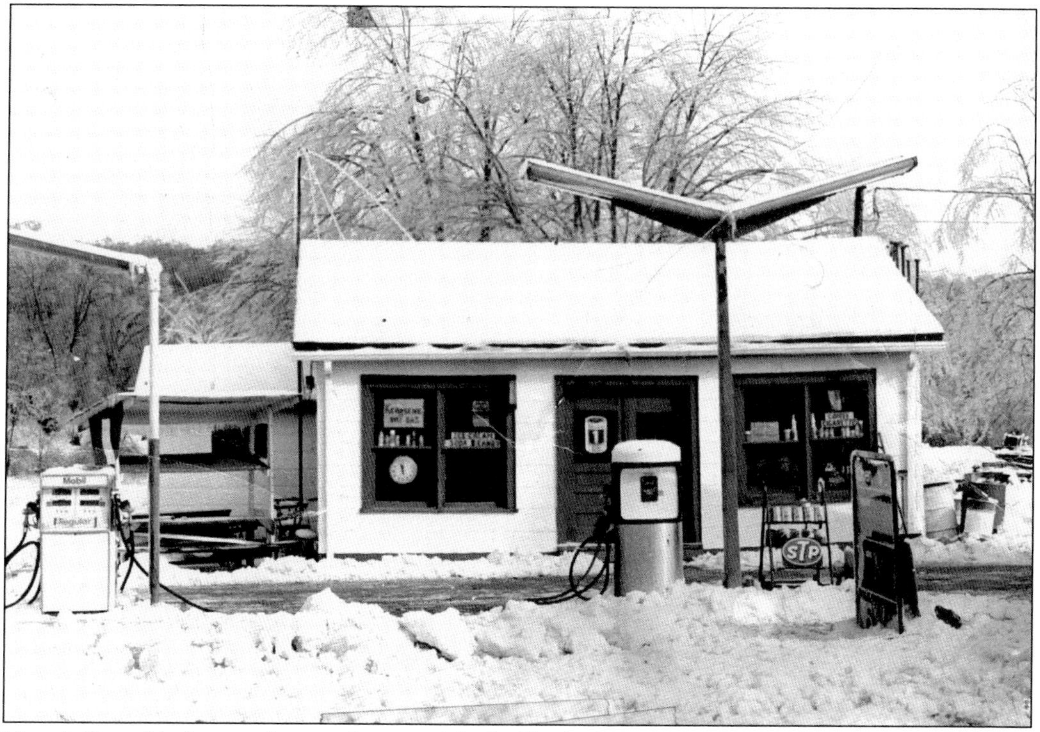

Here is Smuckler's store, later to become Maple Shade Grocery Store, as it looked in the 1950s.

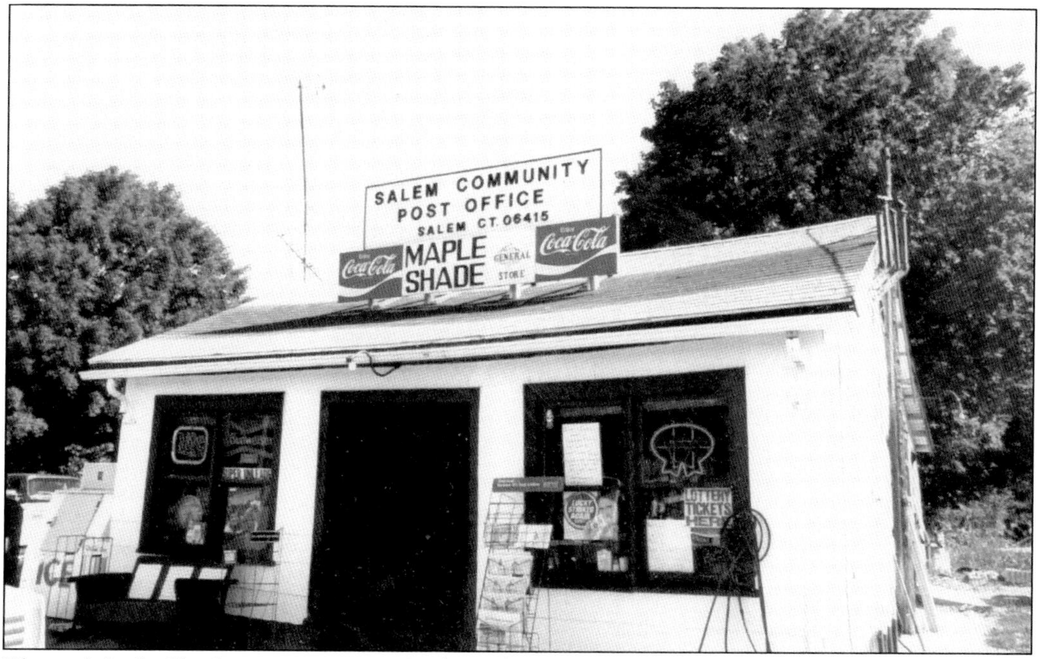

This is Maple Shade as seen in 1983 when the post office was added. After 78 years, Salem again has a post office. It is a popular store for campers, as it is not too far from Witch Meadow Campground and Salem Farms Campground.

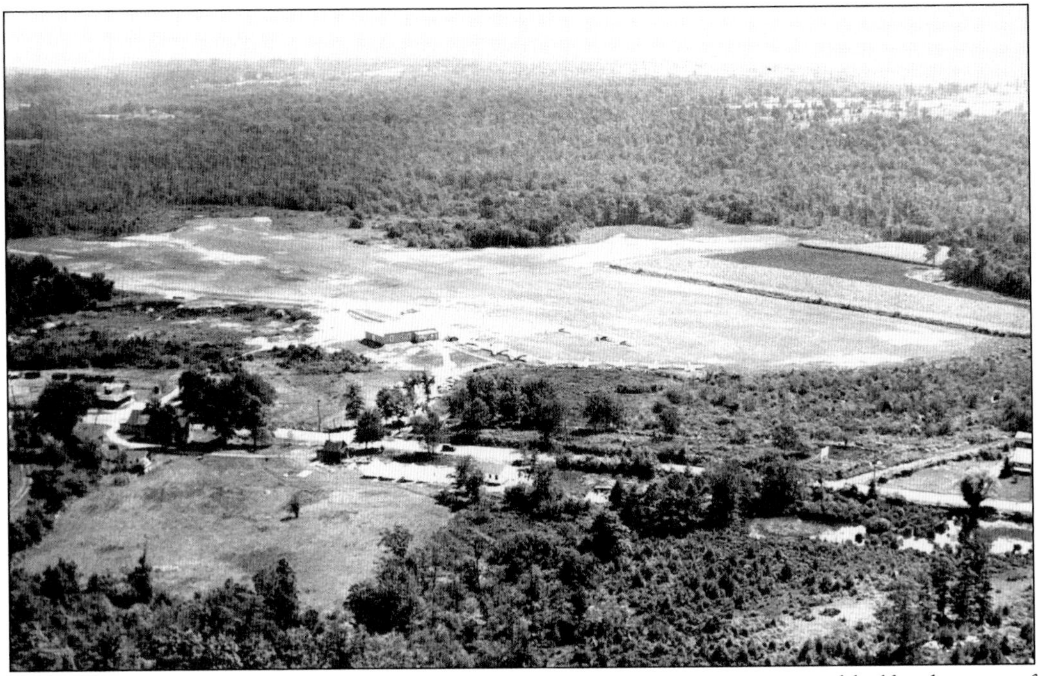

This aerial view shows the Salem Airport in 1946 on Route 82, just one and half miles east of Salem Four Corners. During the war, a small airport had to be 10 miles away from the coast. Raymond Gannoe leased the land from the Arrowitz family, who had used the land as a chicken farm. It is now an airport for remote-control planes.

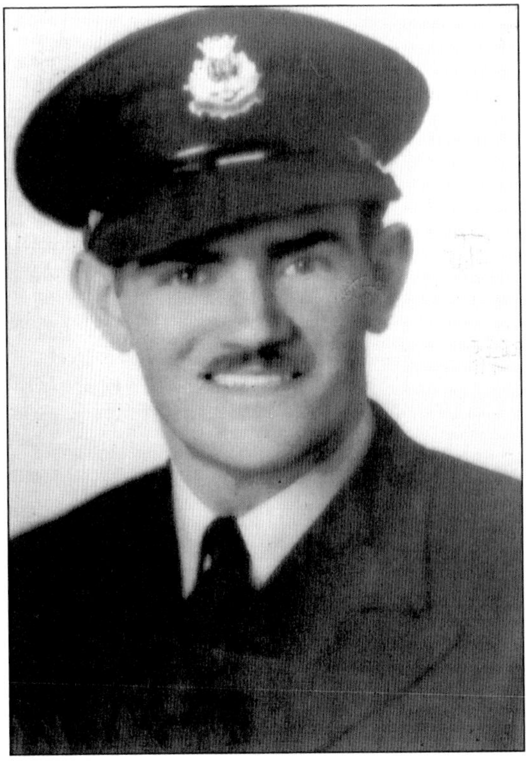

When Raymond Gannoe left the Royal Air Command in 1994, he decided he wanted to be a pilot in Boston; however, he realized it was like driving a bus in the sky. He enjoyed flying the smaller planes, and before World War II, he had operated a small airport in Southington in 1939. He decided to open up his own airport once again with the financial help of Paul Dustin and James T. Moore.

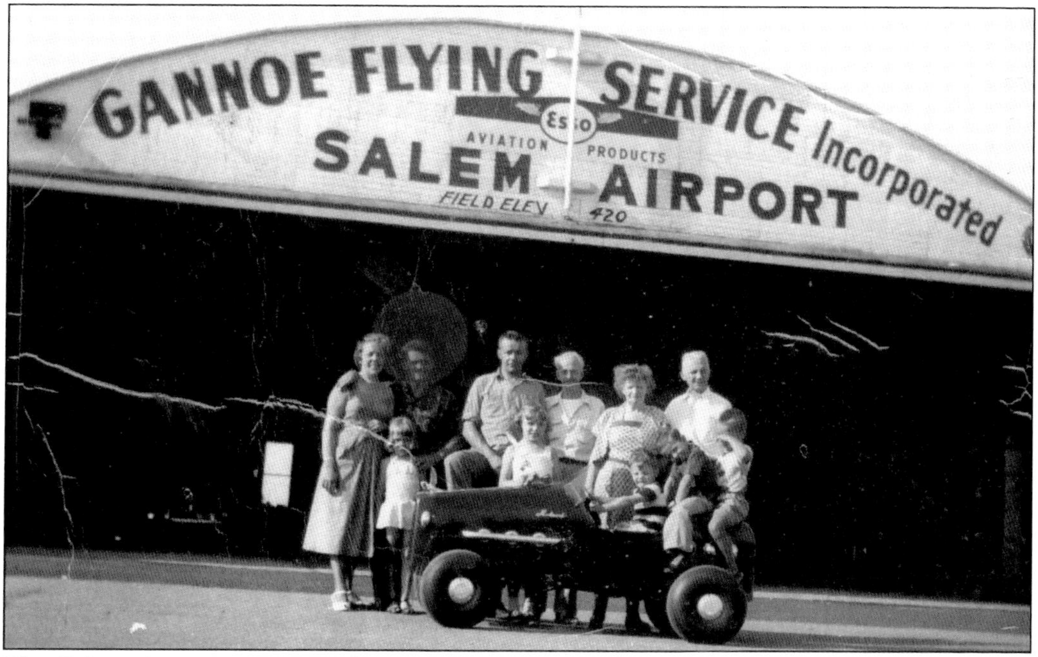

The Salem Airport was opened in 1944. In 1947, with government sponsorship, Raymond Gannoe turned the airport into a flying school, and it became known as Salem Airport and Gannoe Flying Service Incorporated. The first chopper to land at Salem Airport in the summer of 1946 was the HAT, which stood for Helicopter Air Transport Incorporated. This must have been an exciting time for Salemites that were interested in flying. This is a view of the front of the hangar with Gannoe second from the left with family and some of the workers.

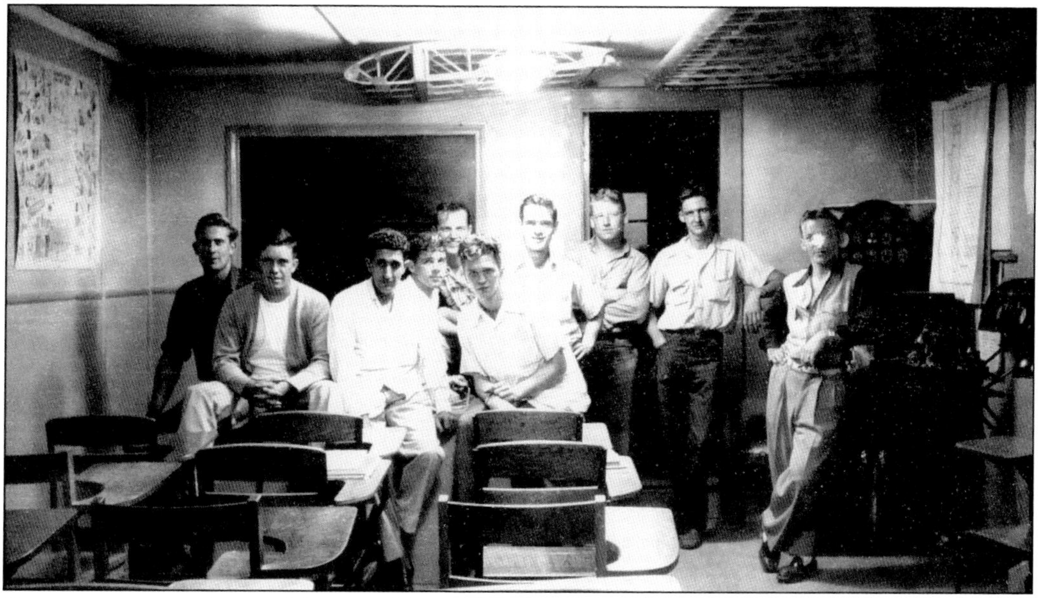

Here are some students of Gannoe Flying Service Incorporated. Paul Zarinder of the Putnam branch of the New London Savings Bank was one of the flight instructors. In 1949, the government rescinded on its support of the flying school, and the airport fizzled out and closed in 1951.

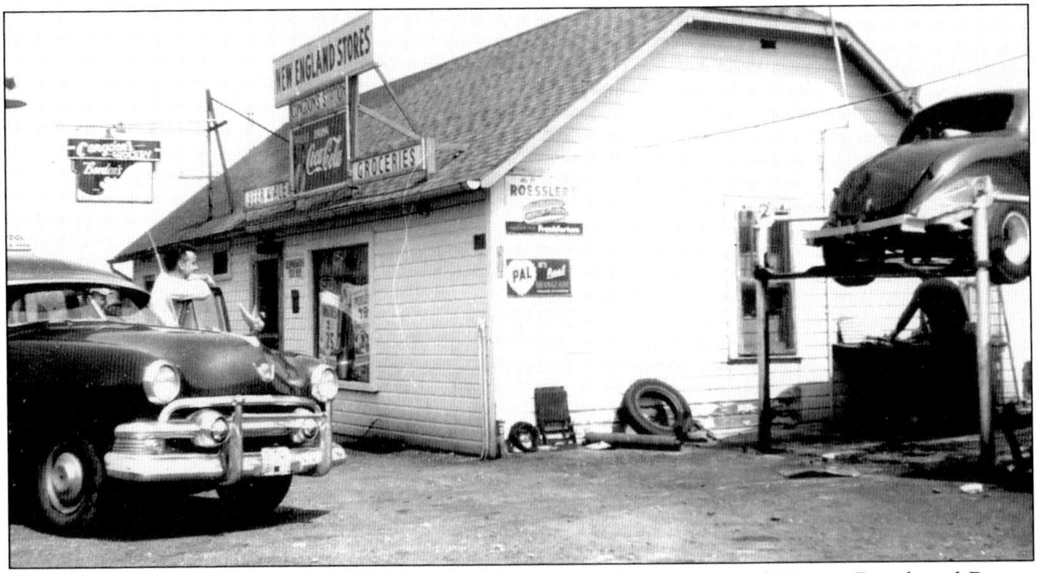

Congdon's Grocery Store, pictured in 1952, was located on corner of Witter Road and Route 354. It was purchased by Edith and Bill Congdon in mid-1940s. Edith and Bill lived in the apartment in back of the store with their three children, Carolyn, Bill Jr. (Buster), and Roger, until the mid-1950s. Edith ran the store, and Bill added on the garage. In the photograph, Bill built the race car that is sitting on a lift. Ed Snarski bids adieu from his sporty vehicle.

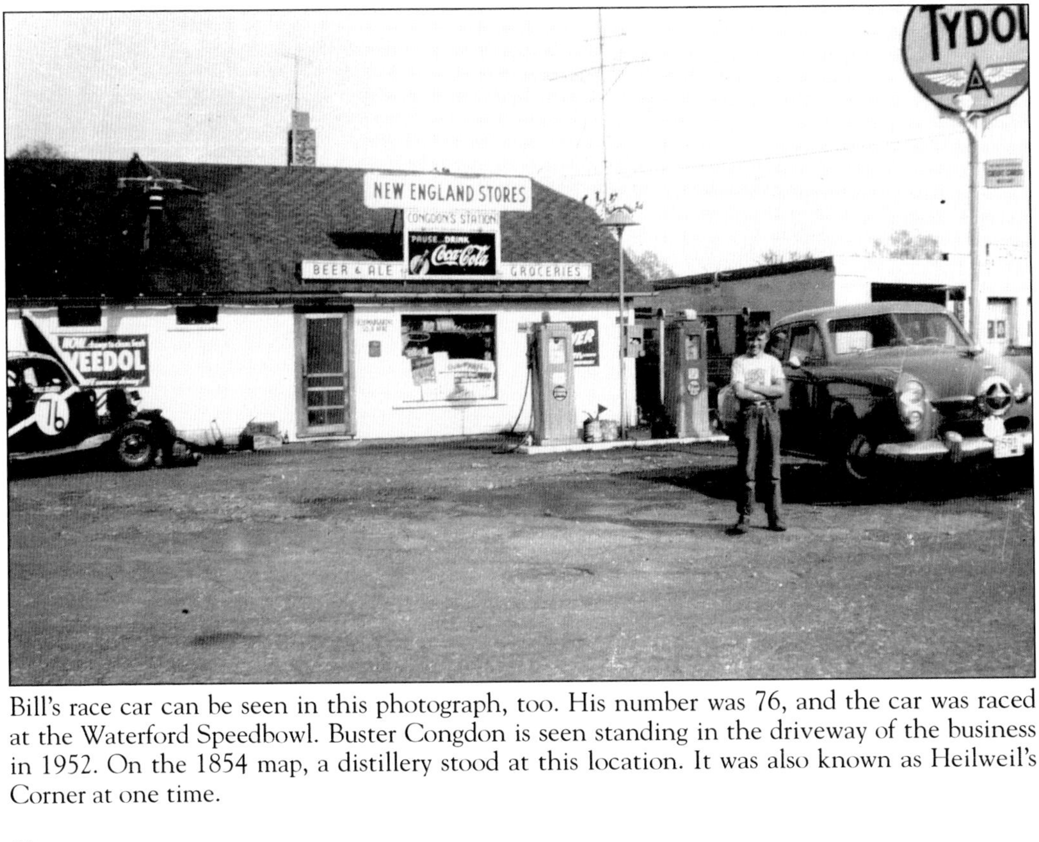

Bill's race car can be seen in this photograph, too. His number was 76, and the car was raced at the Waterford Speedbowl. Buster Congdon is seen standing in the driveway of the business in 1952. On the 1854 map, a distillery stood at this location. It was also known as Heilweil's Corner at one time.

Six

Gardner Lake

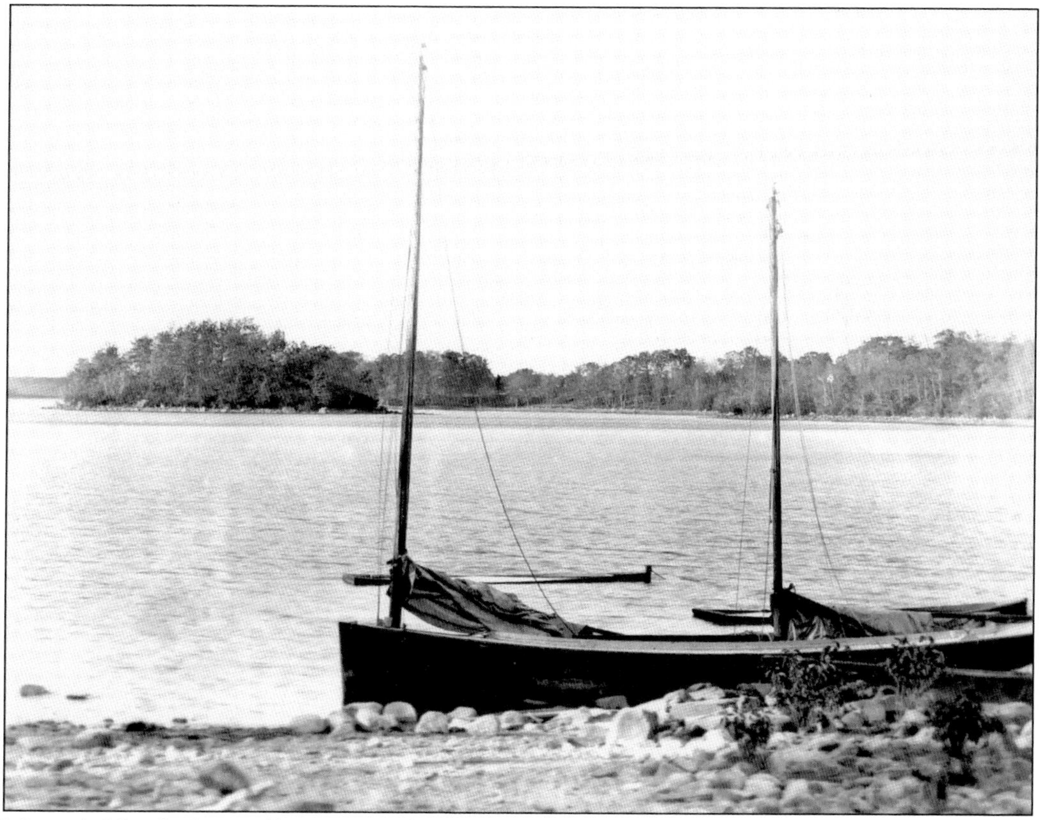

Minnie's Island, the smallest state park in Connecticut, is located in Gardner Lake and actually lies half in Salem and half in Montville. The one-acre island is on the south side of Gardner Lake about 100 yards off the east shore. It is a popular place for boaters to picnic, but no fires are allowed. Oramel Whittlesey owned the island at one time and named it after his niece, whose nickname was Minnie. Minnie's Island can be seen to the left in the background of this photograph.

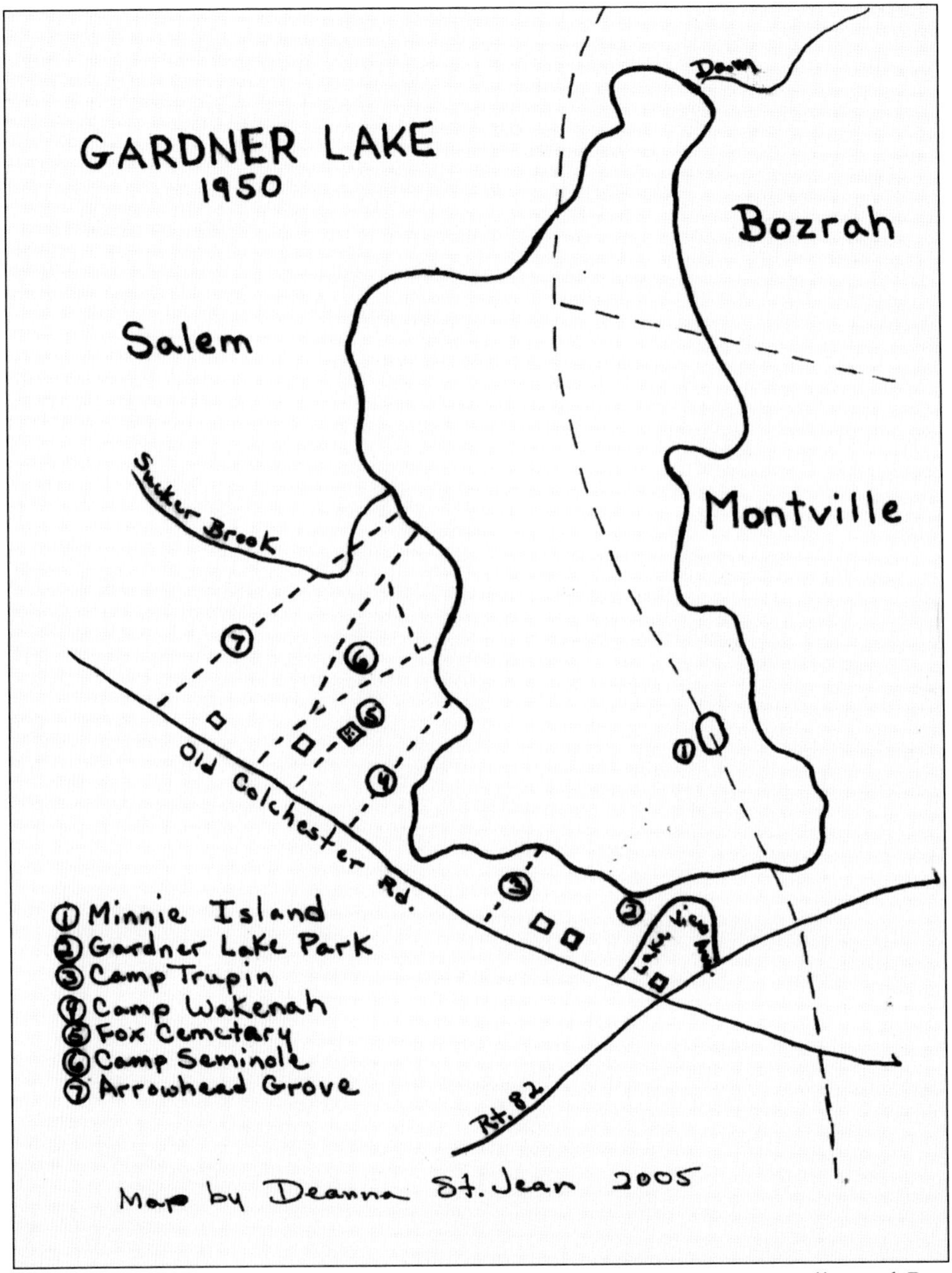

Gardner Lake, located in southeastern Connecticut, borders Salem, Montville, and Bozrah. Gardner Lake was an attraction for visitors as well as locals, and there were many camps. Large war canoes, which carried about 20 children and two adults, a few sailboats, and small fishing boats, with a seven-and-a-half-horsepower limit were the main vessels allowed on the lake. The lake was also used for ice cutting and ice fishing. In the 1960s, most of the camps were sold, and the building boom started around the lake. Campground owners requested higher speed limits to allow for speedboats and water-skiers. A state boat launch was added, and summer homes were winterized. Here is map of the Salem side of Gardner Lake. All that is not marked on the Salem side was privately owned.

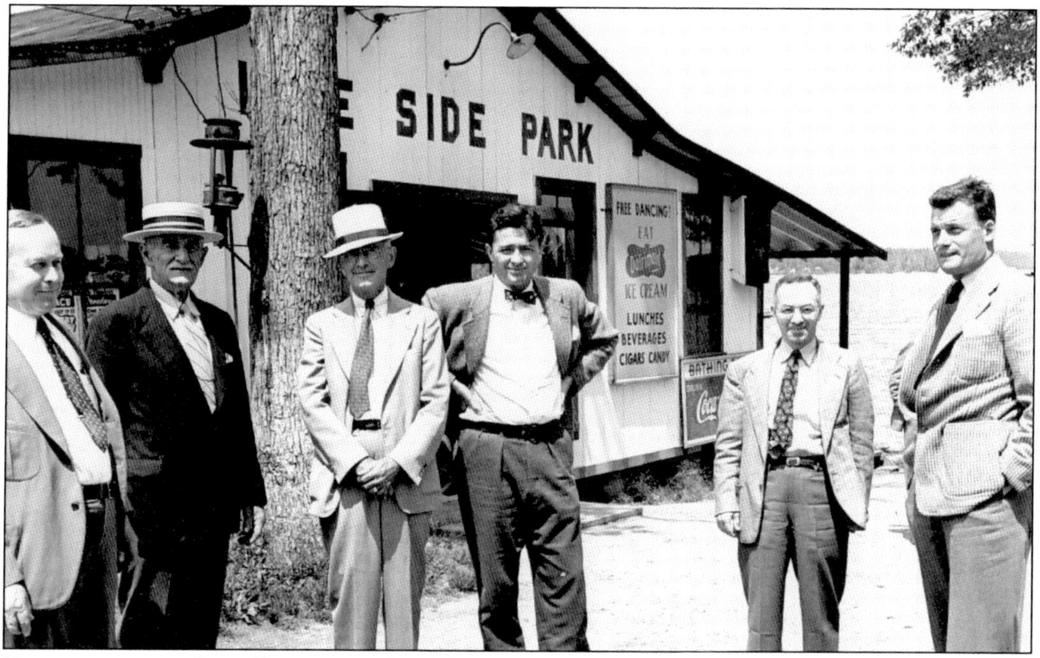

Some men are gathered here around 1935. Mr. Brown owned the Lakeside Park Pavilion, which would later be called Gardner Lake Park when owned by Samuel Shecter. It burnt down in the mid-1960s. It was later owned by Carmen Bolardo and Donald Bordeau Sr. The state now owns the property but has not opened it to the public as of yet due to state budget cuts.

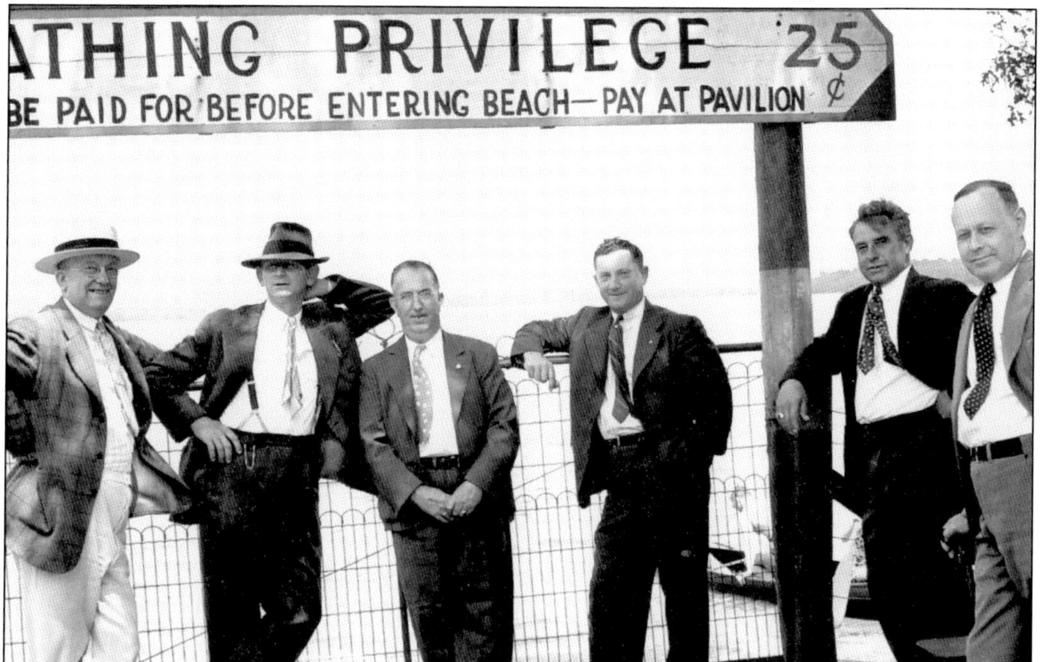

This is the entrance to Lakeside Park beach around 1935. The 25¢ bathing privileges at the park lasted through the 1950s. By 1998, it cost $2.50 per person. The beach, lake, and canoe in the background appear to be just beyond the gate.

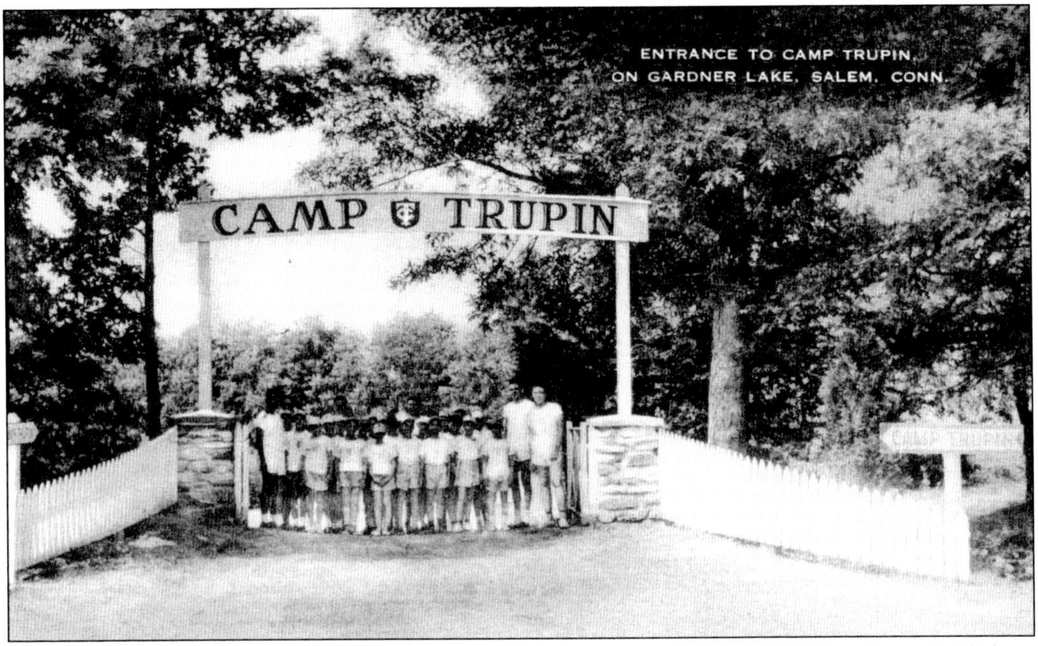

Camp Trupin was in operation from the 1920s until the 1960s. Mr. And Mrs. Trupin and their two daughters were native New Yorkers who owned a summer home in Salem. They lived in the house next to what is now the boat launch. This was a coed camp for ages 7 to 15. There were separate lodging quarters for the girls and boys.

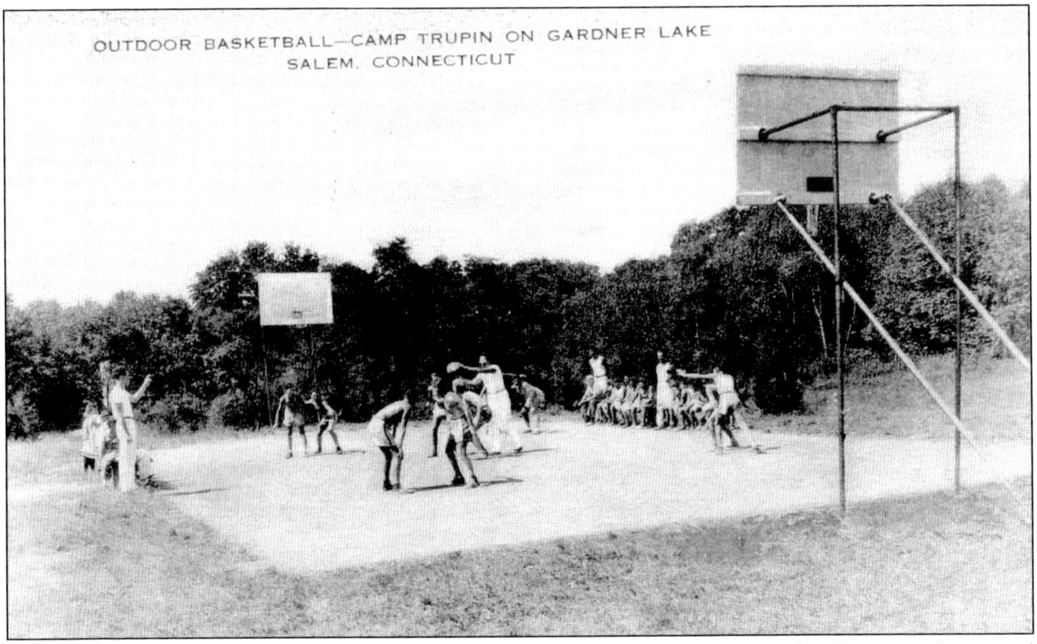

Camp Trupin was specifically a camp for Jewish children from New York who came here and spent the entire summer swimming, canoeing, playing basketball, volleyball, tennis, and doing arts and crafts. War canoes were raced across the lake in competition with some of the other camps on the lake. In this picture postcard, the boys are playing a heated game of basketball.

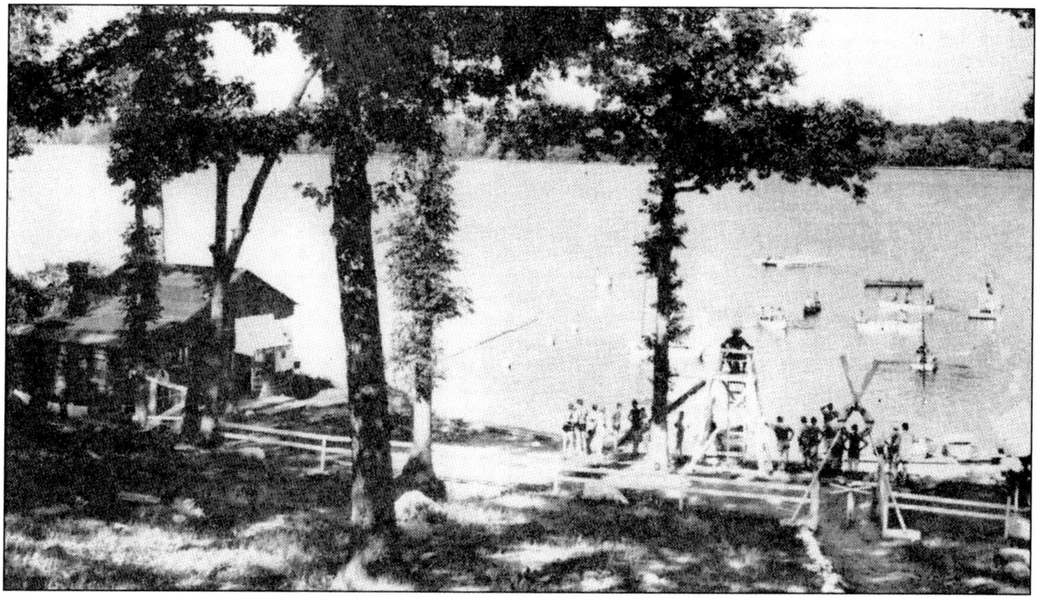

This is a postcard waterfront view of Lake Wakenah, the eighth-oldest Boy Scouts camp in America. It opened in 1918 and closed in 2005 and was sold. The camp included a large clubhouse/dining hall and cabins. Scouting weekends, overnighters, day camp, and award ceremonies were popular activities for the Boys Scouts at this camp. Official flag retirement ceremonies were performed on the shore. Awards activities were viewed by the parents from log bleachers set on a hill facing the lake.

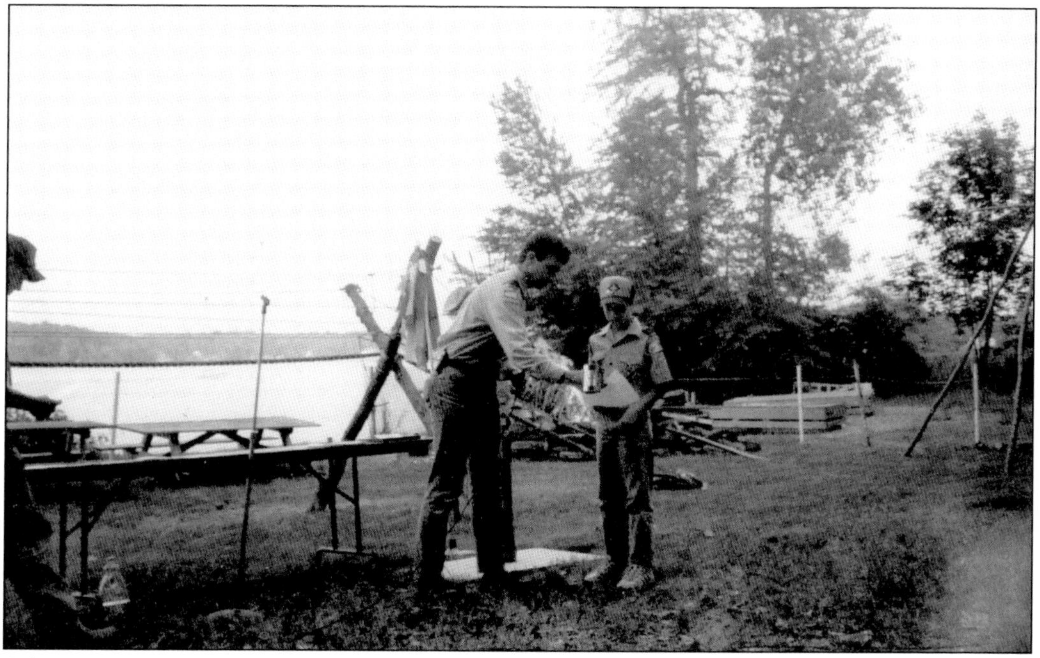

Salem scoutmaster Jeffrey Moore presents an award to his son Jeremy Moore for crossing the bridge from Cub Scouts to Boy Scouts at Camp Wakenah around 1997. Awards and ceremonies have taken place at Camp Wakenah for nearly 87 years. Note the ceremonial fire in the background that burns at all Boy Scouts events.

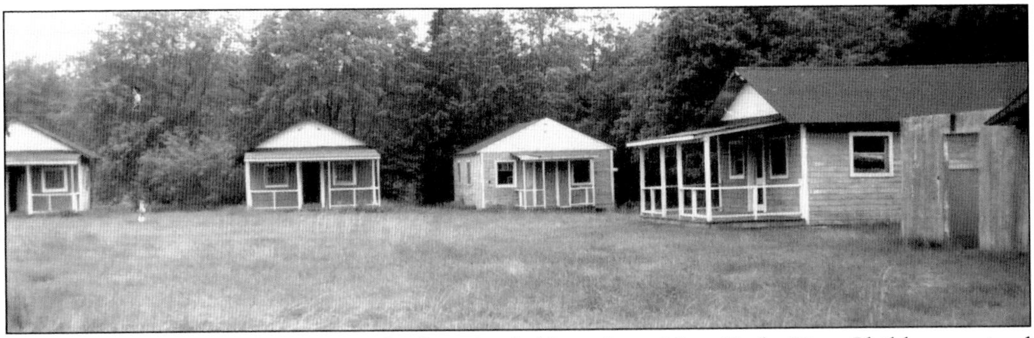

Camp Seminole was also a camp for Jewish children from New York City. Children arrived by charter bus in June and left the last week of August. The camp was started by Henry and Octavia Kendall. The Kendalls lived in Salem most of the year and wintered in Florida. The camp was divided into to two separate camps, a boys' camp and a girls' camp, each having their own waterfront with a patch of woods with about 1,000 feet separating the two. Here are several of the cabins in the boys' camp.

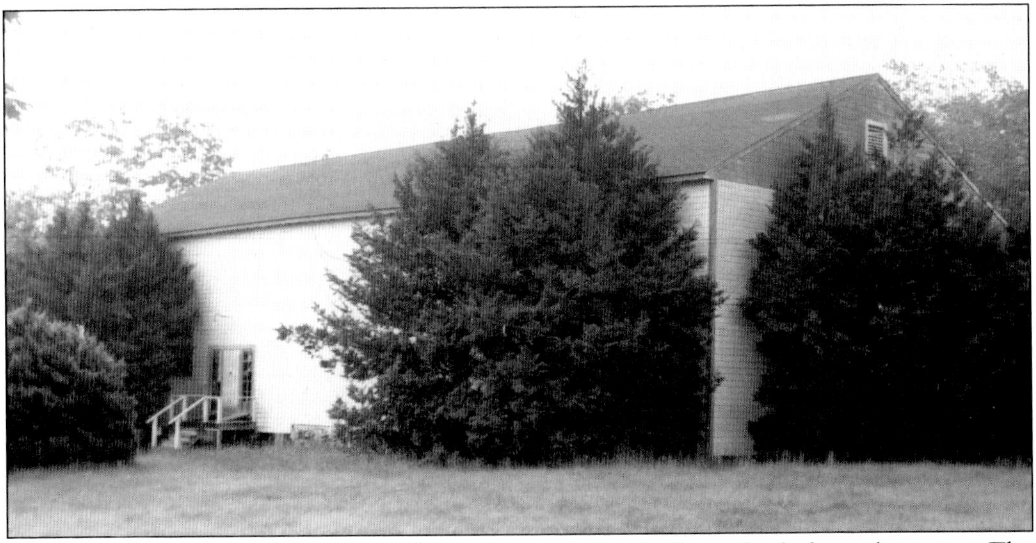

Here is a photograph of the Camp Seminole recreation hall, set back from the water. The building was utilized by both girls and boys, especially on rainy days. The building had a stage and piano and an indoor basketball court. It was probably used at night as well. Besides regular camping activities, horseback riding was also available. The entire camp was sold to a Mr. Rabino, who ran the camp for several years before selling the girls' camp to developers, then becoming what is known today as Forest Drive. The boys' camp was sold to Joseph Leitao, who turned it into Indian Field Campground. It has been sold several times since.

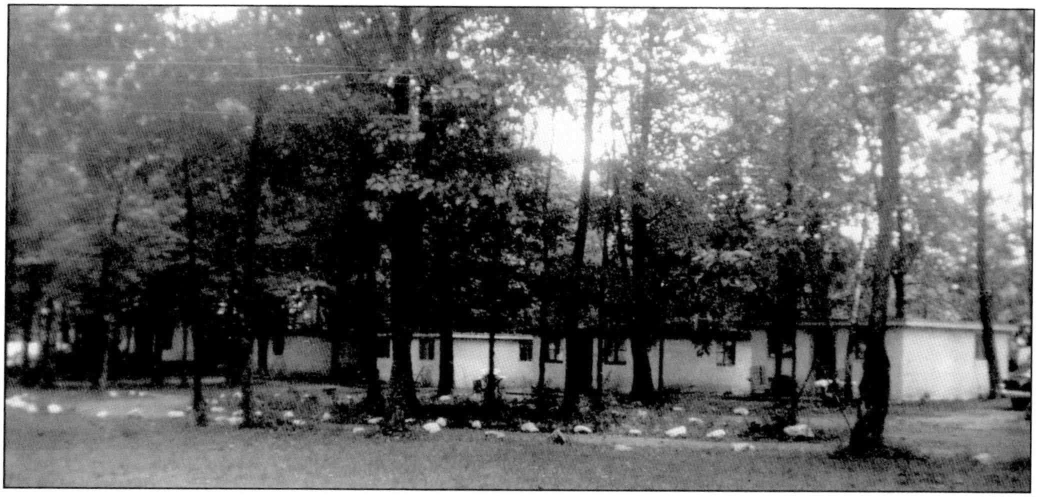

Joseph Eugene and James Thomas Moore purchased this property and one wooden cottage in 1947. Four cement cottages were built, and all were rented by the following year. Luella Moore named the cottages Arrowhead Grove for the arrowheads that were found along the shore and the beautiful setting of trees. The cottages were rented by the week, the month, or the season. Since there were no bathrooms in the individual cottages, there was a large communal bathroom divided for ladies and for gentlemen that also included showers. Each cottage had a kitchen, one bedroom, and a pull-out couch on each end of the living room. The cottages were sold in 1954 to Mr. and Mrs. Bailey of Hartford and then again in 1972 to Charlotte and Bernie Stone. The cottages are now owned individually in a co-op.

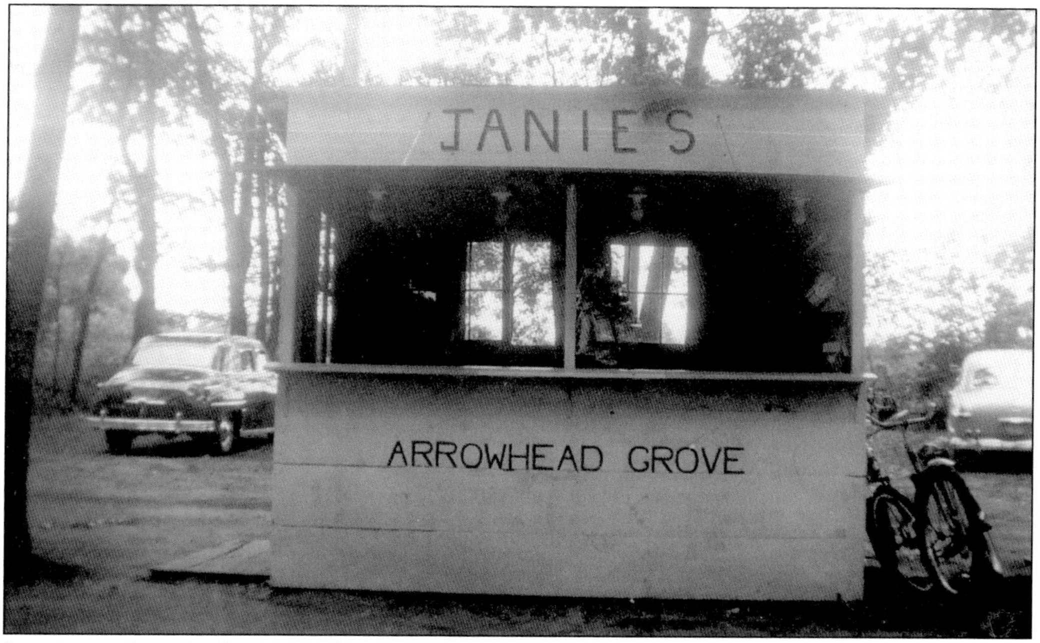

Janie's stand was built to provide access to a telephone for the vacationers at Arrowhead Grove. The eleven-year-old Janet Moore, daughter of Joseph T. Moore, saw this as an opportunity to sell chips, soda, and other snacks to the campers. The young entrepreneur occasionally needed a break, so she allowed her two sisters, Deanna and Peggy, to watch the stand. It was more than likely that in Janie's absence, Deanna and Peggy had devoured some of the profits.

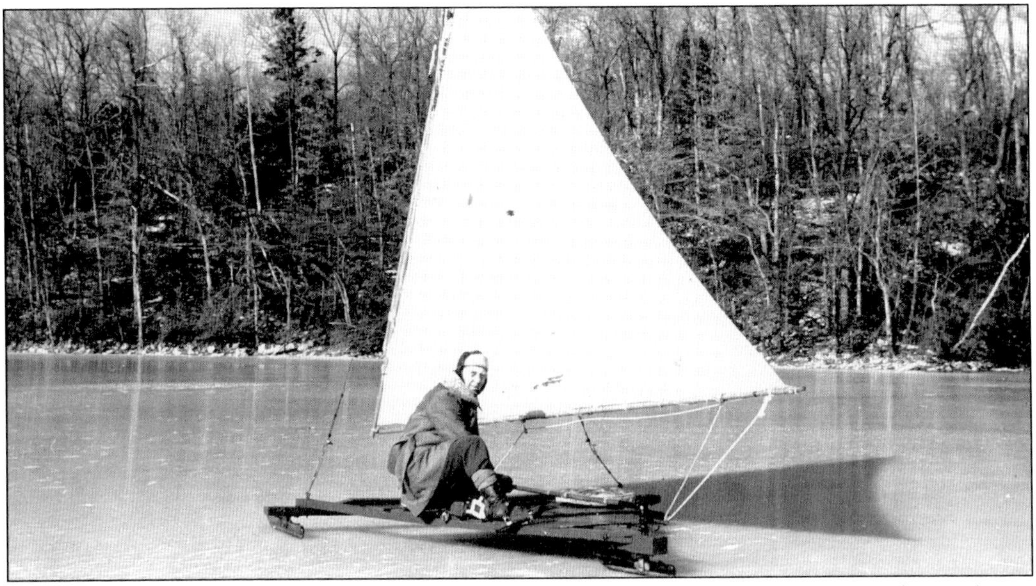

Bill Ricker, a retired pharmacist from Norwich, loved ice sailing, "flying" across Gardner Lake on his iceboat, as shown in this photograph. For this reason he was known as the "Flying Druggist" of Gardner Lake. At his Salem summer cottage on Gardner Lake, he also spent the summers canoeing. Unfortunately he drowned near Minnie's Island in January 1953 while sailing his boat on thin ice that gave way.

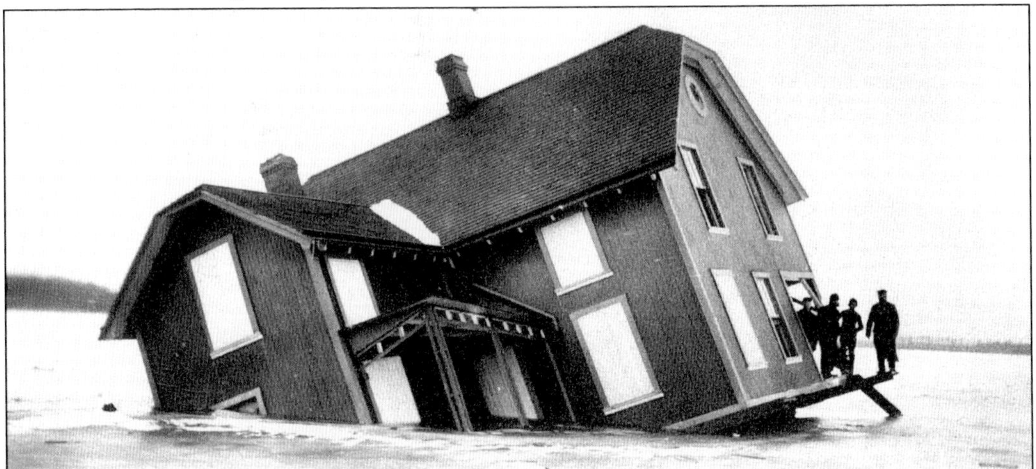

In the winter of 1895, Thomas LeCount hired a Mr. Woodsmansee of Norwich to move his two-and-a-half-story, 28-ton house, fully furnished, from his lot on Gardner Lake to another spot on the lake's east side about a half mile away. After the 18 draft horses pulled the house out about 100 yards onto the lake, it got stuck. As temperatures got warmer and a mill on the other side began draining water from the lake, rendering the ice fragile, the house wedged into the ice farther. It soon began to sink. All effort was made to remove most of the furniture, so only a stove, sideboard, and piano remained. Folks came from all over to view the "house on the lake." There was fishing from the upstairs and ice-skating through the hallways. LeCount sued Woodsmansee and received $1,500 in a settlement. LeCount died at 48 years old. In the spring of that year, the house sank to the bottom, where it remains to this day. Fishermen still can hear the faint tinkling of piano keys on a quiet day.

Seven

FAIRY LAKE FARM

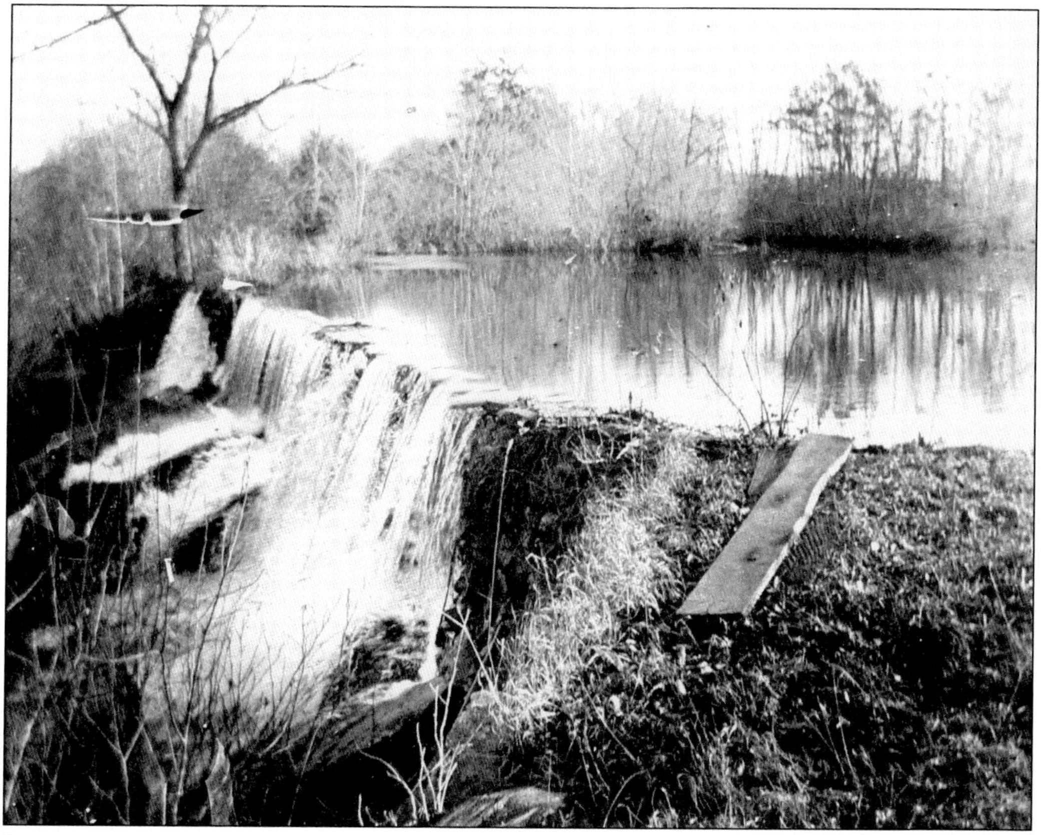

Between 1917 and 1924, Frederick Rawolle purchased 10 farms amounting to 2,800 acres of land completely surrounding Mountain Lake and Fairy Lake. This land, once called Paugwonk, had once been owned by Sanhop, a Niantic sachem, Chappattoe, a Mohegan, and another, a kinsman of Uncas. Frederick Rawolle amassed a fortune in a glycerin-like substance that was used to fracture oil wells. With this fortune, he set sights and succeeded in building his own hydroelectric plant to light his estate on Maynard Hill with views of Long Island Sound. Prior to the Fairy Lake Farm, this area had a candlewick factory owned by Jesse Maynard. Sixty feet above and 450 feet away from the powerhouse, water was pumped in through large pipes from Mill Pond, also known as Lilly Pond. A 50-horsepower Pelton waterwheel rotated at 1,200 revolutions per minute. Coupled to the GE generator, it created 2,300 volts. Moving all equipment was not an easy task, so much of the time, it was moved on skids after snowfall. This is the Mill Pond dam next to Fairy Lake.

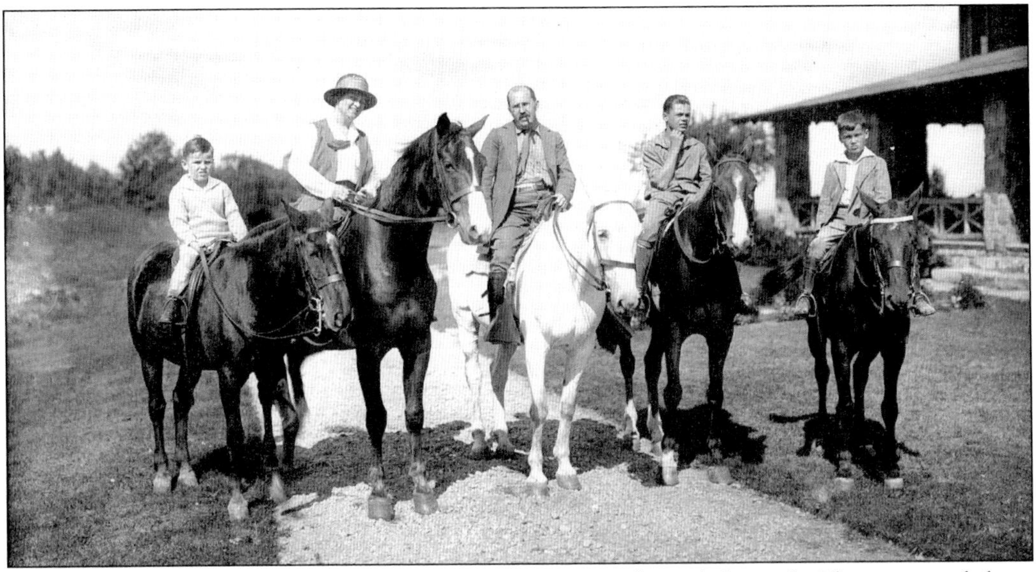

On the road in front of the "Big House" is Frederic Rawolle with his wife, Florence, and three boys, from left to right, Charles, Frank, and Freddy. This main house had two master bedrooms with bathrooms, two guest rooms with a bath, two sleeping porches, a kitchen, pantry, laundry room, office area, foyer with a fireplace, and large living room with a fireplace that could burn four-foot logs. Deck beams of sailing ships were used for the 40-foot ceiling beams and the mantel over the fireplace. "Chop your own wood and it will warm you twice" was carved into the mantel.

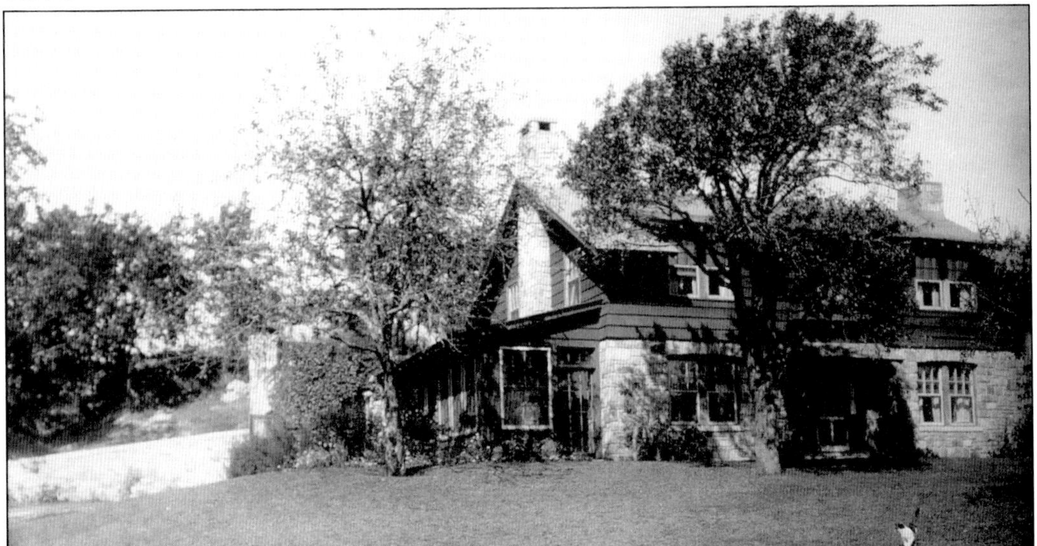

John D. Fraser was the first superintendent and managed the place before he took ill and died a year later. Fraser had cleared acres of land, helped start the famous herd of Ayrshires, and built a road to Rawolle's estate atop Maynard Hill. Later William Brill, who early in 1920 had installed the 50-horsepower hydroelectric plant, became superintendent. A couple hundred feet away and below the main house is the superintendent's home, pictured here. There was an apple orchard and woodshed to the right. The woodshed was destroyed, and some of the apple trees were lost in the Hurricane of 1938. Not too shabby, is it?

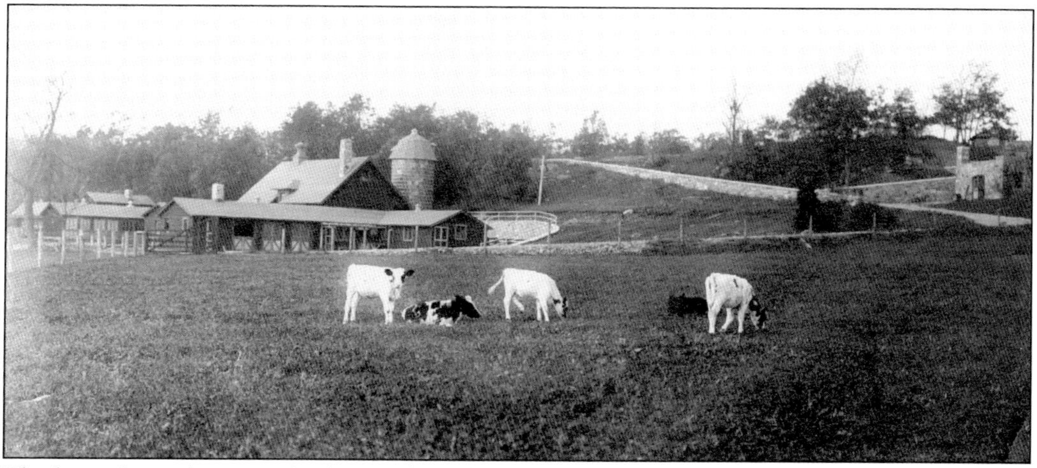

The barn shown here was built into the side of a hill. A ramp was built behind the silo so that hay wagons could drive directly in the hayloft. Efficiency was the key to a successful farm, and Rawolle made sure his was very efficient. The power was turned on by remote control. He had washing machines, mangles for ironing clothes, two large electric stoves, refrigeration, and heating and cooling systems. He lit up Fairy Lake for the local hockey team, the Bears, that would play at Madison Square Garden.

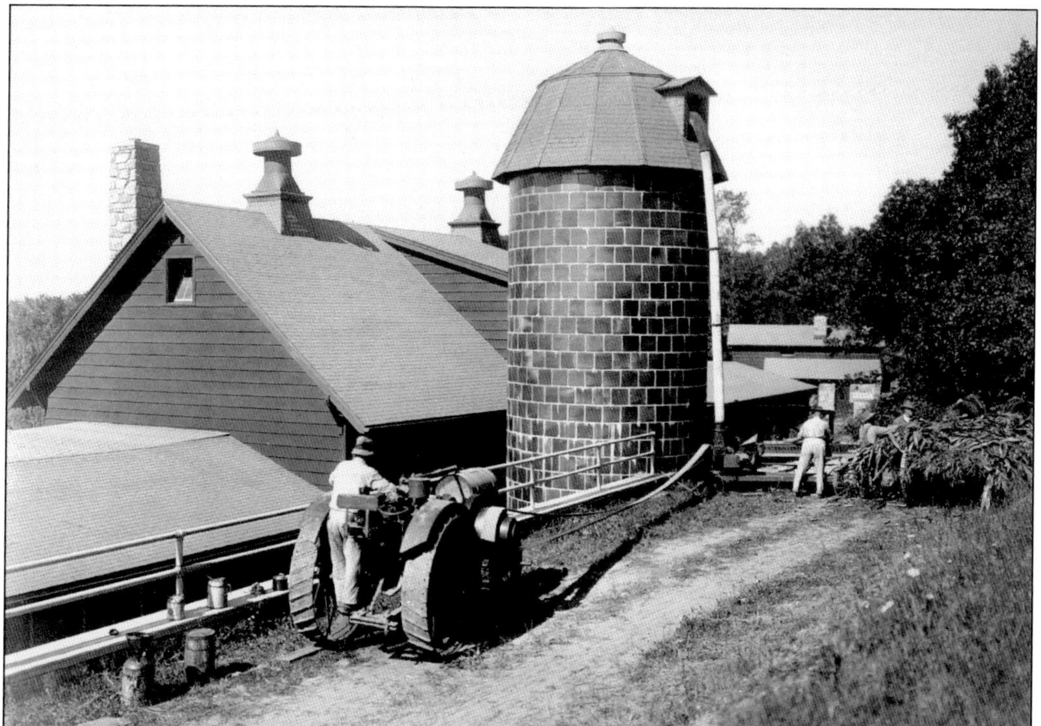

The farm of 22 acres of field not only raised Ayrshire cattle but also raised chickens and pigs. The Rawolle farm also grew produce such as peas and corn. Walt DeWolfe helped to cut the corn. Later Rawolle's vegetables were among the first frozen vegetables and were shipped to his store at Salem Four Corners, to New London, and to fine restaurants in New York City. Here a close-up of the barn and silo shows the men loading corn into the silo.

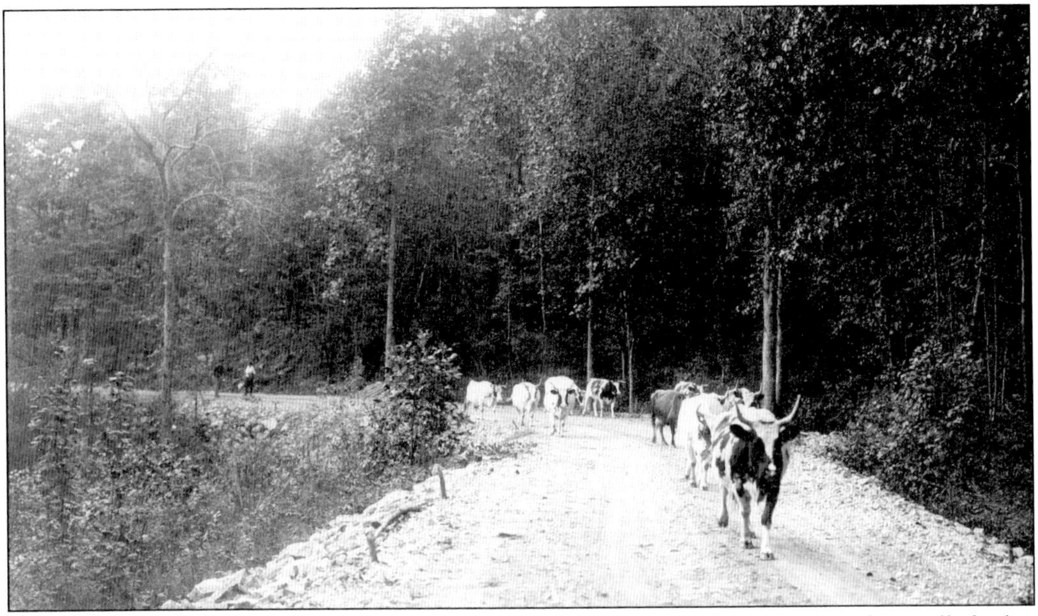

The famous Alyshire herd was purchased because Frederic Rawolle desired quality milk for his three sons. In 1931, Fairy Lake Farm was one of the eight producers of certified milk in the state of Connecticut. It was the only certified milk in New London County at this time. The advantage of electric milking and the consistent temperatures of electric refrigeration of milk was quite evident. University of Connecticut students would visit to see this amazing farm.

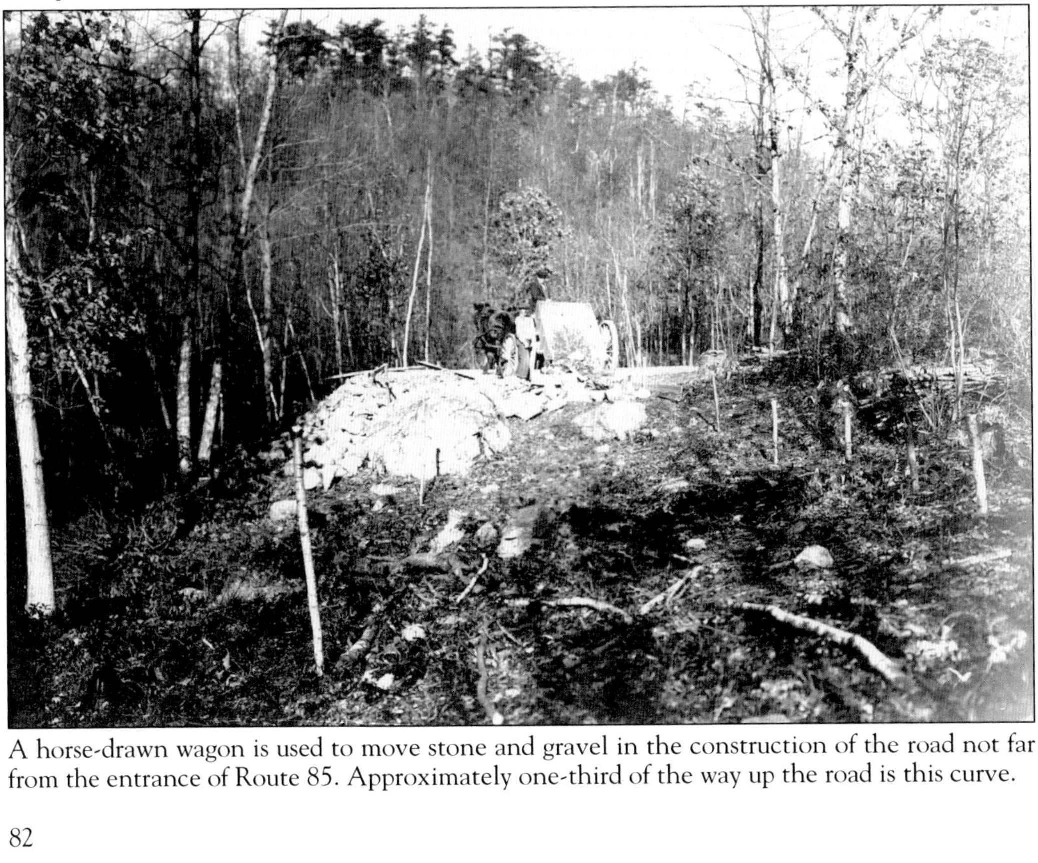

A horse-drawn wagon is used to move stone and gravel in the construction of the road not far from the entrance of Route 85. Approximately one-third of the way up the road is this curve.

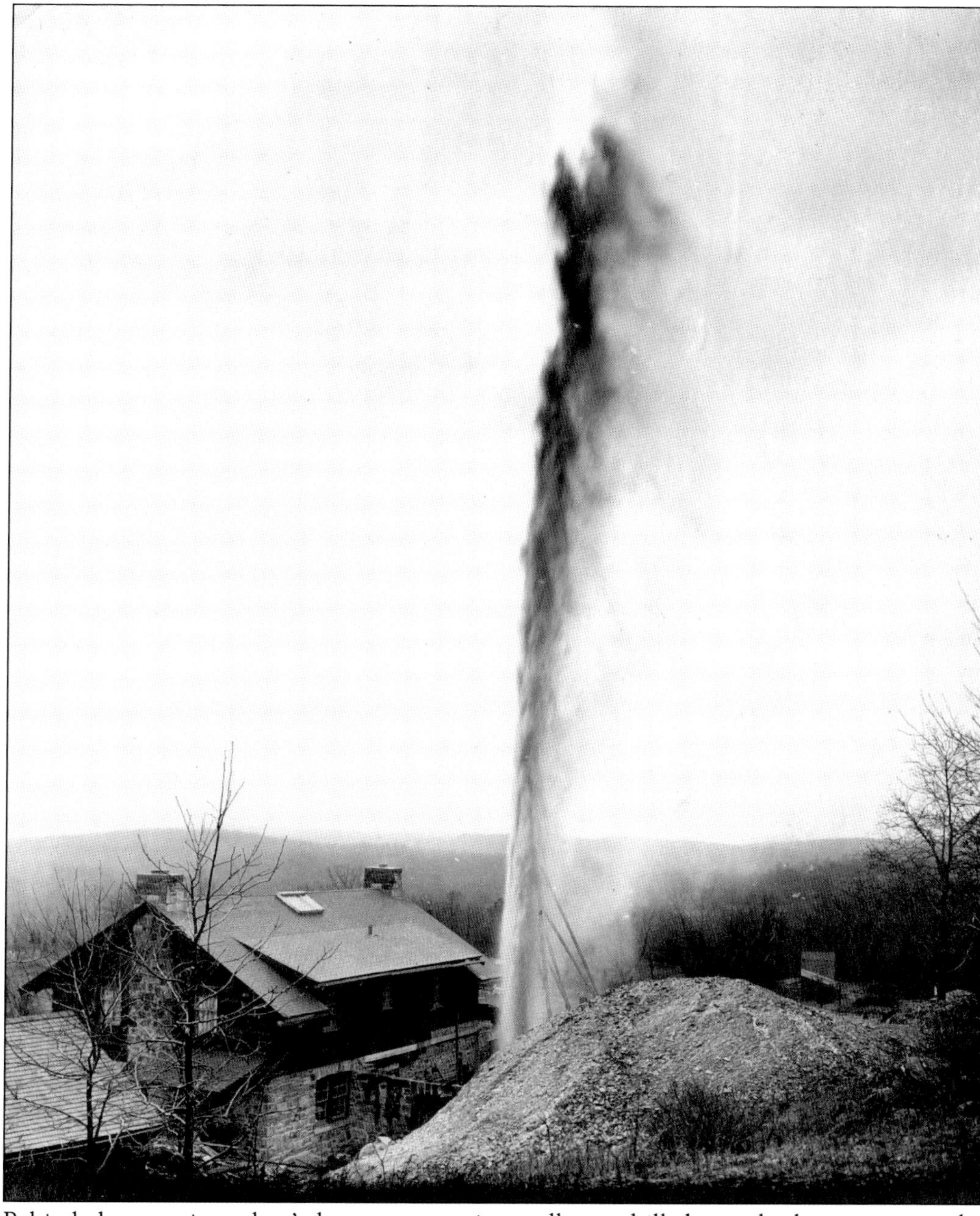

Behind the superintendent's house an artesian well was drilled as a backup water supply. Unfortunately a five-gallon container of kerosene was accidentally spilled into the well just nearing the completion of construction and made the well unusable until the 1960s.

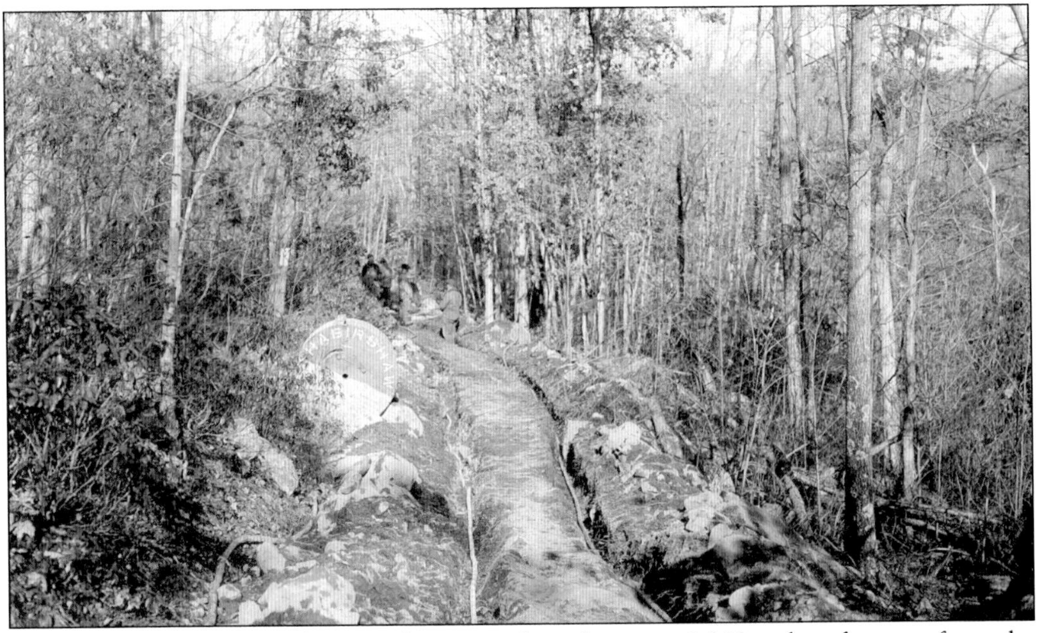

These cables in the trenches are the power lines bringing 2,300 volts of power from the powerhouse to the pump houses. Inside the pump houses are transformers that reduce the voltage. The pump house, constructed of concrete and stone, has a cement-lined reservoir that holds 40,000 gallons of water. A seven-and-a-half-horsepower Rumsy pump motor was used to pump water 2,100 feet up to a second 90,000-gallon reservoir located near the house.

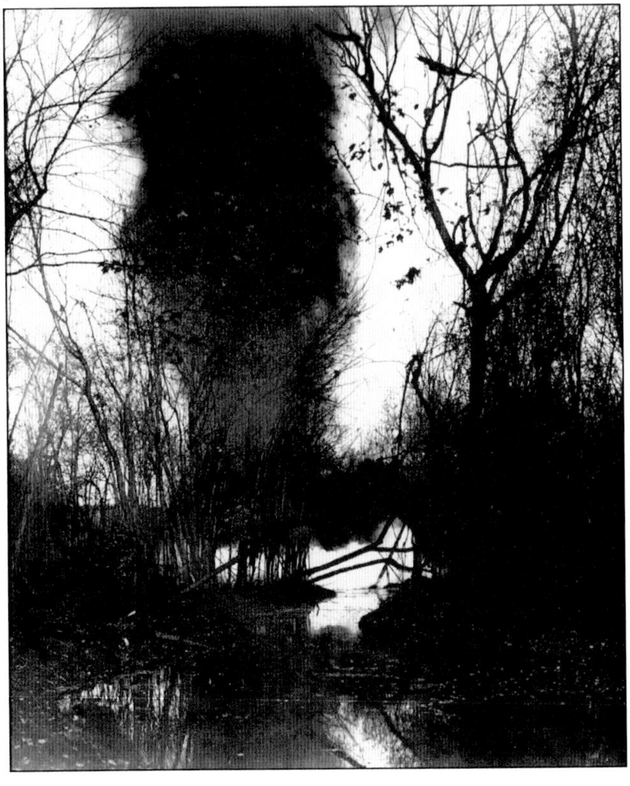

Frederic Rawolle wanted to put his houseboat in Fairy Lake, so with his own dynamite-like invention, he blasted a canal from Carr, or Stump, Pond to Fairly Lake. Carr Pond can be seen from Route 85 just south of Salem Four Corners. The Hurricane of 1938 completely destroyed the boat.

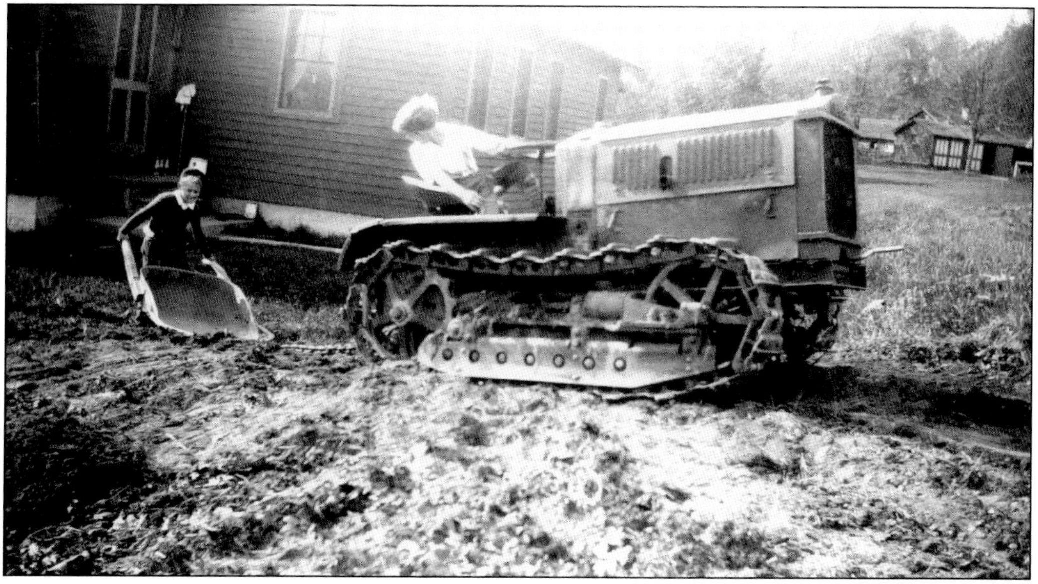

Duncan Fraser (left) and Ralph Mudgett Jr. use a Cleveland tractor in 1935. The Fraser family lived in and ran the Fairy Lake Store built by Rawolle.

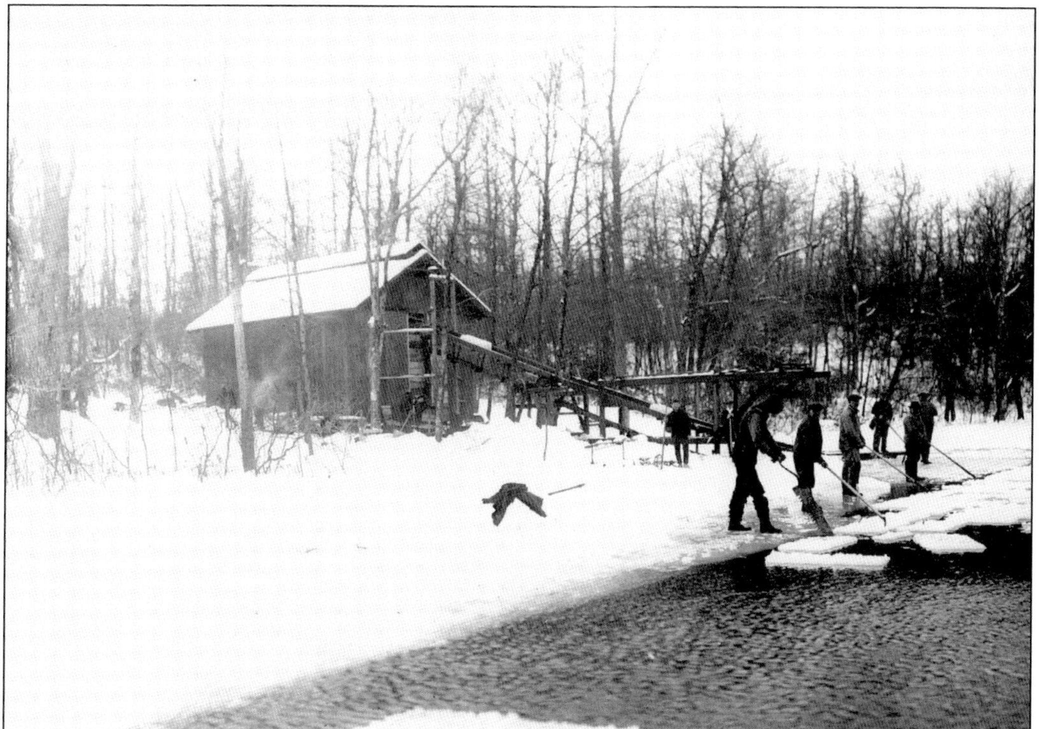

Frederic Rawolle owned Horse Pond and all the land up to Salem Four Corners. Seen here are men harvesting ice on Horse, or Bride's Pond. On the south end of the pond was an icehouse where ice was stored and then redistributed to Rawolle's farm. January, a time when the ice was thick enough, was the usual time for ice harvesting in most of Salem.

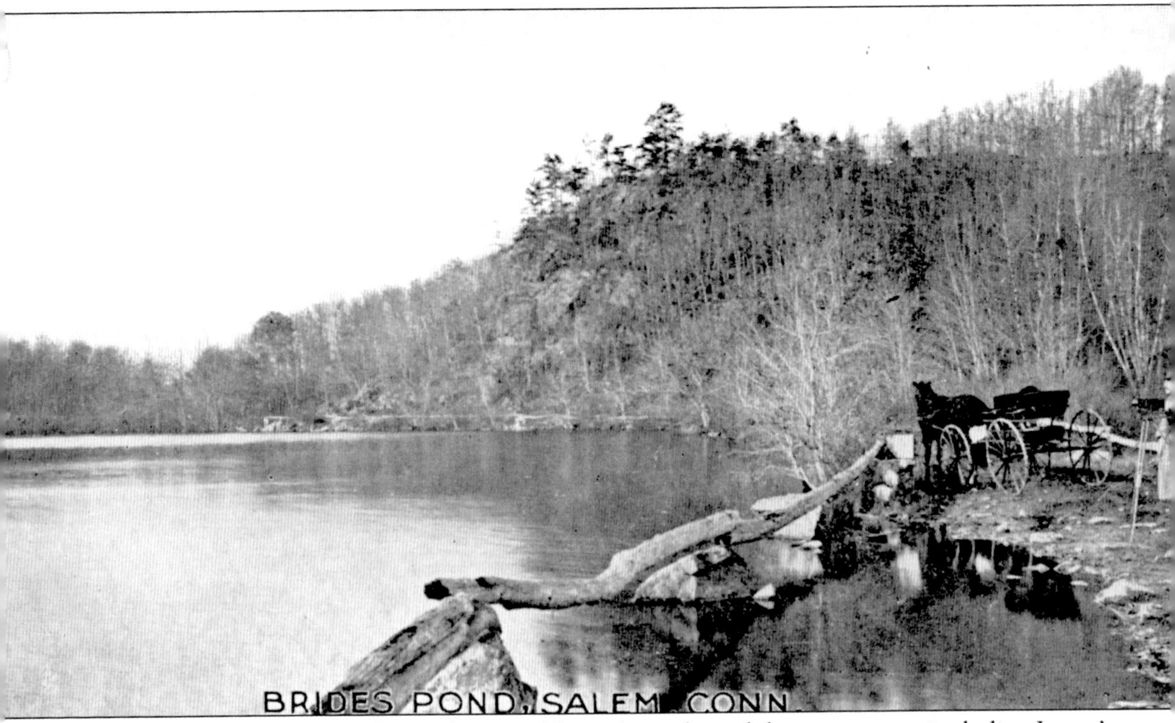

Horse Pond, or Bride's Pond, was also noted for its legends, and there are many, including Lover's Leap. Though legends claim it is bottomless, or 90 feet deep, the state police proved otherwise. On May 1, 1991, the state police, using a depth sounder and underwater video camera, scanned roughly 90 percent of the pond. The deepest spot they found was dead center of the lake, which was only 19 feet deep. However, they were not able to scan areas less than 30 feet in width, so they did say there could be holes as large as 30 feet wide that they could somehow miss. One of the many legends of Horse Pond is of a Native American girl and her lover. While camping at Paugwonk Pond (Fairy Lake), the lovers were discovered by tribe members. On horseback, fleeing the disapproving tribe, they leapt to their deaths into the water from the top of the cliff now called Lover's Leap. Before Route 85 was completed, the old Governor's Road was on the west side of Horse Pond, so the water came right up to the cliff. It is said if one stands on top of the cliff on a moonlit night, one can still see the horses' manes in the water.

Eight

FARMS AND PEOPLE

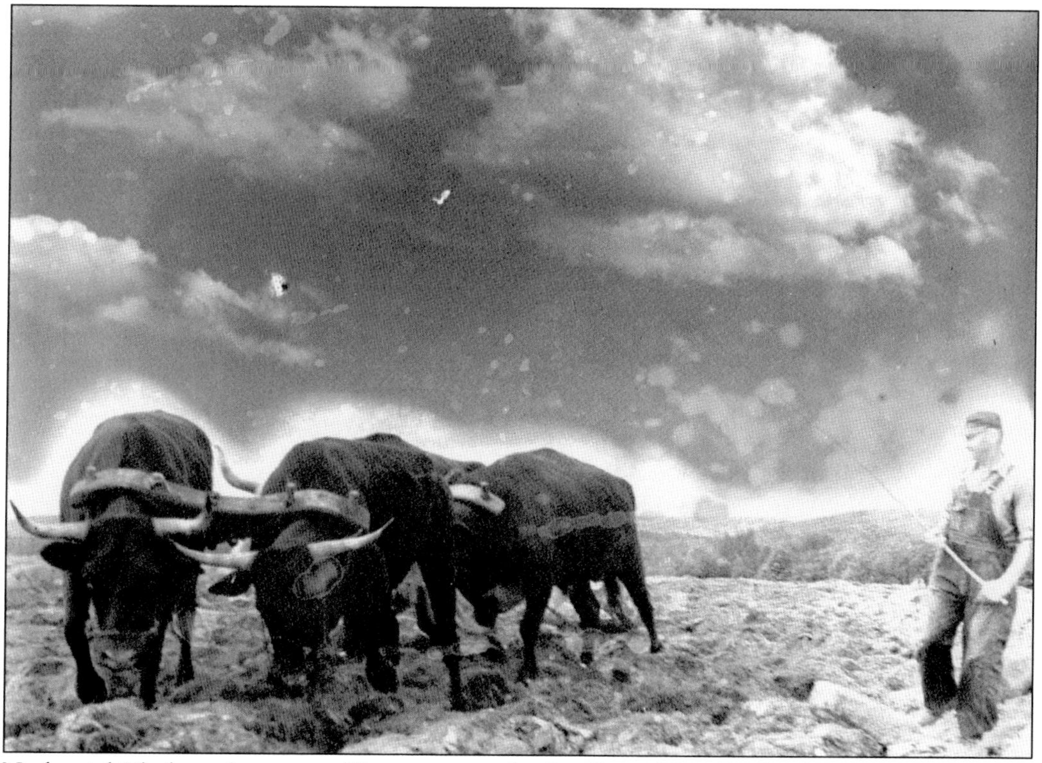

Nathaniel Clark works oxen pulling stone on the Fox Farm. New England seems to grow rocks. After every cold winter, the heaving thaw pushed rocks up to the surface. A farmer had to clear the field of rocks annually before planting. It was also a good time to find arrowheads in the fields of Salem where the Mohegans once hunted.

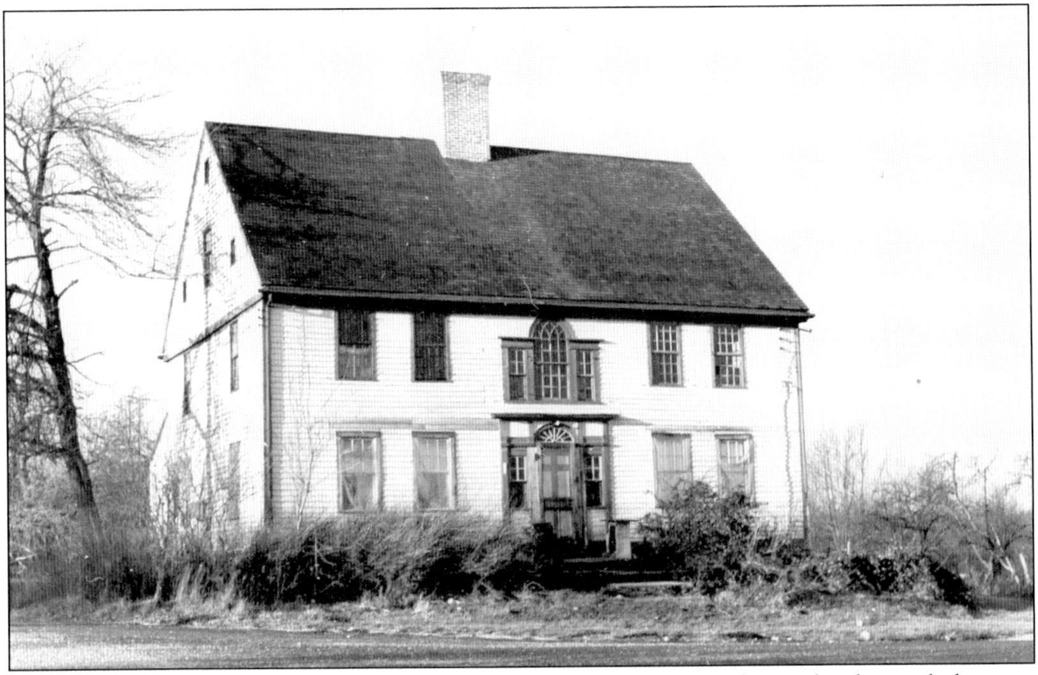

On the corner of Route 354 and Witter Road, across from Congdon's, this house belonging to Mr. Heilweil was taken down by the Congdons in order to build a junkyard. Mr. Heilweil abandoned the house in the mid-1840s when he built the house kitty-corner, which is on the corner of Rattlesnake Ledge and Route 354. In earlier times, it had been the Witter house, in 1868, and the Lathrop house in 1854.

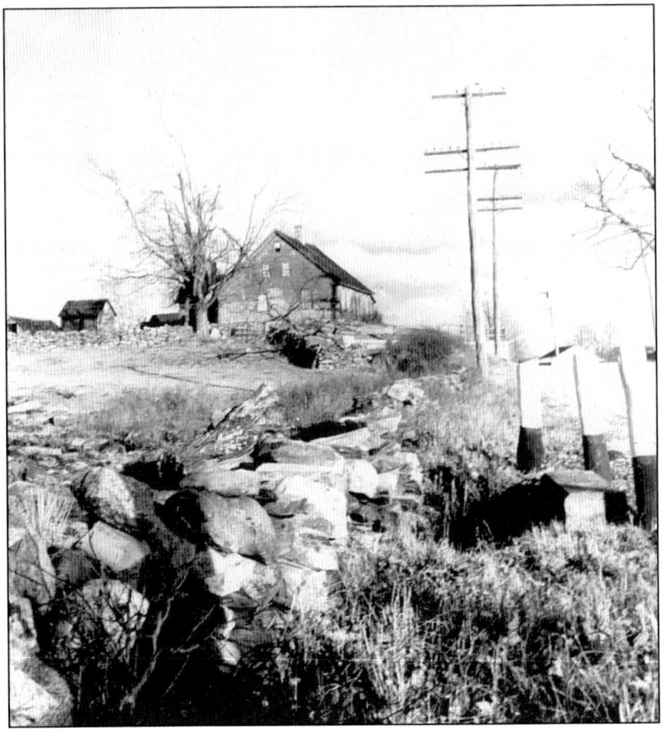

People were often times identified with their homes and land. Since farming was so important to the folks of Salem, when a farm was bought or sold the name seemed to go with the property; identification of the kind of crops they grew and the farm animals and the acreage involved could all be determined by the owner's name since most people knew one another. This is Fred Winchester's house on the left and Del Winchester's house on the right around the 1930s or 1940s. They were located on Route 82 heading toward Norwich just after Harris Road. Fred's house burned down in the early 1960s.

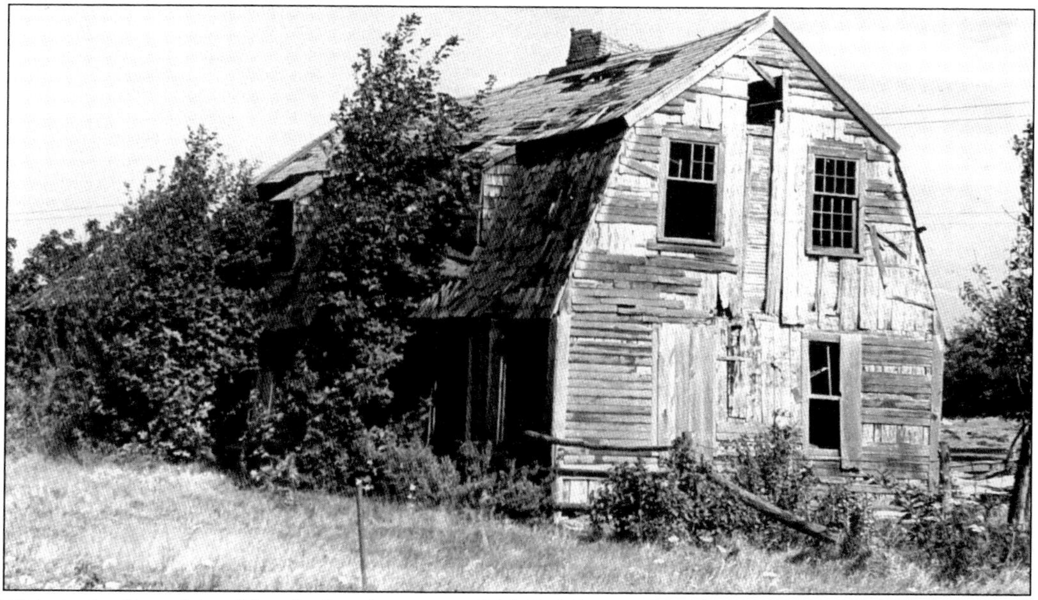

This is the Josephine Kotula farmhouse on Old Colchester Road in Salem, just south of Route 82. She was the mother of John Yaworski. John Yaworski lived in this home, just as it is seen in this photograph, until he built a new home over on Harris Road.

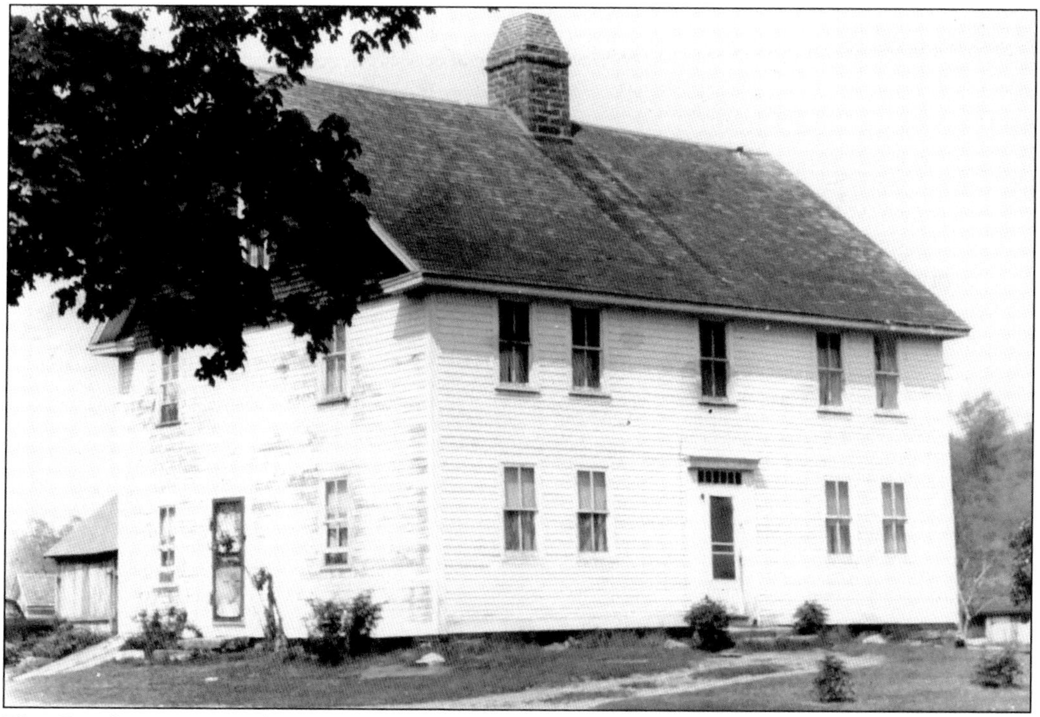

This Day house was earlier a Treadway house. Located on Route 85 across from Maple Shade Grocery Store, it was taken down piece by piece and moved to New Hampshire and rebuilt. A driveway can still be seen there. The Fishers lived in this house, renting it from the Days during the 1950s and 1960s. The DeWolf home located on Beckwith was another home that was moved. It was moved to Lebanon, Connecticut.

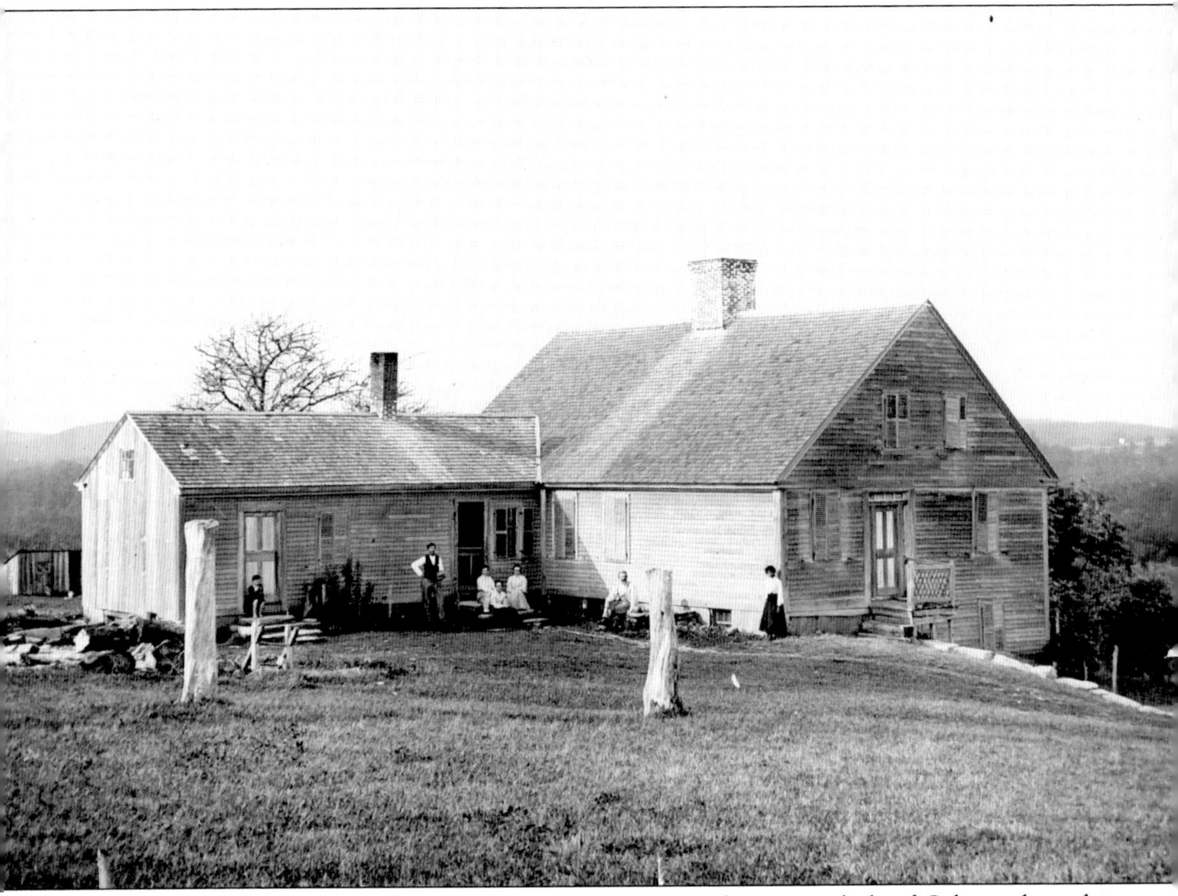

This home was the home of Charles A Williams Esq., the town clerk of Salem when this photograph was taken in 1902. It stood on the old Governor's Road when the road circled around Horse Pond. The old road was abandoned when the new one was built. The Captain Gilbert home, according to *Chronicles of a Connecticut Farm*, was located 30 rods west of this house. The boy on the left is Harold Peit. Standing is Frank E. Williams (truant officer for Salem). The women sitting are identified as Mable C. Williams (Iowa city), Harriet (Goldie) Williams, and Mrs. Charles A Williams. At the far right is Jennie Tossit.

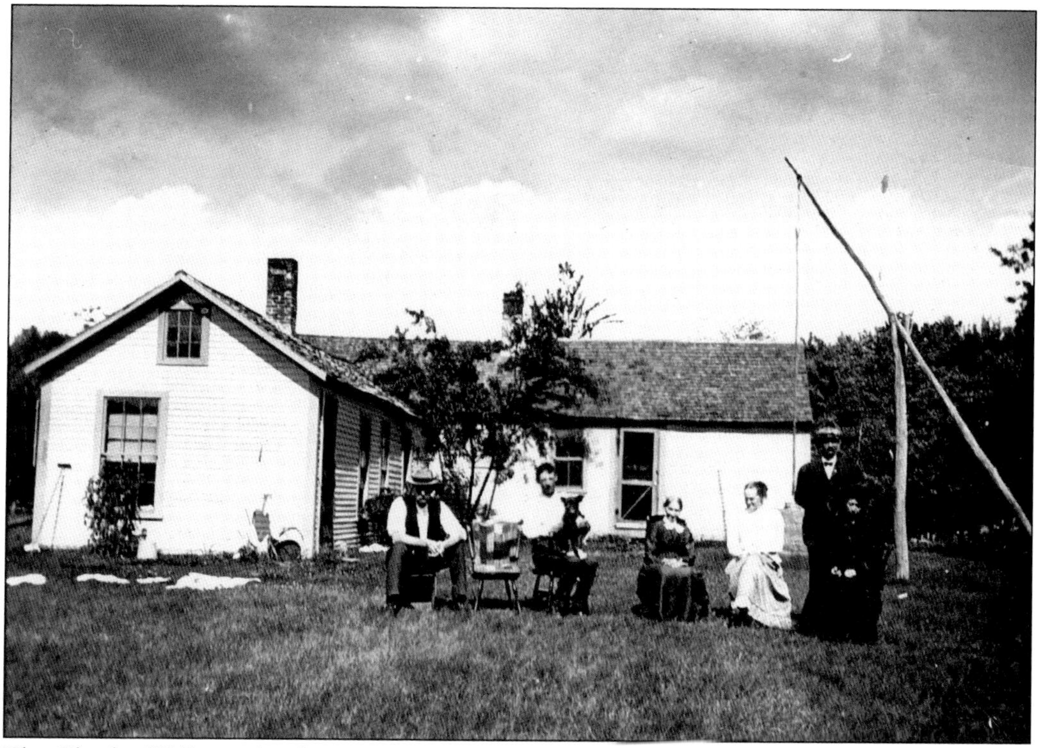

The Charles Williams family enjoys time outside. Notice the strange contraption to the right. It was used to dip water from the well. It was called a well sweep.

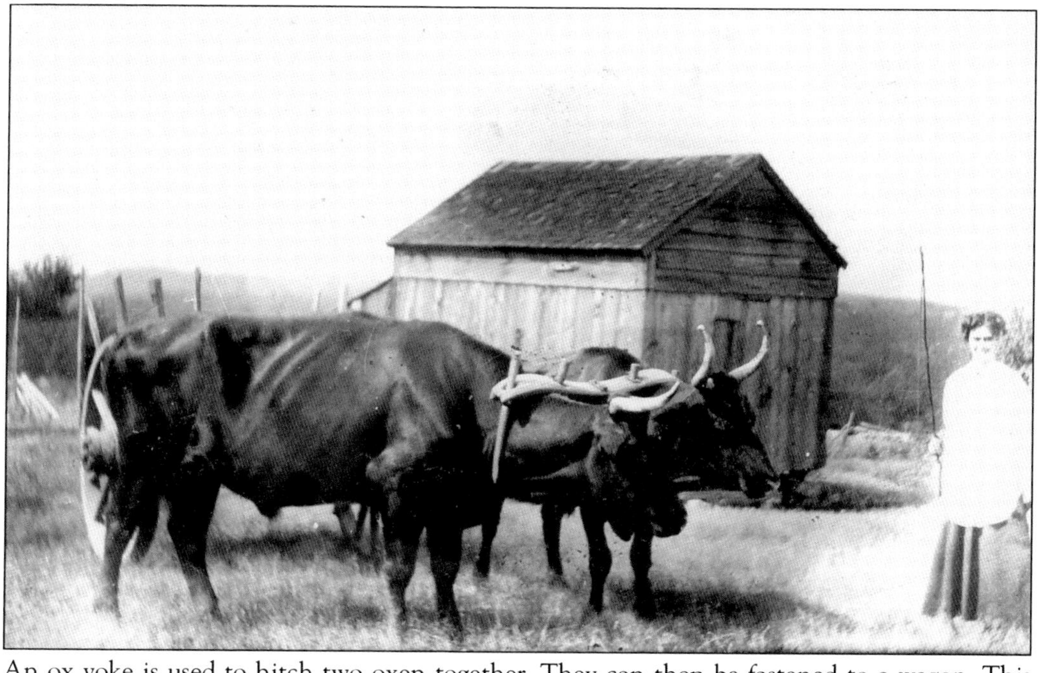

An ox yoke is used to hitch two oxen together. They can then be fastened to a wagon. This photograph shows Harriet Williams, daughter of Charles, tending to oxen pulling a wagon, probably of hay.

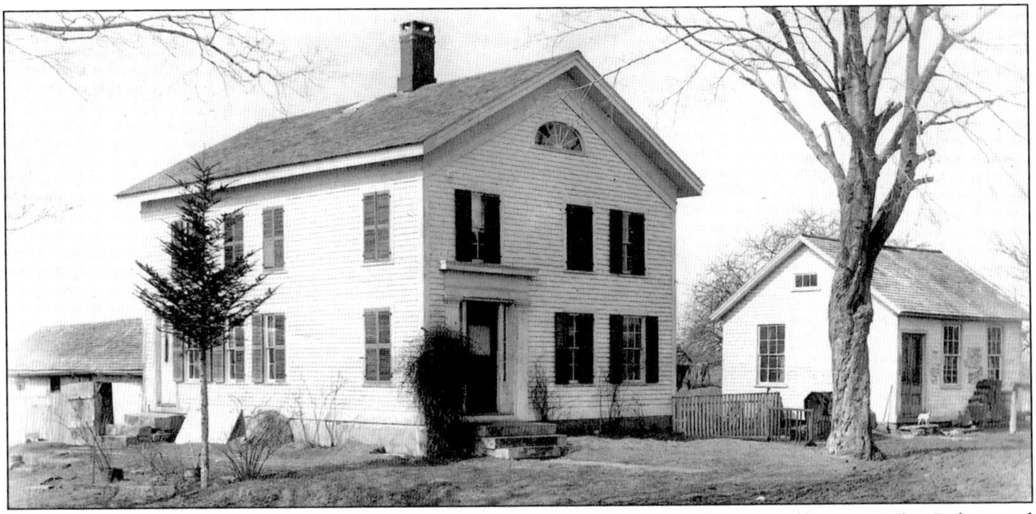

The Greek Revival house to the left originally belonged to Salinda M. Fuller in 1851. It burned down in 1974. During the 1940s and 1950s, it was the home of Victor Cannell, whose wife was a Rathbun. The small store to the right later became the home of John Rathbun. It is now occupied by a daughter of the Rathbuns and is located across from Salem School.

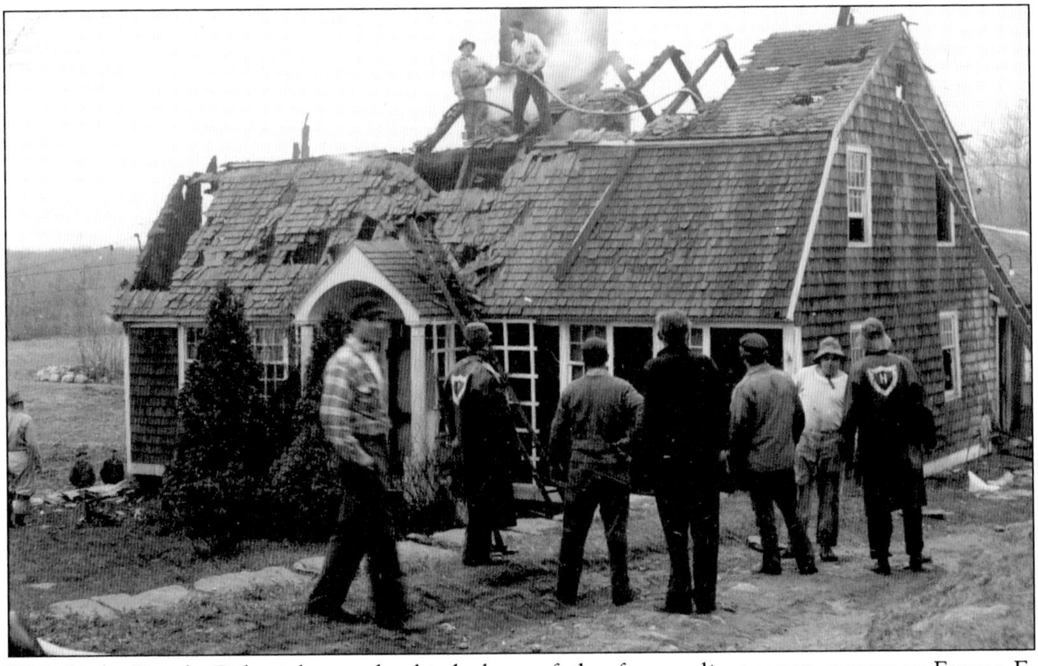

This little Dutch Colonial was the birthplace of the former lieutenant governor Ernest E. Rogers, who was in office from 1929 to 1931. The Fletchers also owned this property for many years. At one time, it was the last house on the left going north on Route 85 toward Colchester. Herr, a devastating fire around 1946–1947 is tended to by early firefighters and shows the lack of equipment and sophistication of today's fire firefighting. In this photograph, there are no special uniforms, but the *H*, maybe Hayward Fire Company, is shown on their clothing. With hoses, they pumped water from the well and from the brook. The house was severely burned, and another home was built at the same location.

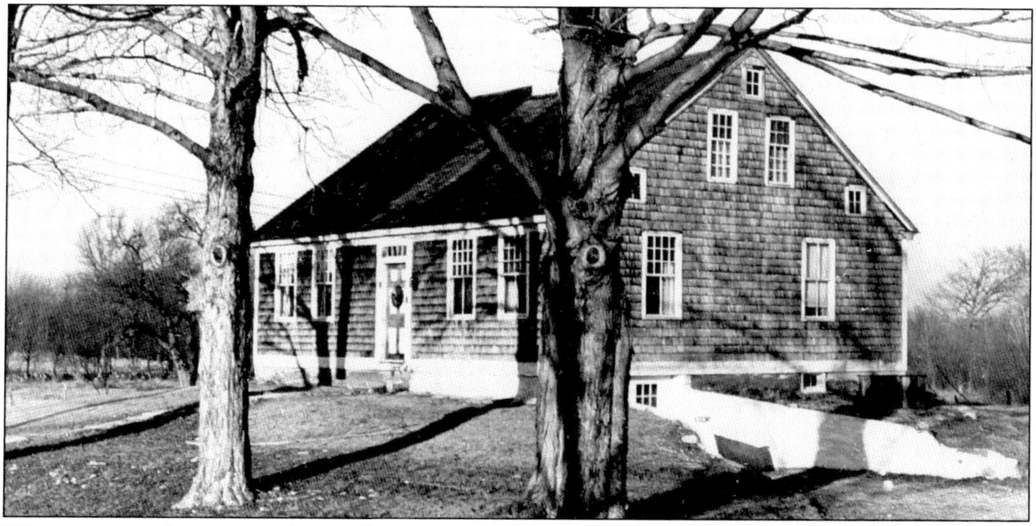

Three or more houses similar to this one were built for the workers who worked in the sawmill at the top of Gardener Lake. This particular one, built around 1790, is located on Route 354 across from the Gardner Lake Firehouse.

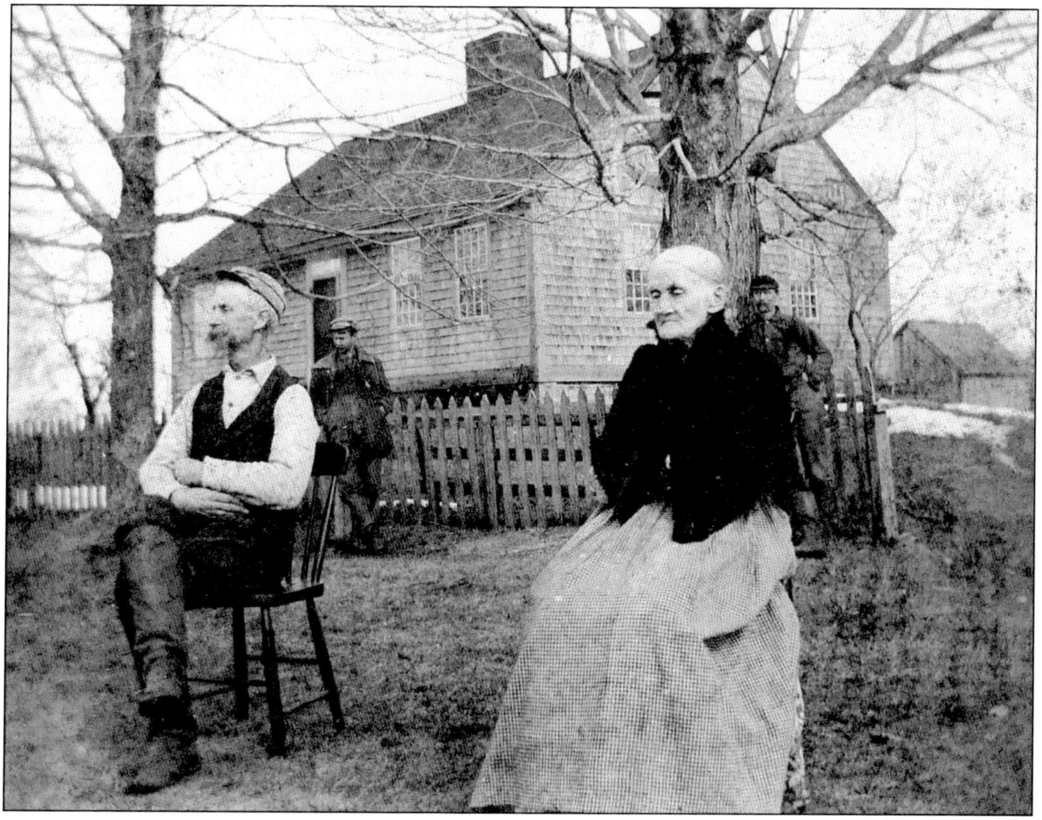

This is another photograph of the same mill house, taken around the 1890s with Horace and Tabitha Stoddard Chapman. Tabitha appears to be wearing a mourning cape, which was a small black lace cape that had a high collar and covered the shoulders and down to the elbows. The other two men in the photograph are unidentified.

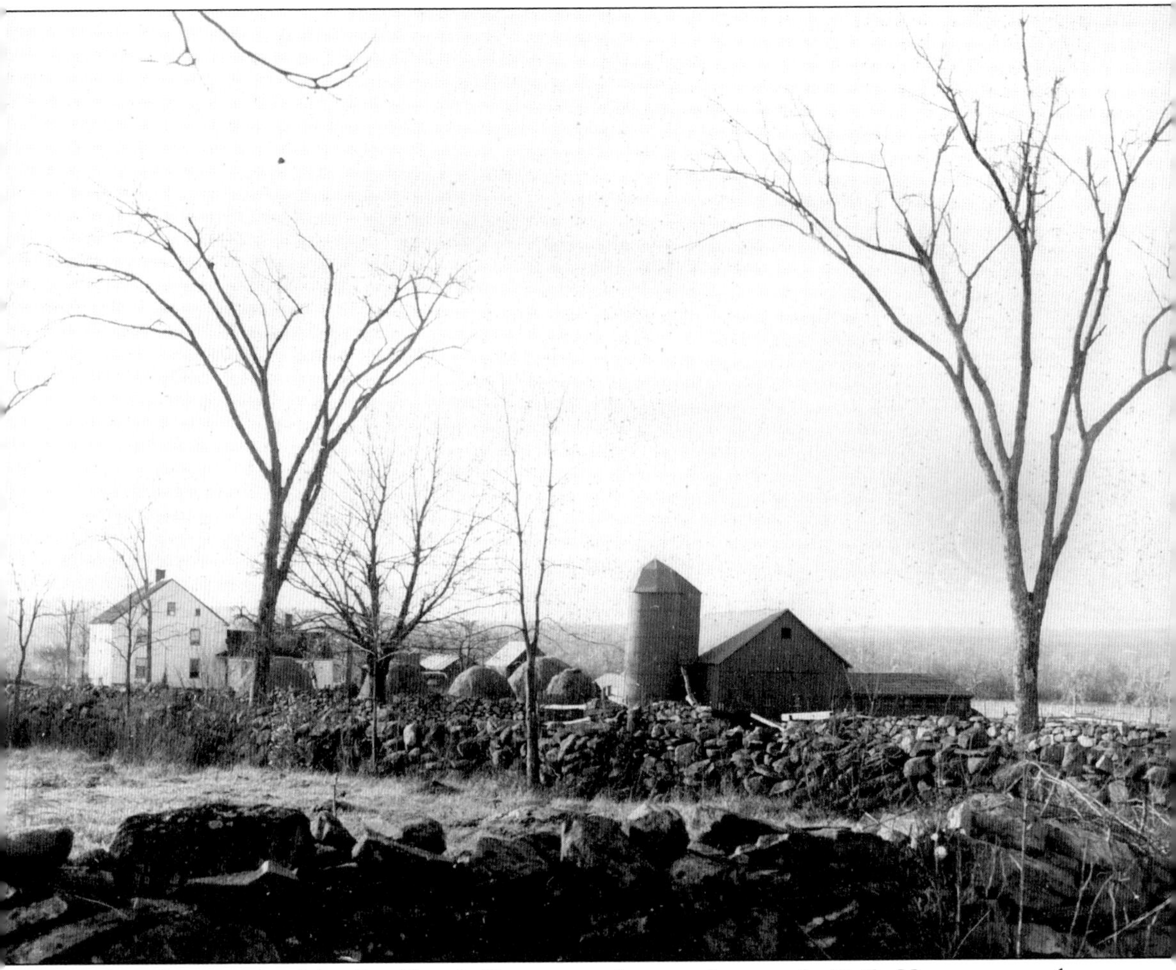

This photograph of the Fox Family Farm was taken on January 3, 1942. Hay was not always baled; it was often put into haystacks and cut with a hay knife. Restoration took place in 2005 on Music Vale Road. Elmer Chappell, first selectman for two terms, resident for 18 years, and dairy farmer, lived in this house until 1972.

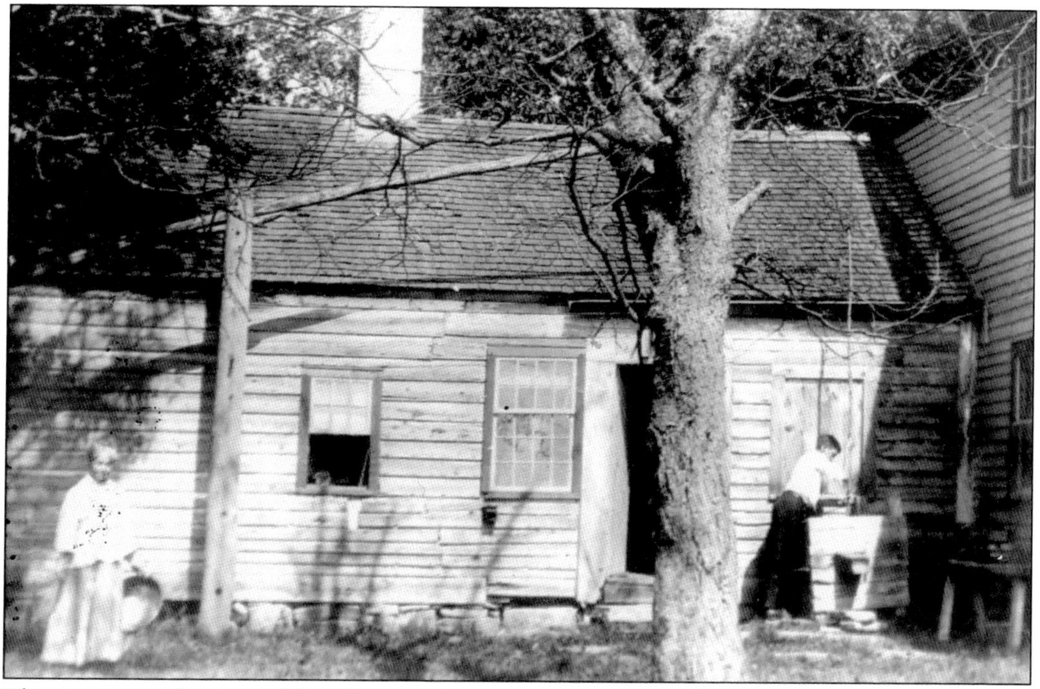

This is a rear side view of Fox Farm with a woman using a well sweep. It appears to be chore time for these folks.

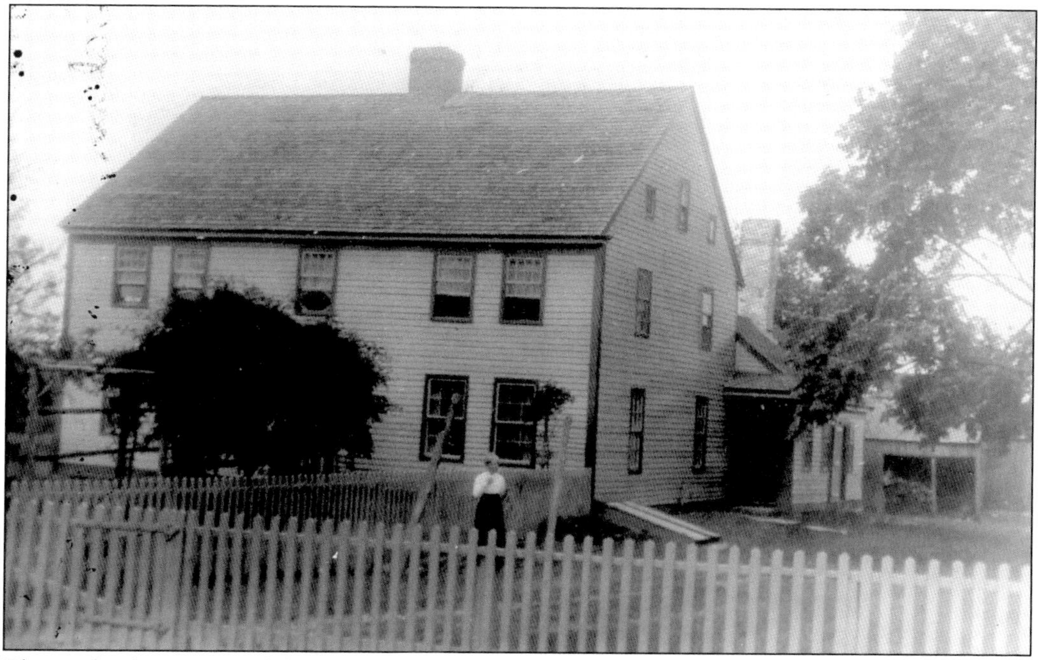

This is the front view of the Fox Farm as it looked in August 1913. As of 2005, this home was being restored and painted yellow.

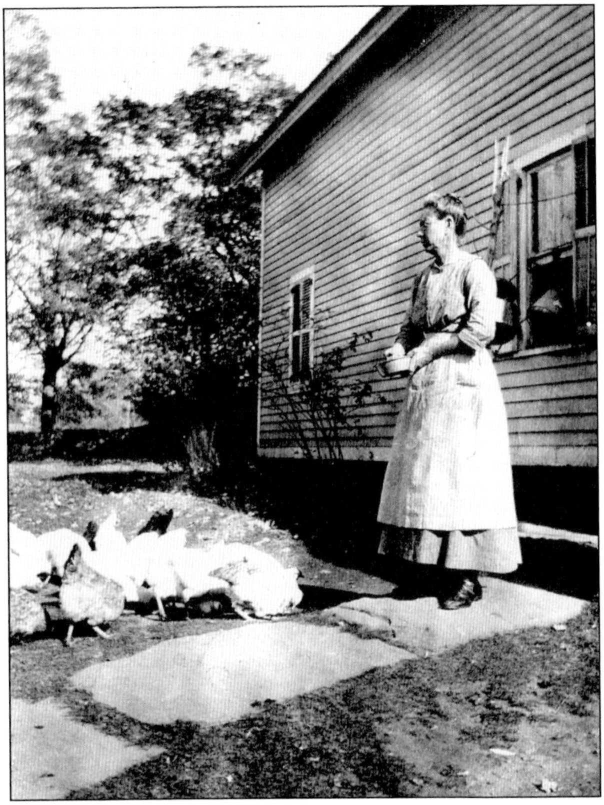

Ora Clark, wife of Nathaniel Clark, feeds the chickens in the yard. In those days, women grabbed a fresh chicken and butchered it for Sunday dinner. The feathers were plucked, and the remaining feathers were singed.

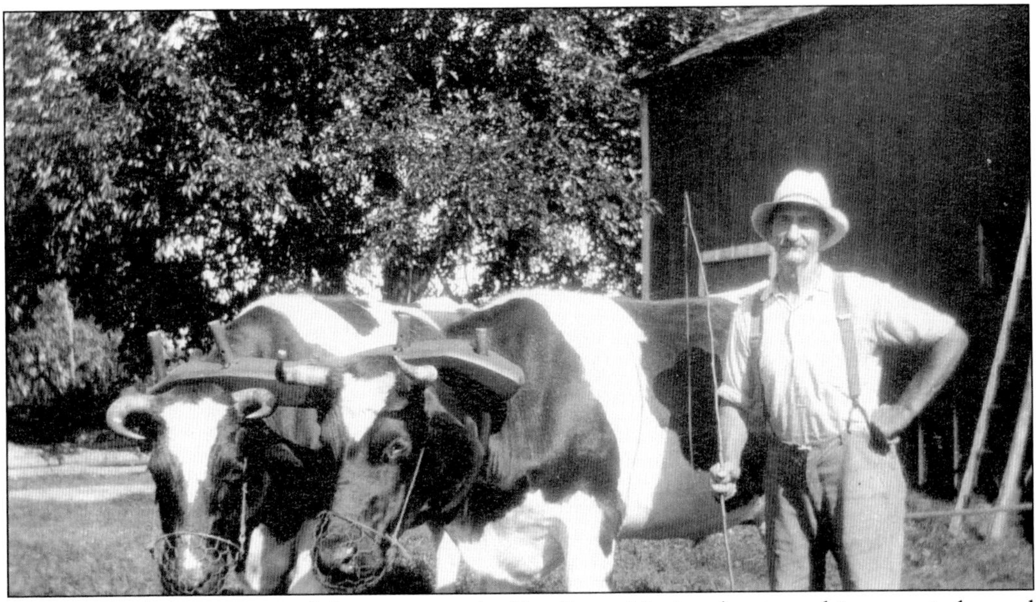

Nathaniel Clark appears with his oxen on the Fox Farm. Notice the tiny whip, or switch, used to control and steer the oxen. Clark was known for his coon dog, Jeff, and his great skill at hunting fox, mink, and raccoons.

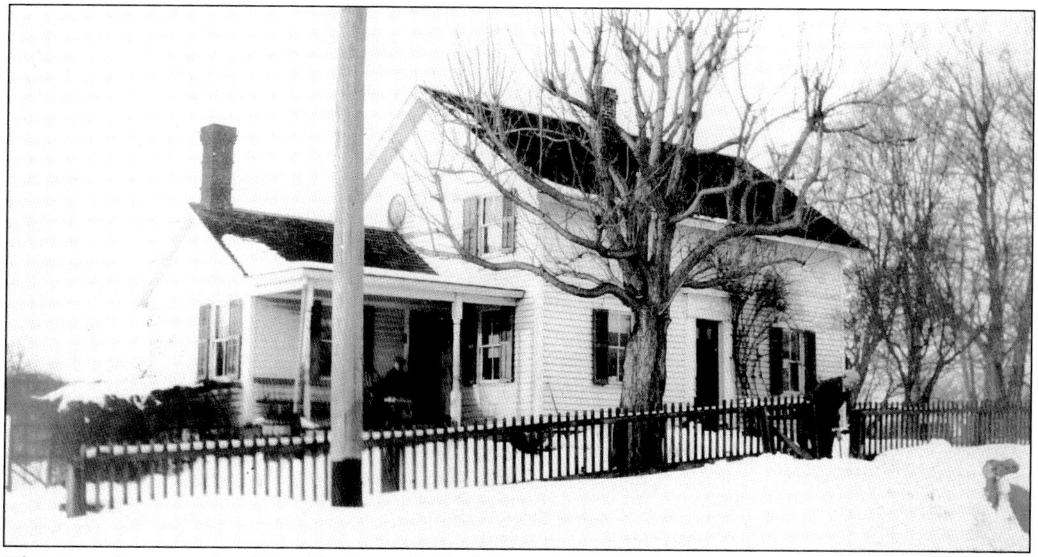

This is a photograph of the Nathaniel Clark home as it looked in 1930. It is located on Route 82 directly opposite of Dolbeare Cemetery near where the Dolbeare Tavern once stood. It was later known as the Coffeys' house.

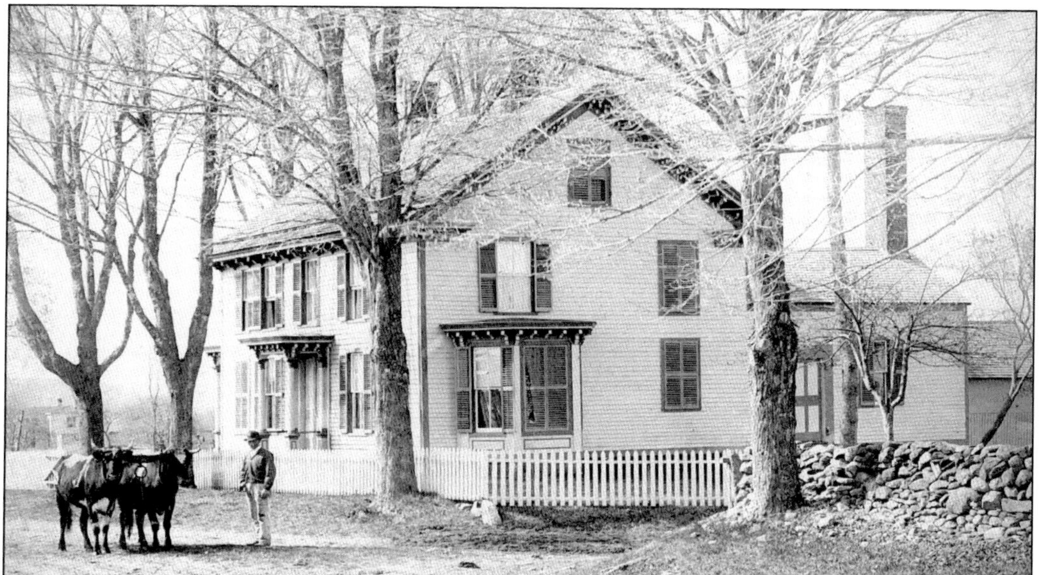

The Simon Ray house, mid-1800s, is pictured here. This house still stands and is located on the corner of Route 85 and Round Hill Road. After the McRaes, the Darling family lived here and then the Donald Fraser family in 1945 after they moved from the store at Salem Four Corners.

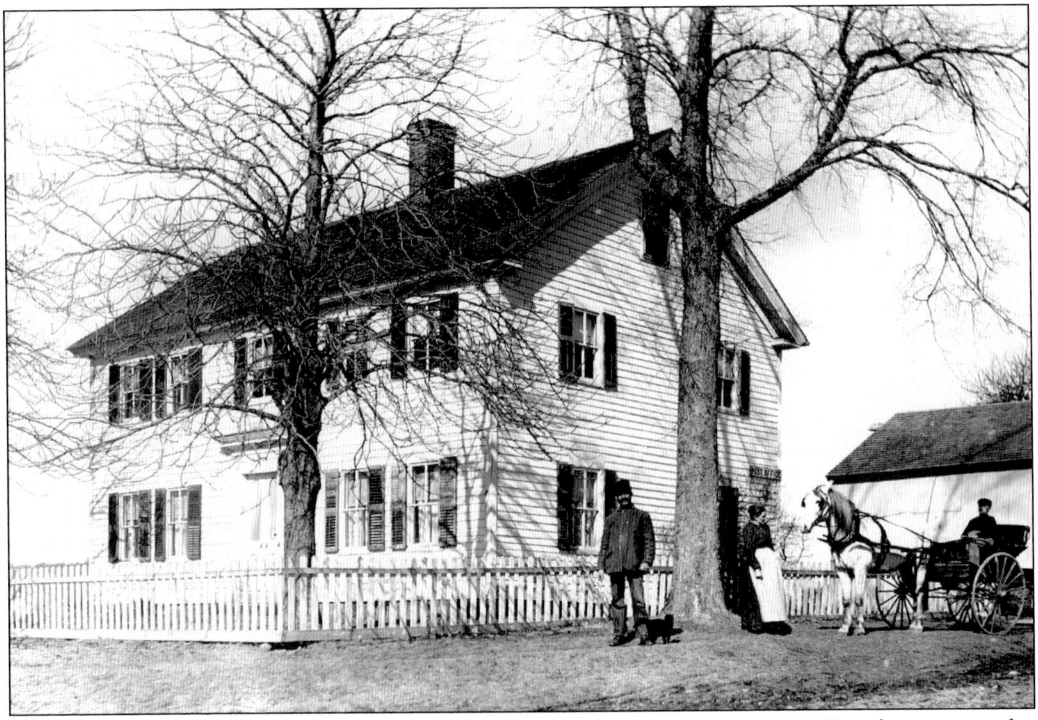

From April 11, 1899, until it closed on September 30, 1905, the Simon Ray house was the Salem Post Office. Donald McRae was the postmaster. Prior to this, the post office was located at Chadwick's store at Music Vale Road. Seen here is McRae with family and a postal carriage. The small post office sign can be seen just above the woman's head in this photograph.

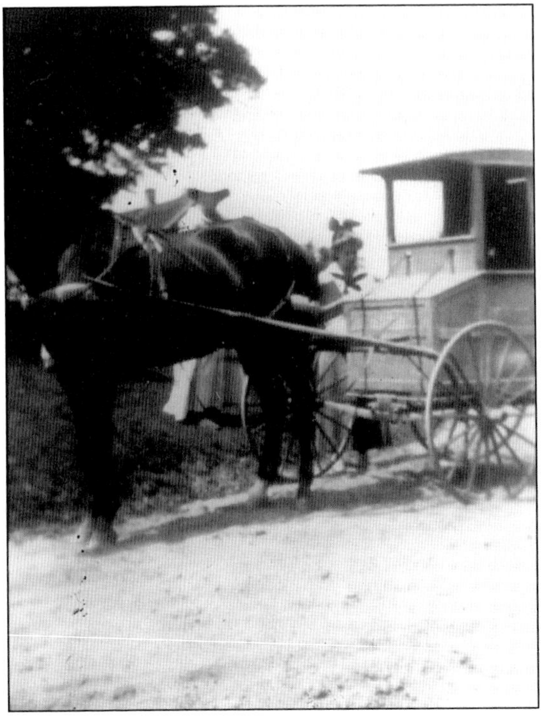

In 1902, Salem consisted of two postal routes: RFD 3 (rural free delivery) Colchester for the west side of Salem, and RFD 4 Colchester for the east side of Salem. Mail was delivered by the RFD and the recipient's name. Later street numbers and street names were added to the mailing address along with the town name, Salem. Entered by a door in the rear, Mr. McIntosh's delivery wagon is seen here in 1913. He was postal carrier for RFD 3 from the Colchester office from 1902 to 1919.

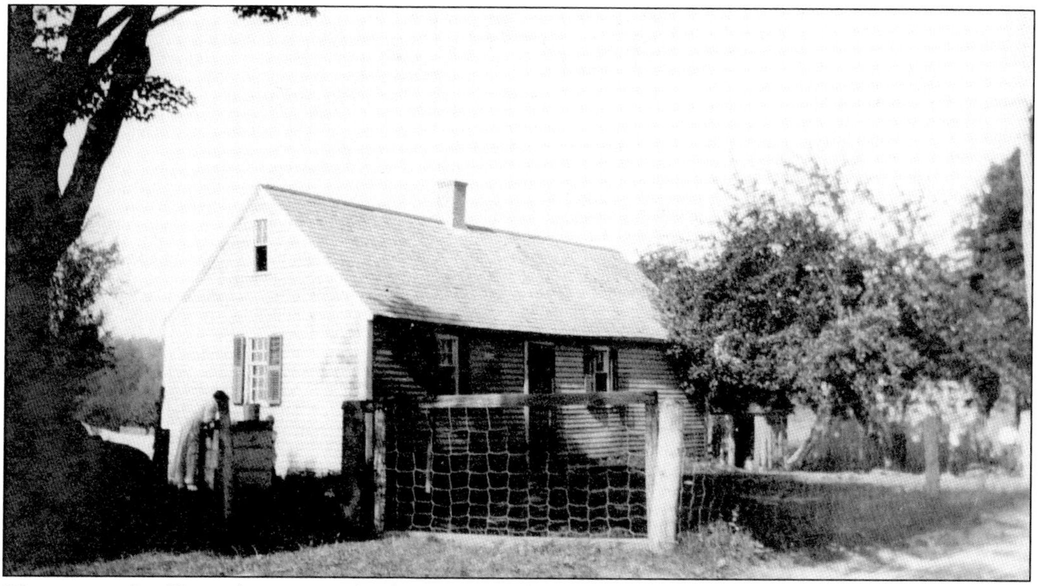

The original tollgate house was built in 1800 when the Hartford New London Turnpike took over the old Governor's Road and was straightened and fixed. This is the tollgate house as it looked in 1917. It is very close to the road. At one time, there was a turnpike in the road where, manually, a person had to turn a crank to put up spikes. This would stop traffic so that they would pay their toll money. This toll operated from 1800 to 1865. Legend has it that Captain Kidd crossed the turnpike with several men. He buried his treasure in a cave in Salem. Upon his return across the turnpike he was alone. The legendary cave has been called Smugglers Cave since then.

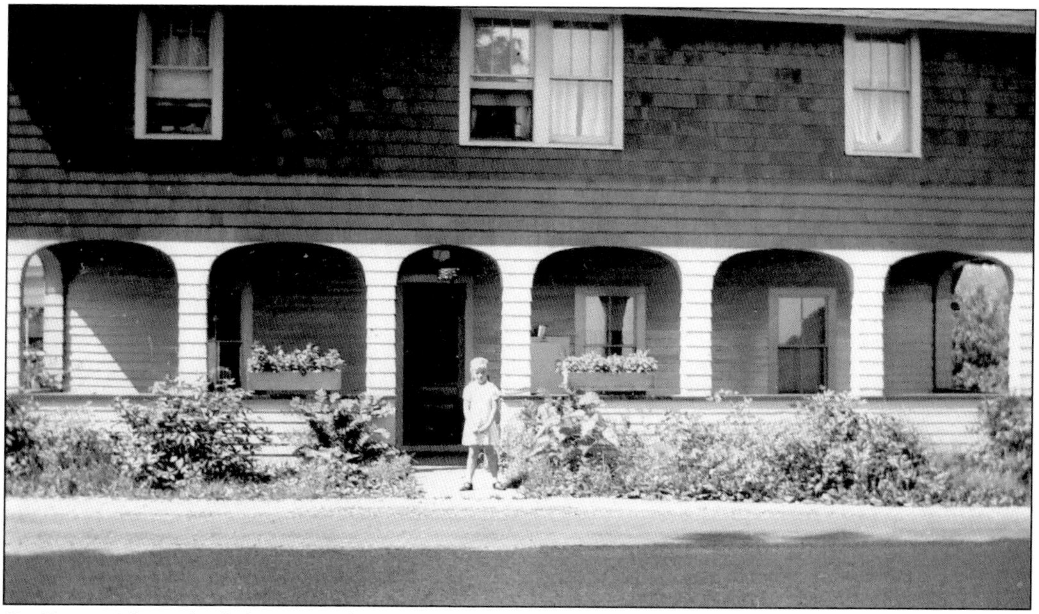

On Route 85, on the left just north of the Salem Town Green, is the same tollgate house as it looked in 1942. The house has been changed so many times it may not look anything like the original house of 1800. In the 1970s, the porch was closed to become part of the inner structure of the house. As of 2005, it was under construction once again. Anita Stodolski poses near the flowers.

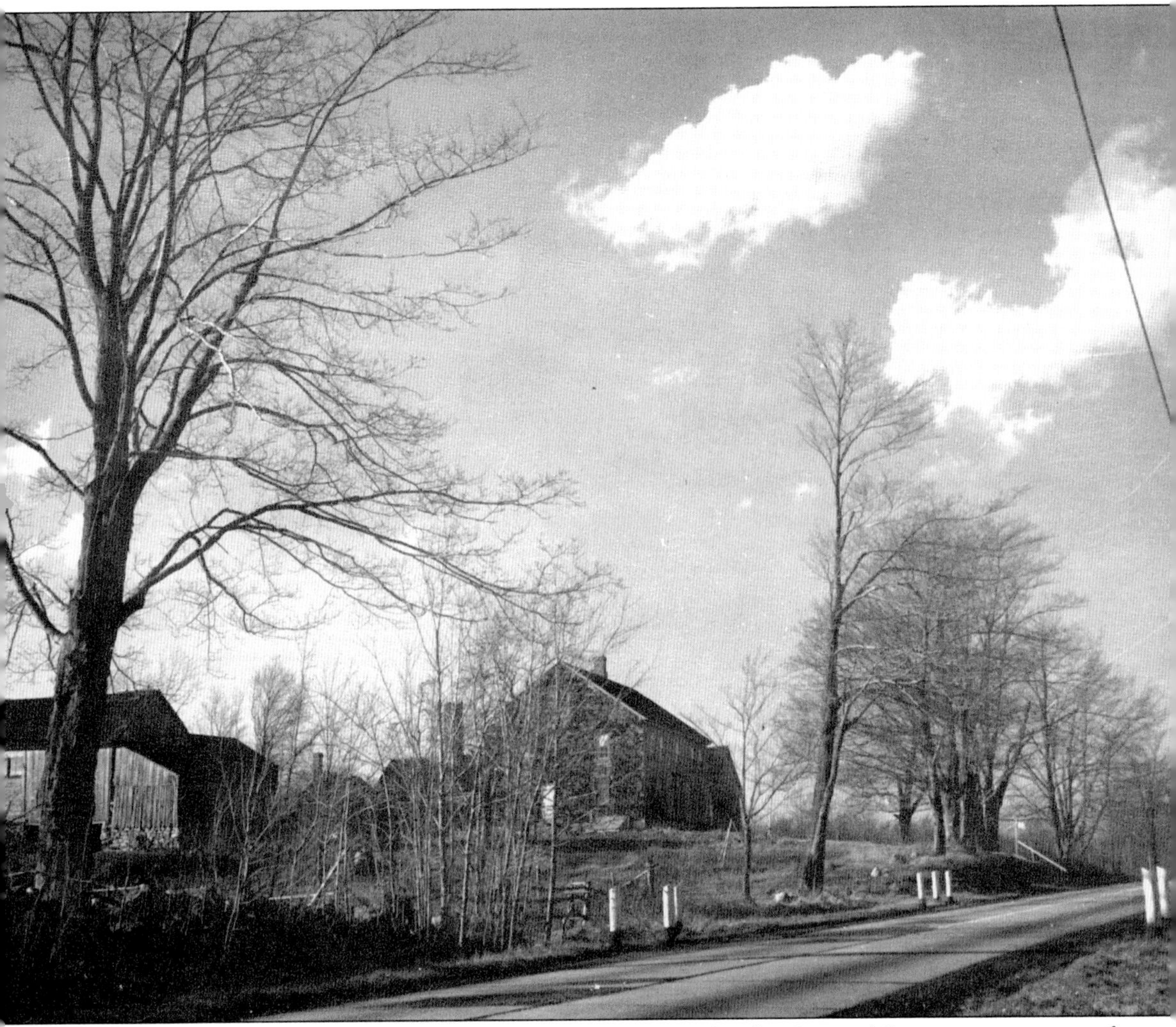

After the confiscation of Col. William Browne's property by the State of Connecticut, some of the previously owned Tory land, in lieu of payment, was distributed to the men returning from the Revolutionary War. Elijah Ransom, lieutenant in the war, received 300 acres of land for his services and built this house around 1783. Located on Route 85 near the Chesterfield line and diagonal to Woodchuck Road, it still stands today. This photograph shows what it looked like in 1942 prior to extensive renovations. A side dormitory had once been used to bunk up to 60 people per week during the 1900s. The dormitory was used by the Cohen family to give New Yorkers an opportunity to live on a farm for a week.

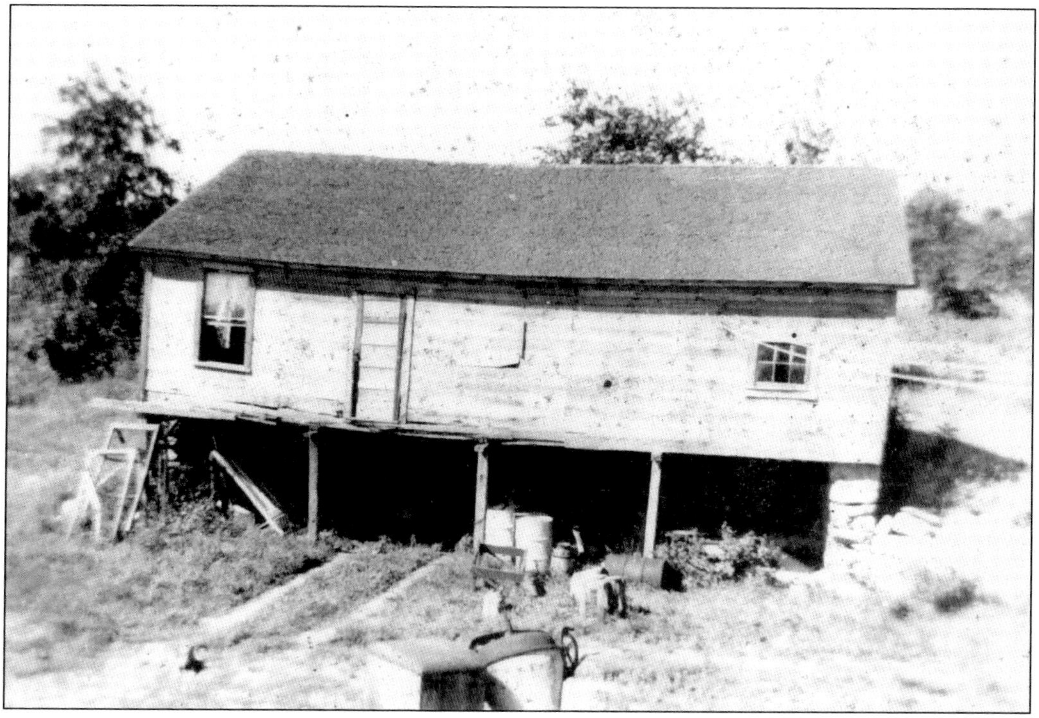

This building was probably used as a carriage shed, as seen in this photograph from around the 1930s. The roof was lowered and made into a modern-day three-stall carriage shed or three-car garage.

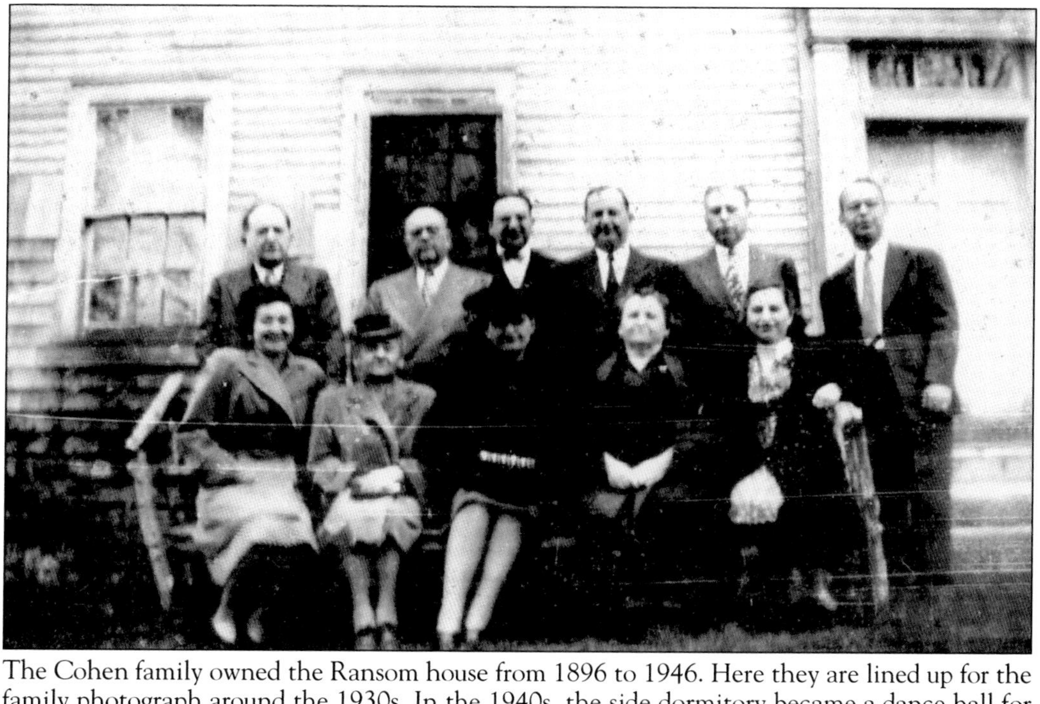

The Cohen family owned the Ransom house from 1896 to 1946. Here they are lined up for the family photograph around the 1930s. In the 1940s, the side dormitory became a dance hall for local Salem people and later was taken down completely around 1950.

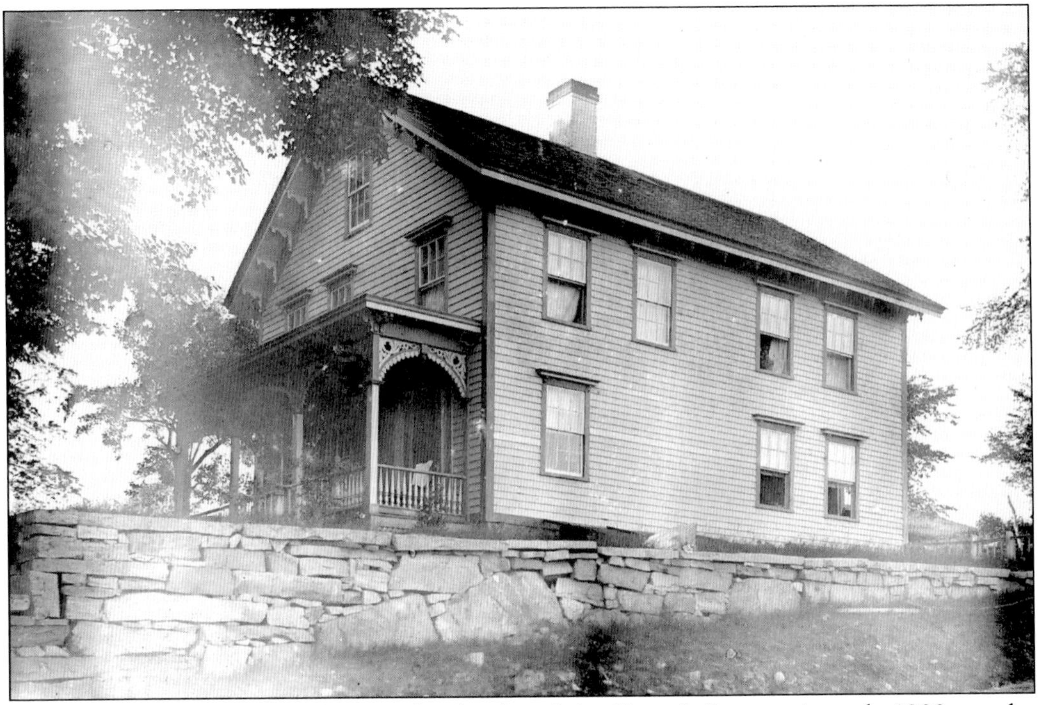

Pictured is the home of Elijah Herrick's daughter Julia Herrick Spencer in early 1900s on the corner of Route 85 and Rattlesnake Ledge. Julia was a teacher at Center School for many years. On the 1868 map, this home was the E. W. Treadway home.

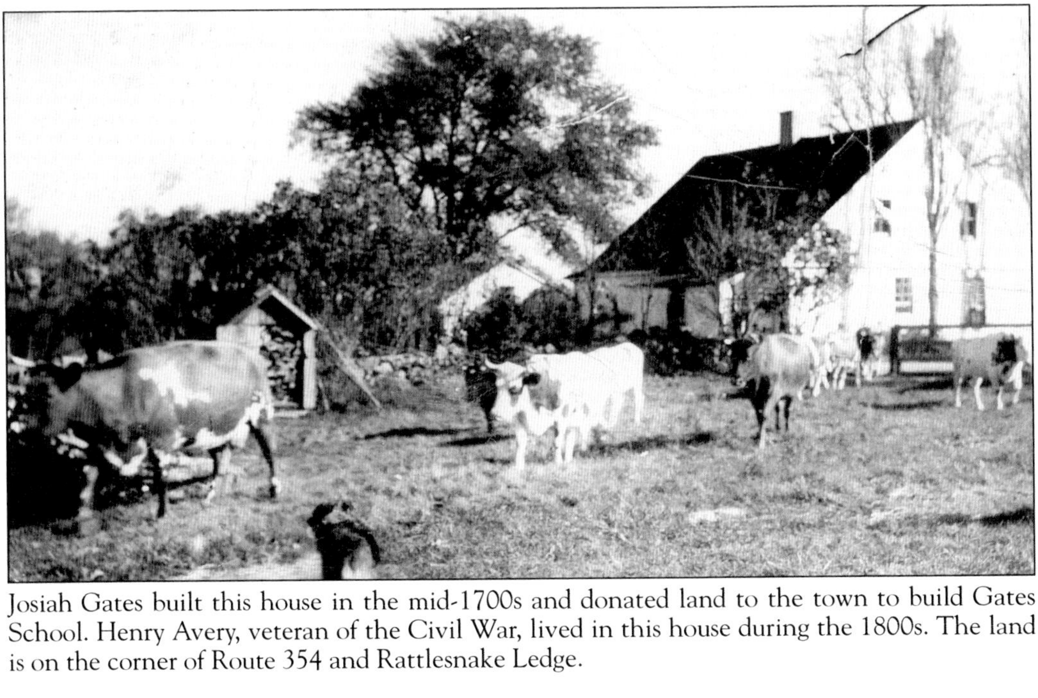

Josiah Gates built this house in the mid-1700s and donated land to the town to build Gates School. Henry Avery, veteran of the Civil War, lived in this house during the 1800s. The land is on the corner of Route 354 and Rattlesnake Ledge.

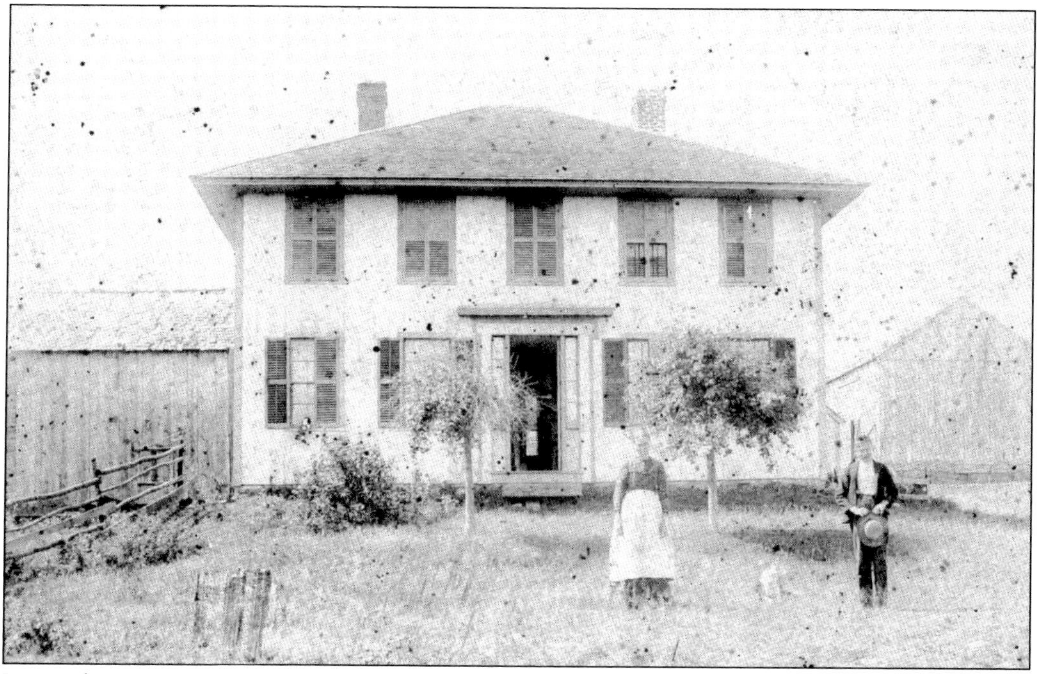

Located on Route 354, this house still stands across from Arrowhead Grove cottages. Sarah Randall and Charles DeWolfe stand in front of the house around 1890. The barn in the background was destroyed by the Hurricane of 1938 and was never rebuilt. The roof of the main house was torn off during the storm and was replaced. It was purchased by Mr. Sellew in the 1920s and was in the family until the 1980s. It has had several owners since then.

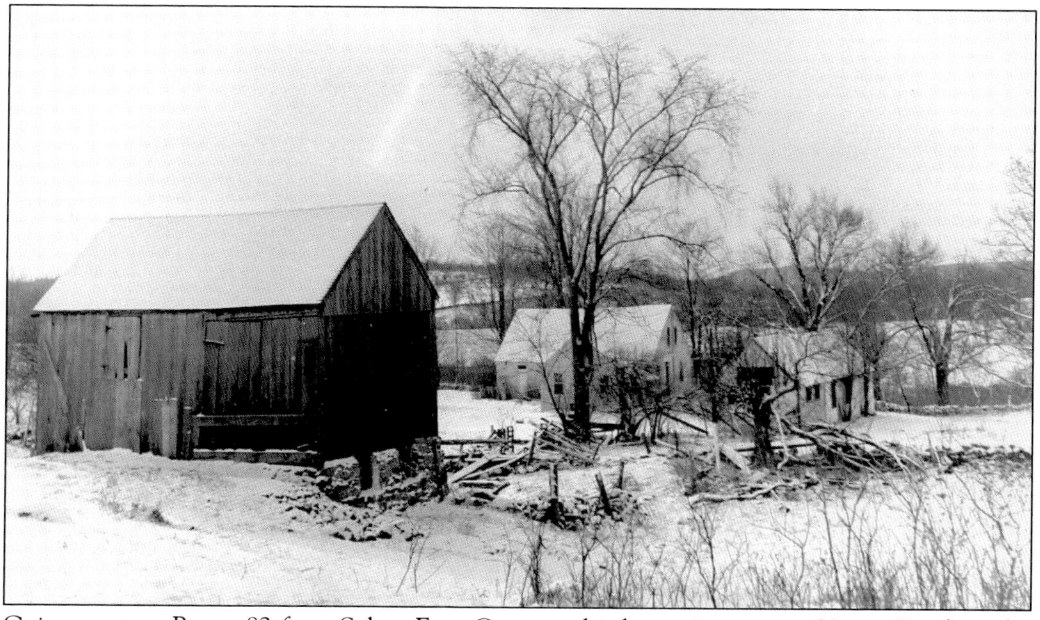

Going west on Route 82 from Salem Four Corners, this house is just past Hagen Road on the right. The barn in the foreground was on the left-hand side of Route 82, but is no longer there. Charles and Catherine Dimmock lived there from the 1930s, and the house is still in the family.

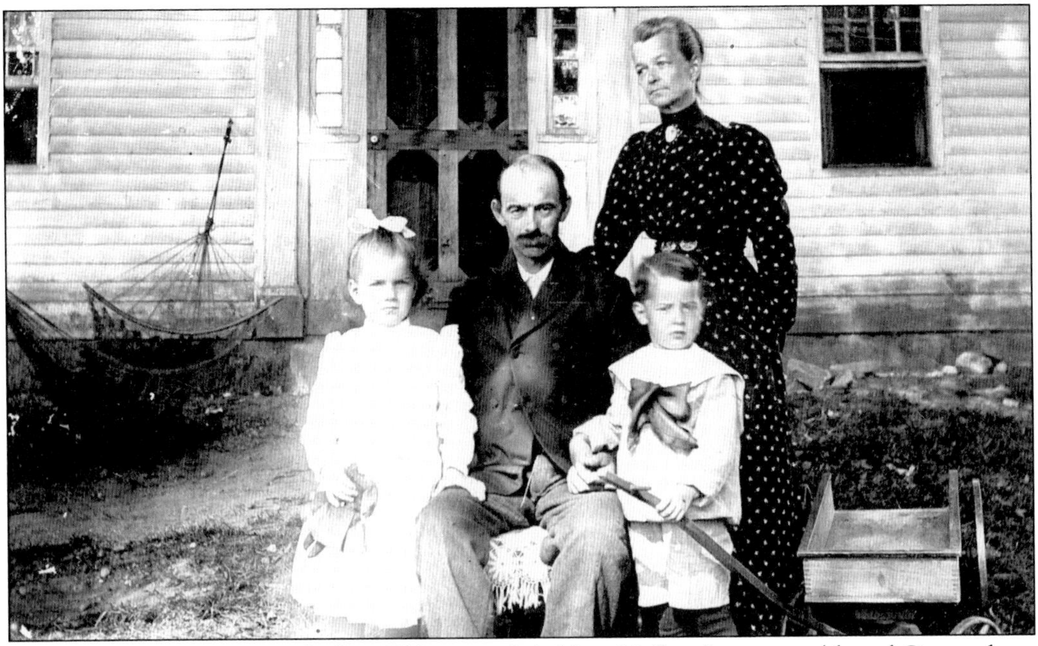

This image shows Elmer and Ellen Tibbetts and children Nellie, five years old, and Grant, three years old, in 1903. It looks as though these folks are going to church, dressed in Sunday best. It is surprising to see a hammock so close to the front door. Children always love wagons no matter what era they are born in. The Tibbetts's house is located on Rattlesnake Ledge. On the 1854 map, it was the home of Judge J. C. Daniels.

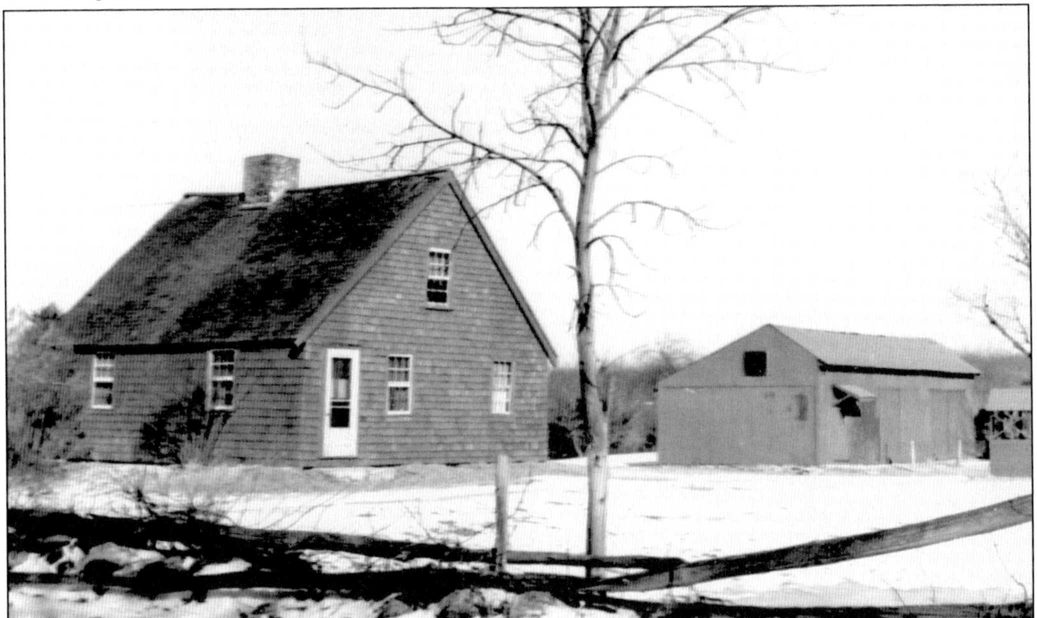

The Tew house on West Road south of Witch Meadow Road was the home of a cooper. The cooper shop is to the right; however, in the winter, Mr. Tew would also make barrels in his attic. Legend says he built a barrel too big to get down the staircase, so he lifted part of the roof to get it out. The home is no longer standing.

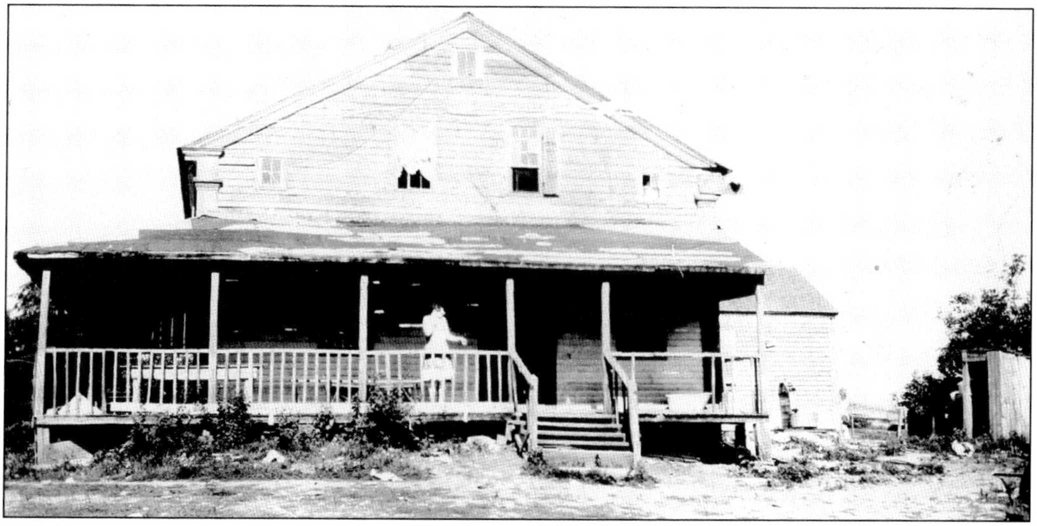

This house was originally the John Way house, built around 1760 with a Way cemetery 500 feet in back of the house, and stayed in the family for many years. In May 1921, 136 acres of land and the house were purchased for $2,000. The Kobylucks purchased the parcel from the Botwinicks, who supposedly kept stolen chickens in the upstairs of the house. For extra income during the Depression era, the Kobylucks rented the children's rooms to summer boarders from New York City. The children were delighted to sleep in the barn during those summers. *The Way It Was: God's Plan*, written by Helen Kobyluck Woronik, documents her life in Salem. She was born in this house in 1931.

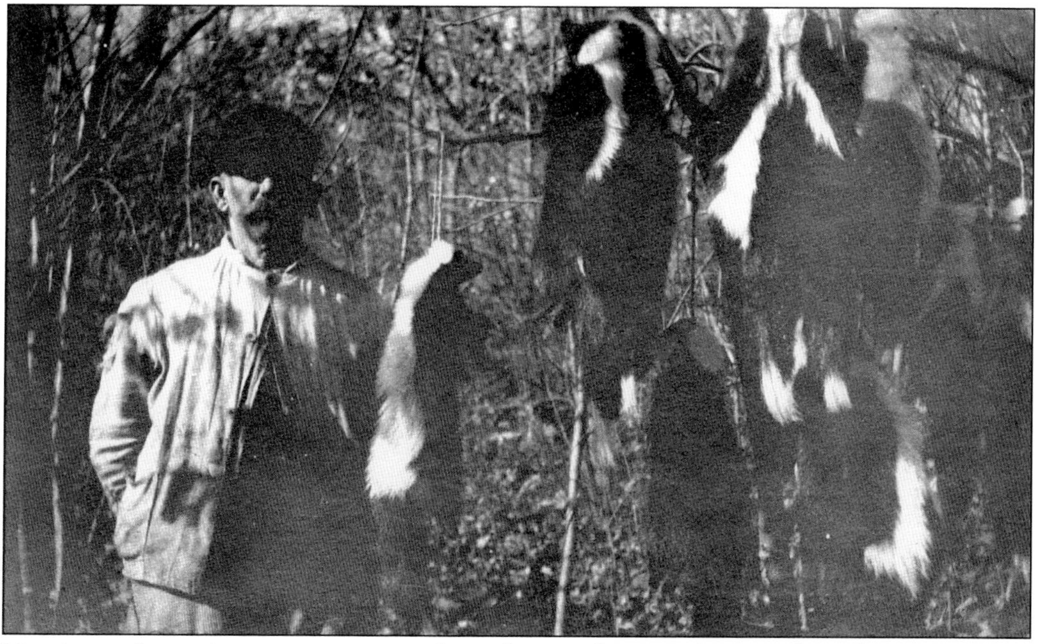

Hunting and trapping was necessary to keep the populations of critters from destroying crops. Pelts such as otter, beaver, and fox brought in $2–$3 in the late 1800s to early 1900s. Mink pelts were worth twice as much as other, more common animal skins. Even rattlesnakes were so plentiful that the town put a bounty on them at one time. Here again is the renowned Nathaniel Clark with skunk pelts. He might be thinking, "It is a stinky job, but someone has to do it."

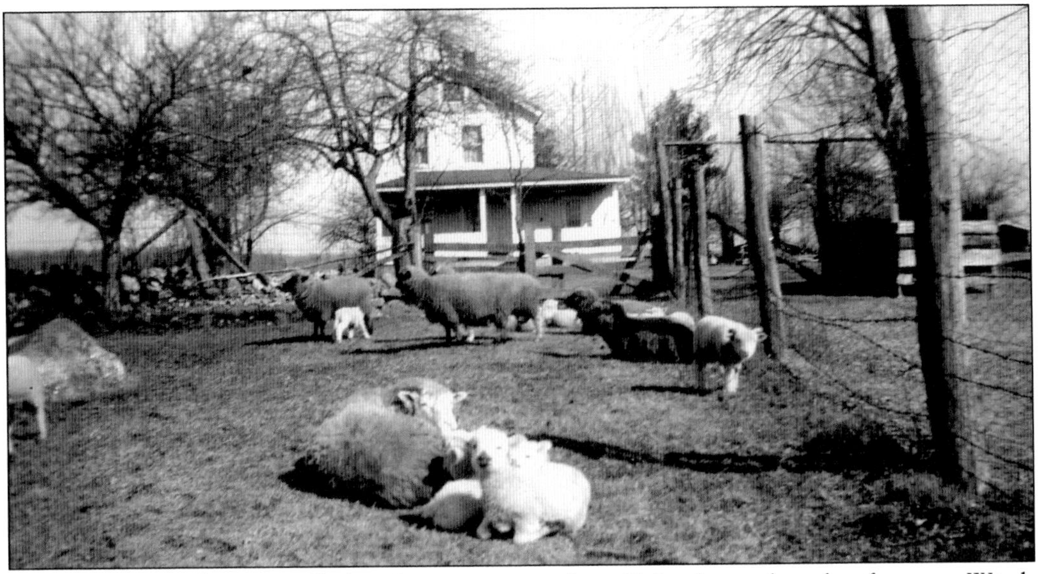

Kashmier and Albertina Wlodarcyk, immigrants from Poland, purchased a farm on Witch Meadow Road (now a horse farm) in 1913. The dairy farm consisted of 35 Guernsey and Holstein milking cows, 50 poultry, 30 sheep, one horse, and some geese and ducks. Farms in Salem were very self-sufficient. Wheat was grown and ground into flour to make bread, which the Wlodarcyks did until the 1930s when they started buying their bread already made.

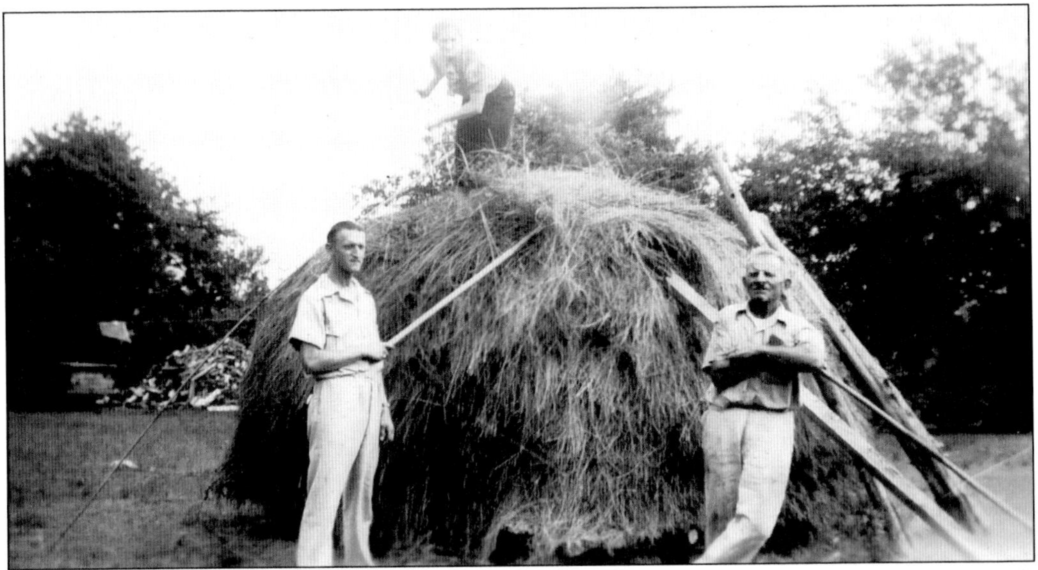

Hay was set in haystacks, not baled in the early days of Salem. Kasmier Jr. and Kasmier Sr., with an unidentified woman, put hay into a haystack on the Wlodarcyk farm on Witch Meadow Road in the late 1930s. They grew their own vegetables and grew grain for feed for the animals. Any surplus of vegetables was then sold. Since there was no electricity until 1930s, milk was lowered to be kept cold inside the well.

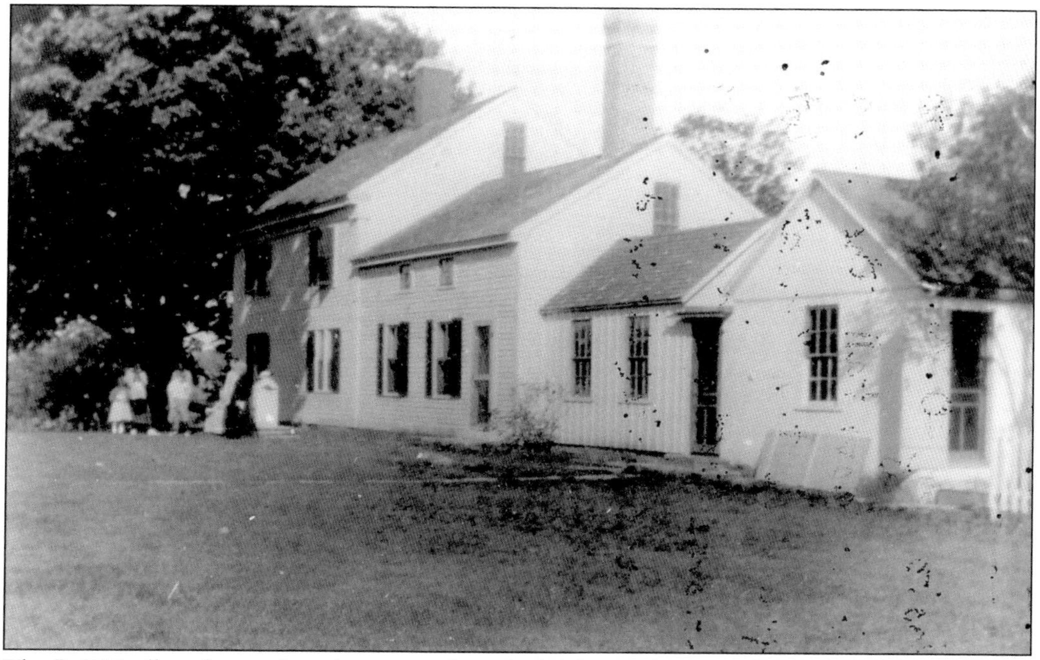

The B. F Hurlburt house, later known as the Alvah Morgan house, still stands today across from the parsonage. Mrs. Beebe, the town clerk from the 1930s through the 1960s, lived in this house for many years. This is a view of the north side of the house.

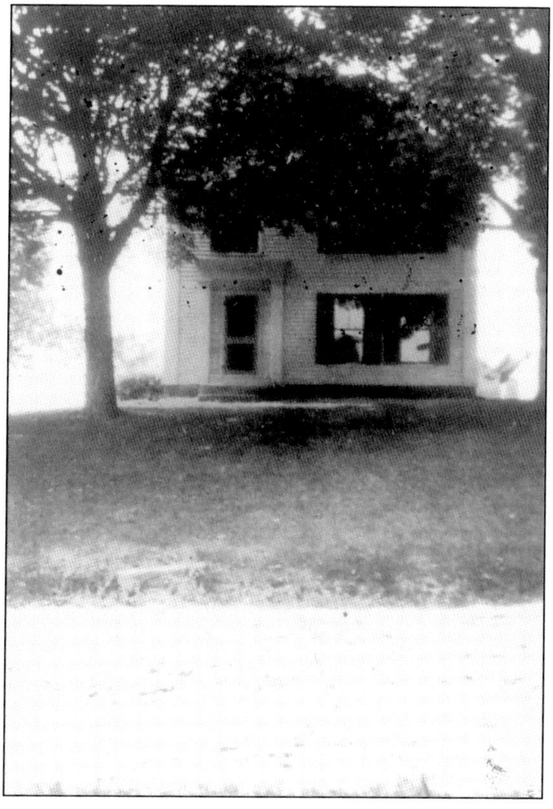

The front view of the Alvah Morgan house is seen here. This house was built in the early 1800s.

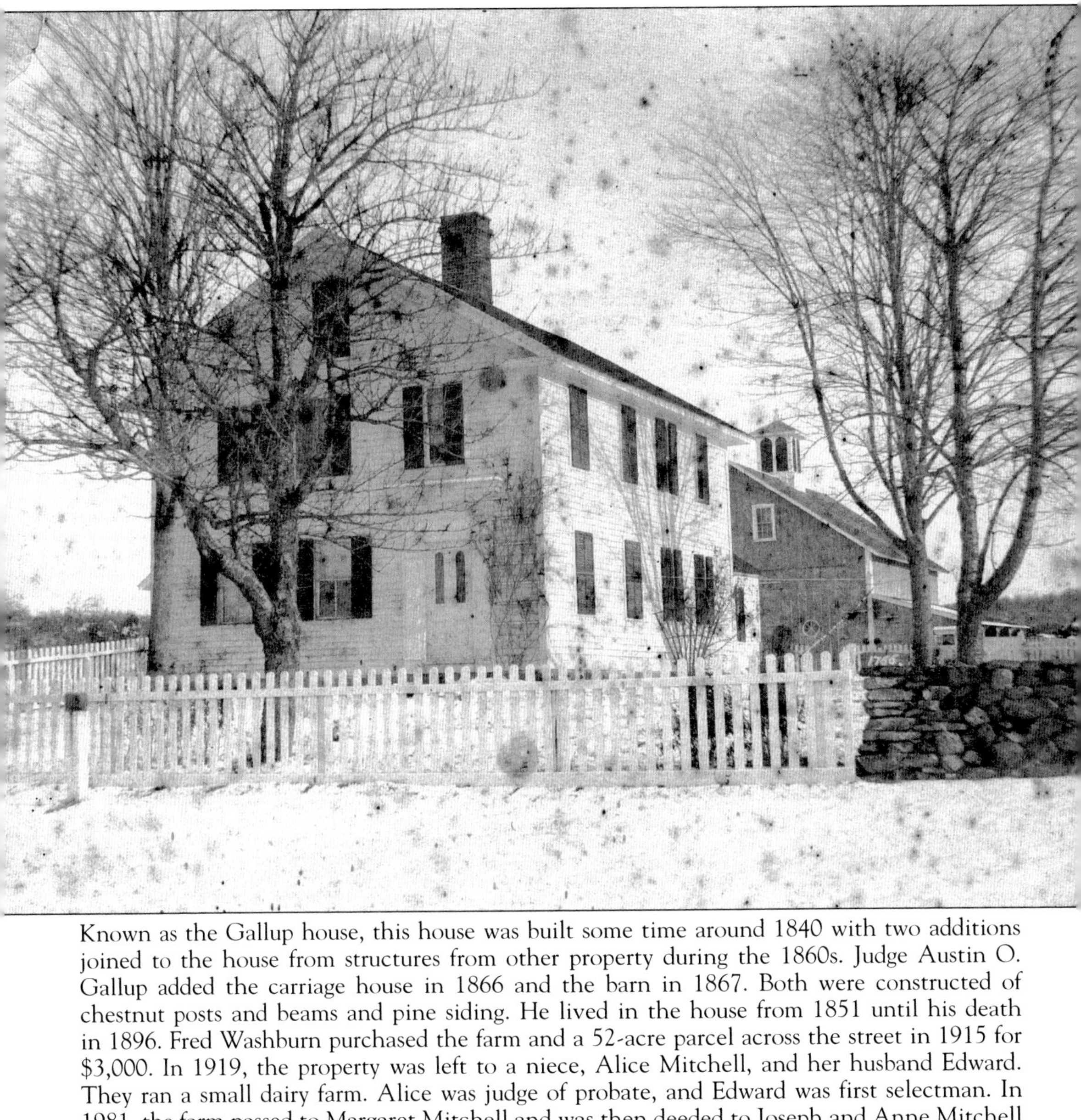

Known as the Gallup house, this house was built some time around 1840 with two additions joined to the house from structures from other property during the 1860s. Judge Austin O. Gallup added the carriage house in 1866 and the barn in 1867. Both were constructed of chestnut posts and beams and pine siding. He lived in the house from 1851 until his death in 1896. Fred Washburn purchased the farm and a 52-acre parcel across the street in 1915 for $3,000. In 1919, the property was left to a niece, Alice Mitchell, and her husband Edward. They ran a small dairy farm. Alice was judge of probate, and Edward was first selectman. In 1981, the farm passed to Margaret Mitchell and was then deeded to Joseph and Anne Mitchell Duncan. In 1997, the Salem Herbfarm was established. In 1998, restorations were made, and a greenhouse was added.

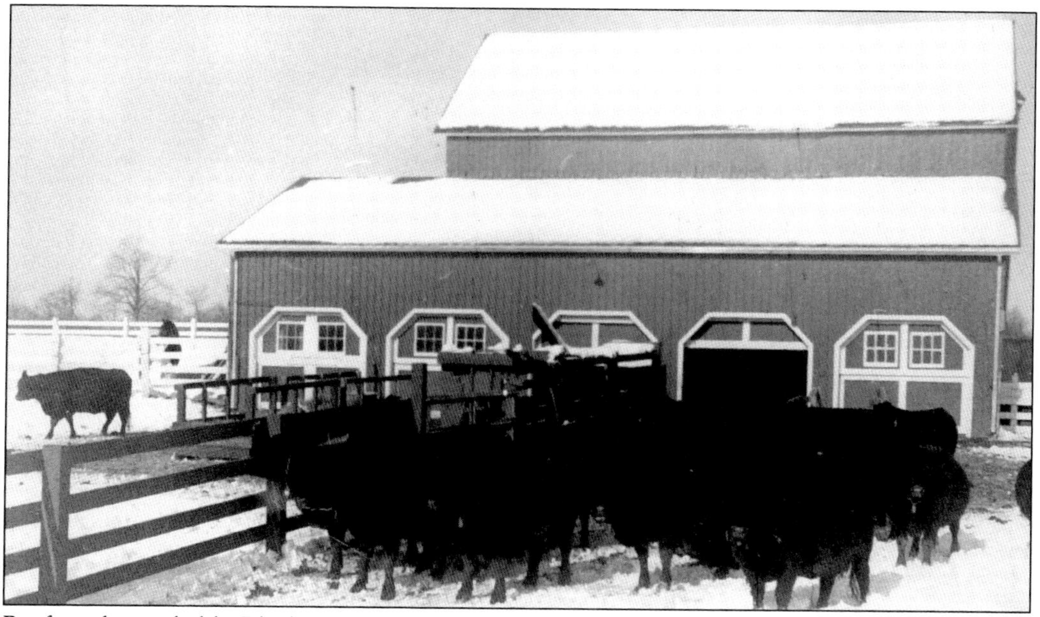

Beef cattle, probably Black Angus, was raised in Salem back in the 1950s and 1960s on the Square D Ranch owned by the Howards. The land and house were previously owned in the mid-1800s by Cpl. John A. Niles, who served in the Civil War. In the past few years, this home has been the host of the Salem Land Trust Fall Fest, a fund-raiser to support the Salem Land Trust's efforts to preserve valuable land and wildlife ecosystems.

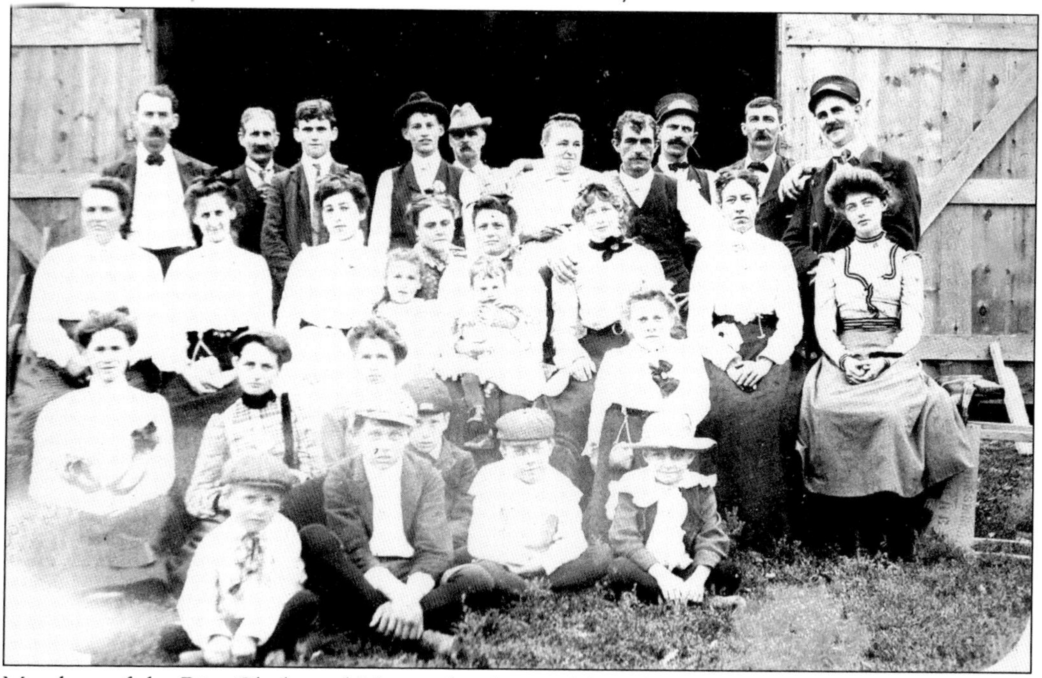

Members of the Rix, Clark, and Murray families and friends are seen here dressed in their best clothes for a special occasion around 1900. White blouses and dark skirts were the fashion at this time in rural Salem. Note the lady on the right, Amy Rix, looks to be dressed a bit differently than the others. The young woman to the right foreground may be Nellie Way.

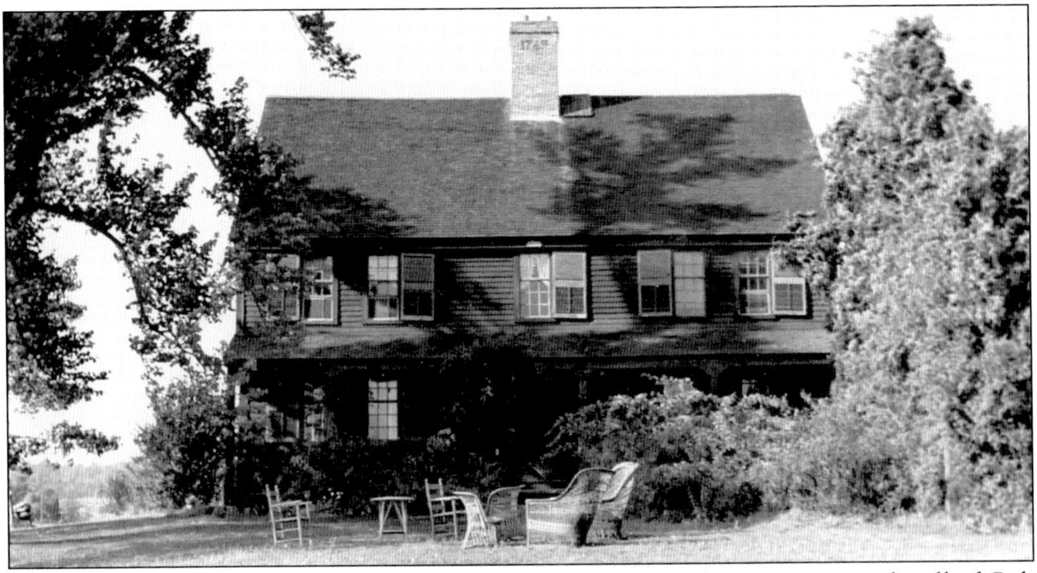

The Mumford house was built in 1769 for John Mumford Sr., who was overseer for all of Col. Samuel Brown's property, largest land owner in Salem. He owned about 9,000 acres. He was an absentee landowner from Salem, Massachusetts.

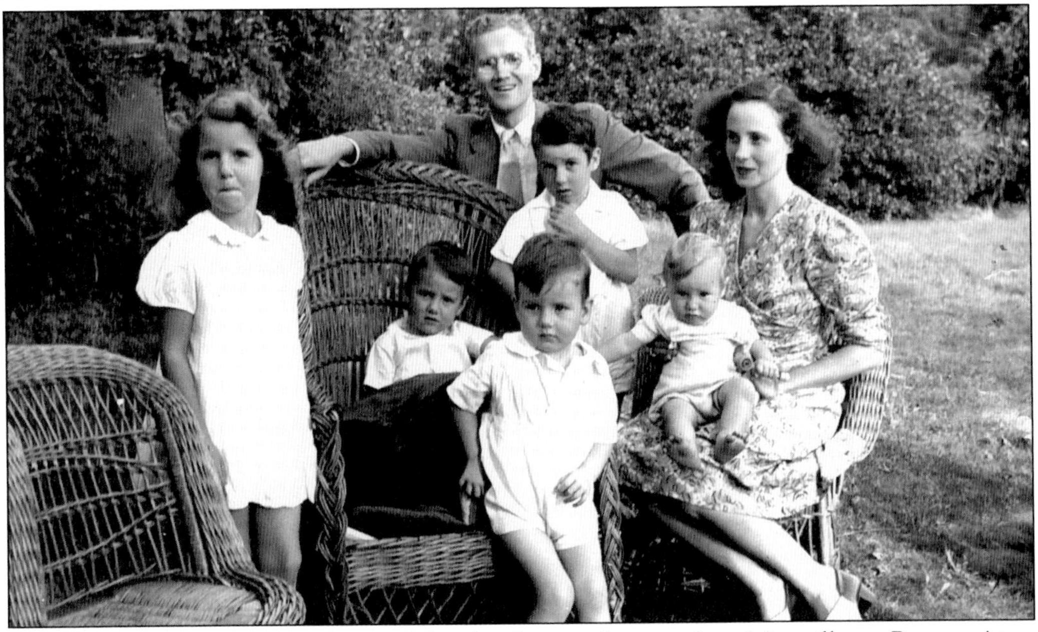

Hiram Bingham IV, seen standing with his family, is on his way from Marseilles to Buenos Aires posts in foreign service. He was issuing visas as a U.S. diplomat during World War II when Germany was invading France. It was not until after his death that his grown children found evidence of his heroism in a dark closet behind a fireplace. After the war, he had refrained from speaking about his service at all. At great personal risk, he had used his government status to help between 2,500 and 5,000 Jewish people escape the Holocaust. For his heroic service in France from 1937 to 1940, he will be issued a stamp in his honor in May–June 2006. From left to right are Tiffany, Thomas (under blanket due to polio), John, Tony, David (on lap), and Rose (Morrison) Bingham. The other six children of Hiram and Rose had not been born yet.

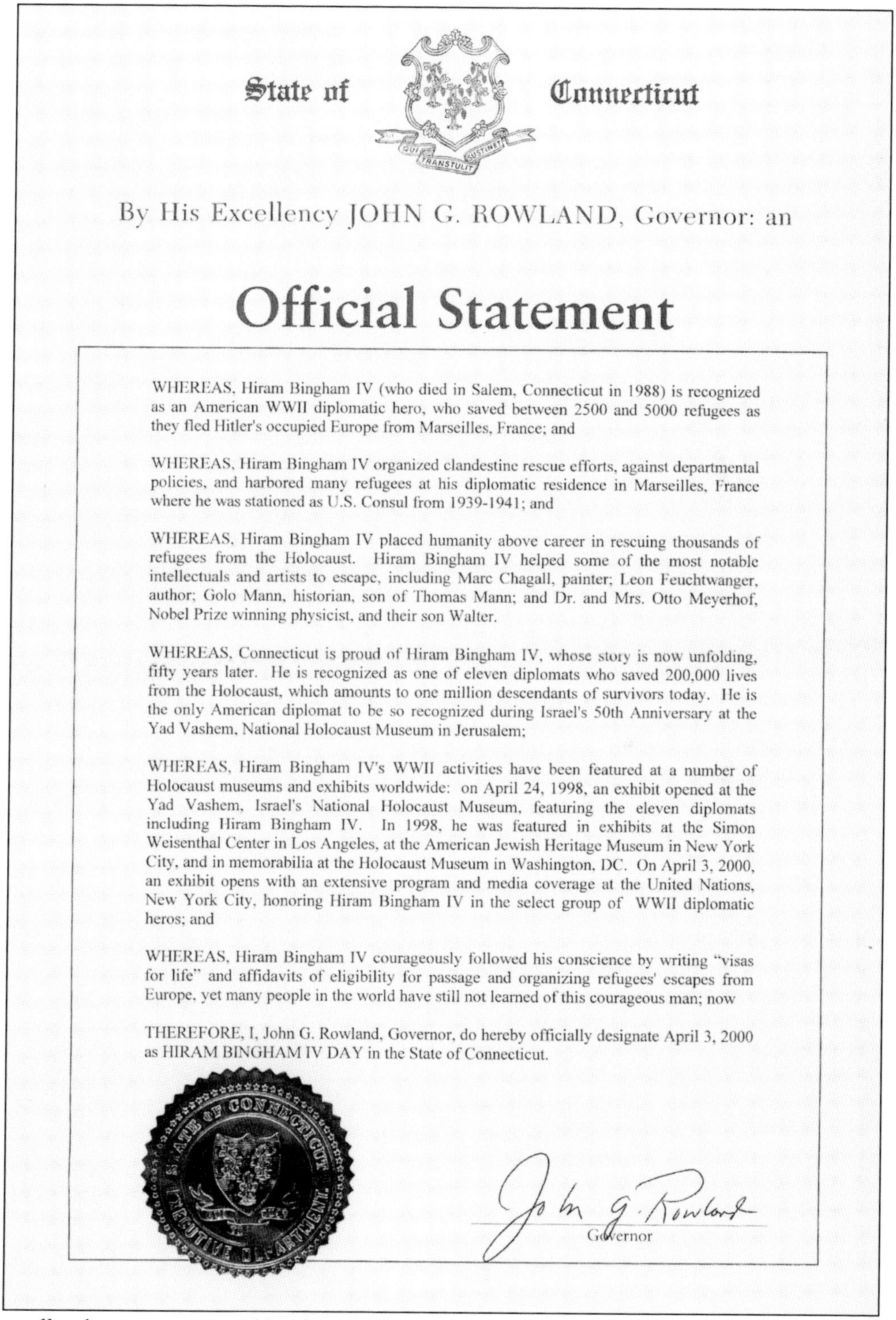

State of Connecticut

QUI TRANSTULIT SUSTINET

By His Excellency JOHN G. ROWLAND, Governor: an

Official Statement

WHEREAS, Hiram Bingham IV (who died in Salem, Connecticut in 1988) is recognized as an American WWII diplomatic hero, who saved between 2500 and 5000 refugees as they fled Hitler's occupied Europe from Marseilles, France; and

WHEREAS, Hiram Bingham IV organized clandestine rescue efforts, against departmental policies, and harbored many refugees at his diplomatic residence in Marseilles, France where he was stationed as U.S. Consul from 1939-1941; and

WHEREAS, Hiram Bingham IV placed humanity above career in rescuing thousands of refugees from the Holocaust. Hiram Bingham IV helped some of the most notable intellectuals and artists to escape, including Marc Chagall, painter; Leon Feuchtwanger, author; Golo Mann, historian, son of Thomas Mann; and Dr. and Mrs. Otto Meyerhof, Nobel Prize winning physicist, and their son Walter.

WHEREAS, Connecticut is proud of Hiram Bingham IV, whose story is now unfolding, fifty years later. He is recognized as one of eleven diplomats who saved 200,000 lives from the Holocaust, which amounts to one million descendants of survivors today. He is the only American diplomat to be so recognized during Israel's 50th Anniversary at the Yad Vashem, National Holocaust Museum in Jerusalem;

WHEREAS, Hiram Bingham IV's WWII activities have been featured at a number of Holocaust museums and exhibits worldwide: on April 24, 1998, an exhibit opened at the Yad Vashem, Israel's National Holocaust Museum, featuring the eleven diplomats including Hiram Bingham IV. In 1998, he was featured in exhibits at the Simon Weisenthal Center in Los Angeles, at the American Jewish Heritage Museum in New York City, and in memorabilia at the Holocaust Museum in Washington, DC. On April 3, 2000, an exhibit opens with an extensive program and media coverage at the United Nations, New York City, honoring Hiram Bingham IV in the select group of WWII diplomatic heros; and

WHEREAS, Hiram Bingham IV courageously followed his conscience by writing "visas for life" and affidavits of eligibility for passage and organizing refugees' escapes from Europe, yet many people in the world have still not learned of this courageous man; now

THEREFORE, I, John G. Rowland, Governor, do hereby officially designate April 3, 2000 as HIRAM BINGHAM IV DAY in the State of Connecticut.

STATE OF CONNECTICUT EXECUTIVE DEPARTMENT

John G. Rowland

Governor

An official statement signed by the governor of Connecticut on April 3, 2000, declares Hiram Bingham Day.

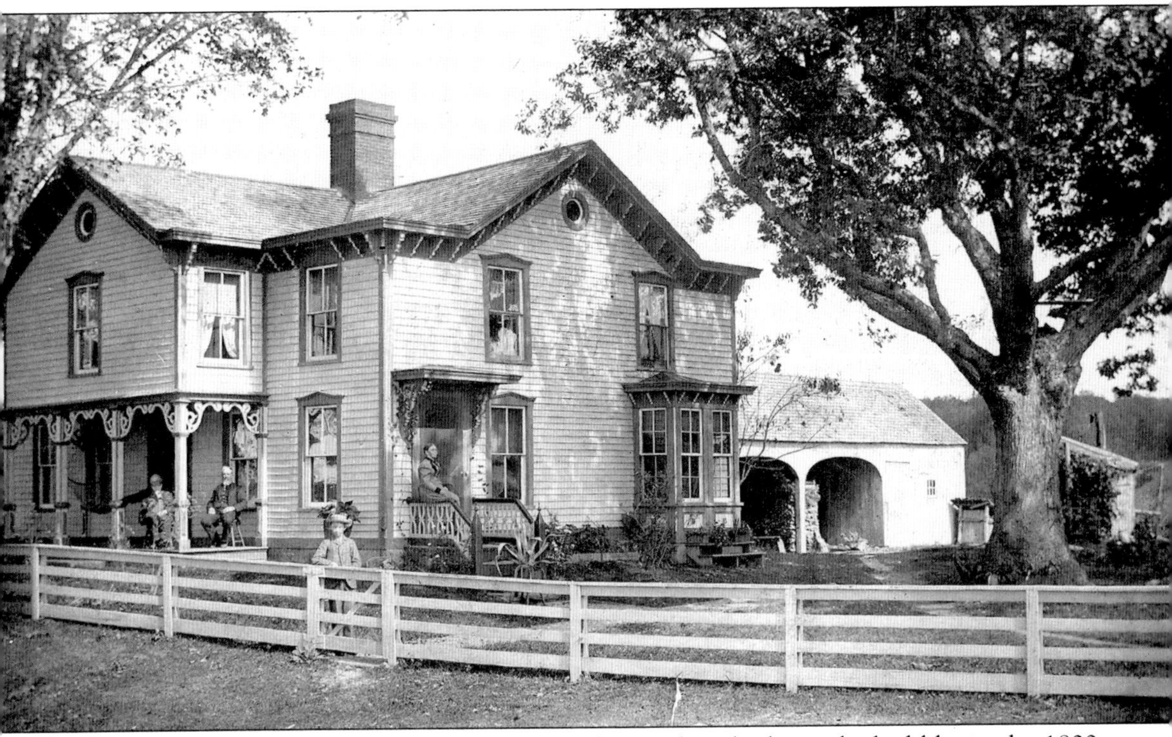

This James Ransom house was built in 1790. This is what the house looked like in the 1800s during the Victorian era.

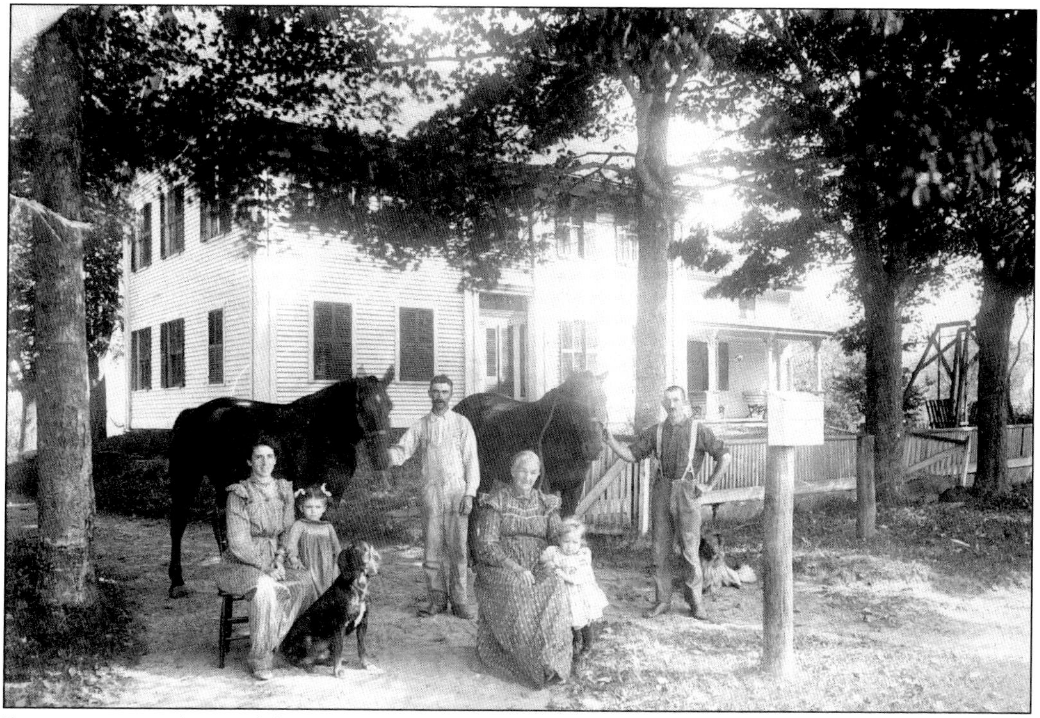

Renovations and remodeling over the years changed the look of this Ransom house. Also called the Darling place, it is located on the same street bearing that particular family name.

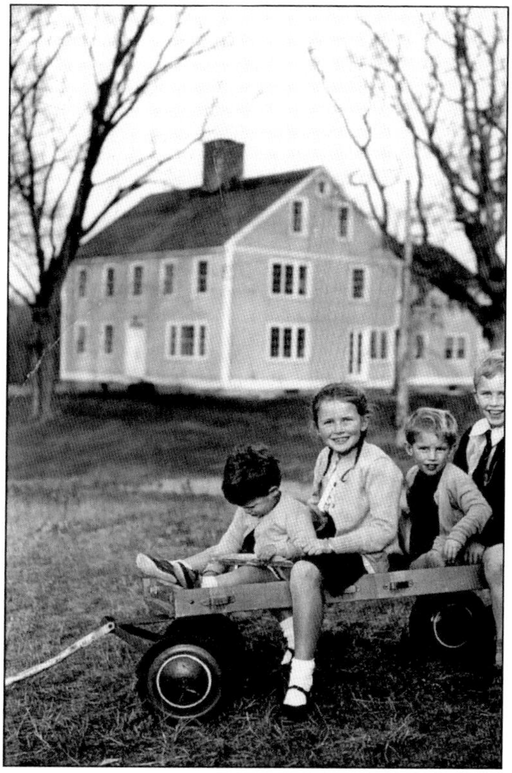

After the renovations of 1938, this is how it appears today. This photograph was taken in early 1940s. From left to right in the wagon are Stephen, Alfreda, Douglas, and Christofer Bingham. Alfred Bingham and Hiram Bingham IV both raised their families here in Salem.

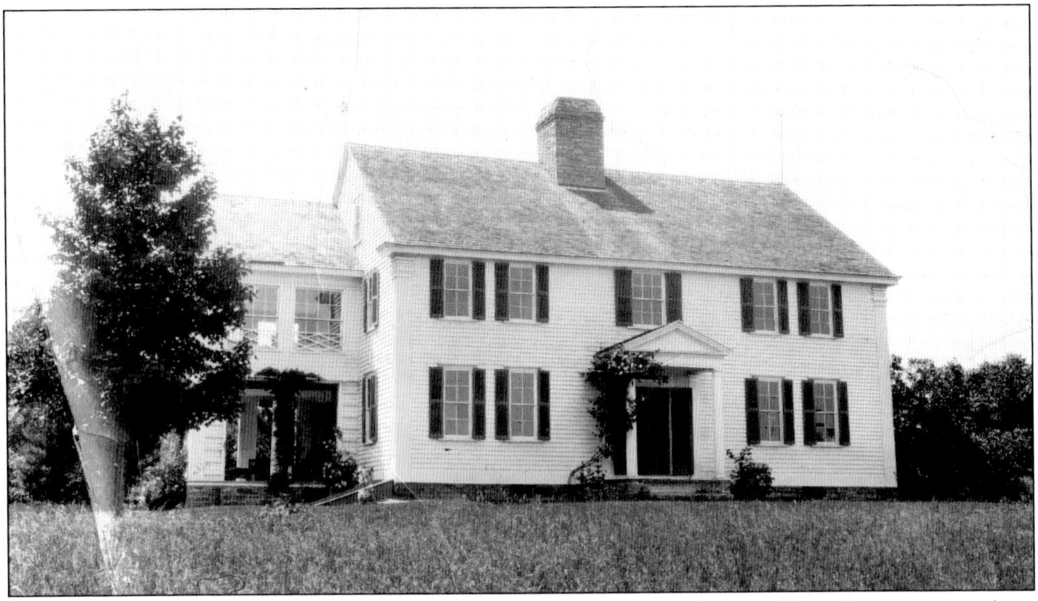

Thomas Shaw had bought large tracts of the confiscated estate of Col William Browne, grandson of Col. Samuel Browne. On June 18, 1791, he built the Woodbridge House at White Oak Hill for his nephew Nathaniel Shaw Woodbridge and his new bride, Elizabeth, daughter of John and Lucretia Mumford. This house was only a mile from Elizabeth's parents' home, the Mumford house. At one time, a red shawl was hung from a window of either house as an indication that visitors were present and an invitation for dinner was being offered. Later the tradition continued again with a red flag being hoisted.

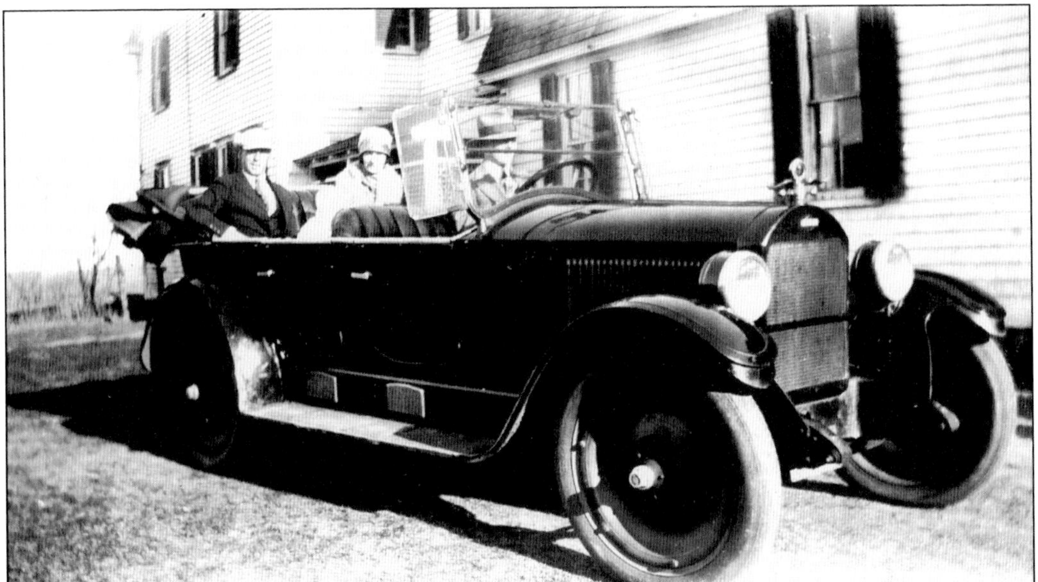

Albert and Jeanie Hampton were caretakers of the Woodbridge House. Here they are seated in their automobile around 1930. The Woodbridge House is on the National Register of Historic Places.

Wallace Maynard, foreman of the Mitchell Farm which was owned by the Bingham family, is seen here in the late 1930s. Since woodchucks were destructive to farms, Maynard would shoot them, collect the tails, and turn them in to his employer for U.S. savings bonds. The Maynards won prizes for horse and cattle at the Hamburg Fair in the early 1900s.

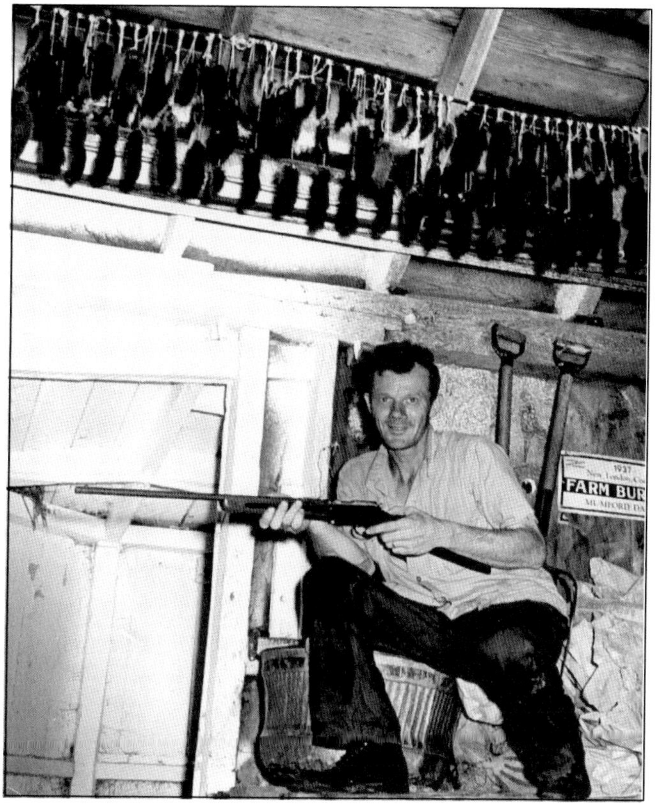

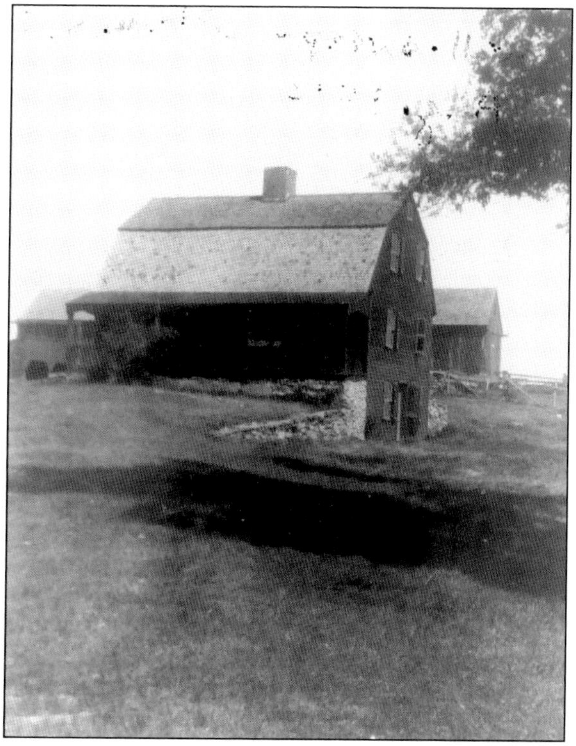

The Charles Henry Bailey farmhouse, better known as the Ike Marvel house, was in the Mitchell family many years before Bailey acquired it. It was in this house that Donald G. Mitchell wrote *Dream Life* and *Reveries of a Bachelor*. Later the Mitchells bought back the farm, and the Ike Marvel house is now part of the Mitchell/Bingham estate.

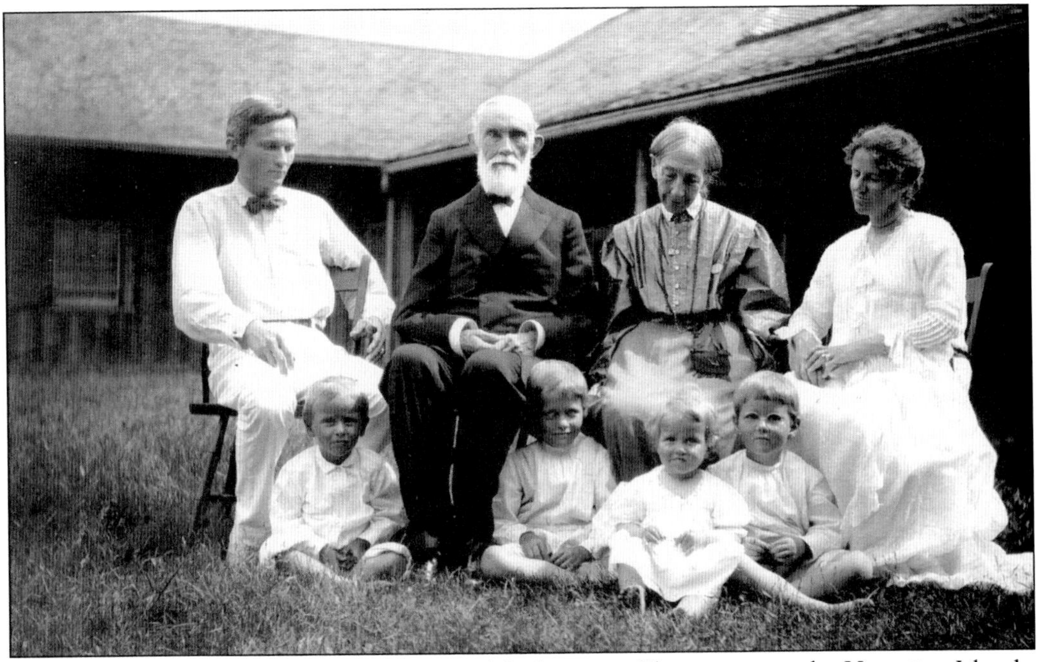

Hiram Bingham I (1789–1869) is most noted for bringing Christianity to the Hawaiian Islands. Hiram Bingham II (1831–1908) created a written language for the Gilbert Islands on the South Pacific. Hiram Bingham III (1875–1956), an explorer, rediscovered the ruins of Machu Picchu, Peru, and was a U.S. senator. Bingham III married the granddaughter and heiress of Charles Tiffany. Taken at the Bingham camp in Salem in 1908, from left to right are (first row) Woodbridge Bingham, Alfred Mitchell, Charles Tiffany, and Hiram Bingham IV; (second row) Hiram Bingham III, Hiram Bingham II, Lydia Bingham Coan, and Alfreda Mitchell Bingham.

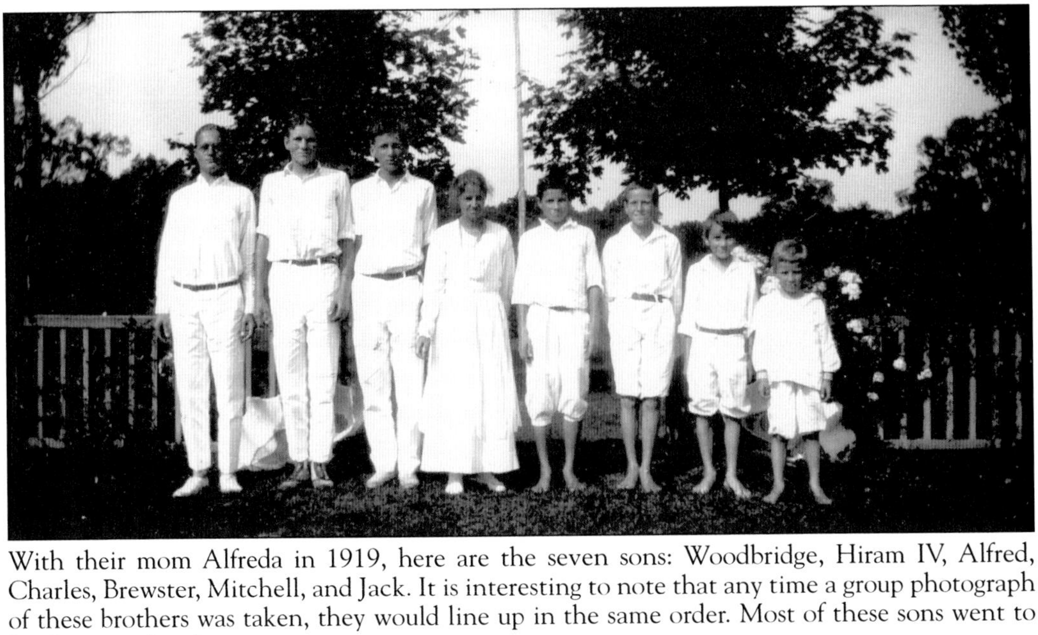

With their mom Alfreda in 1919, here are the seven sons: Woodbridge, Hiram IV, Alfred, Charles, Brewster, Mitchell, and Jack. It is interesting to note that any time a group photograph of these brothers was taken, they would line up in the same order. Most of these sons went to Ivy League schools.

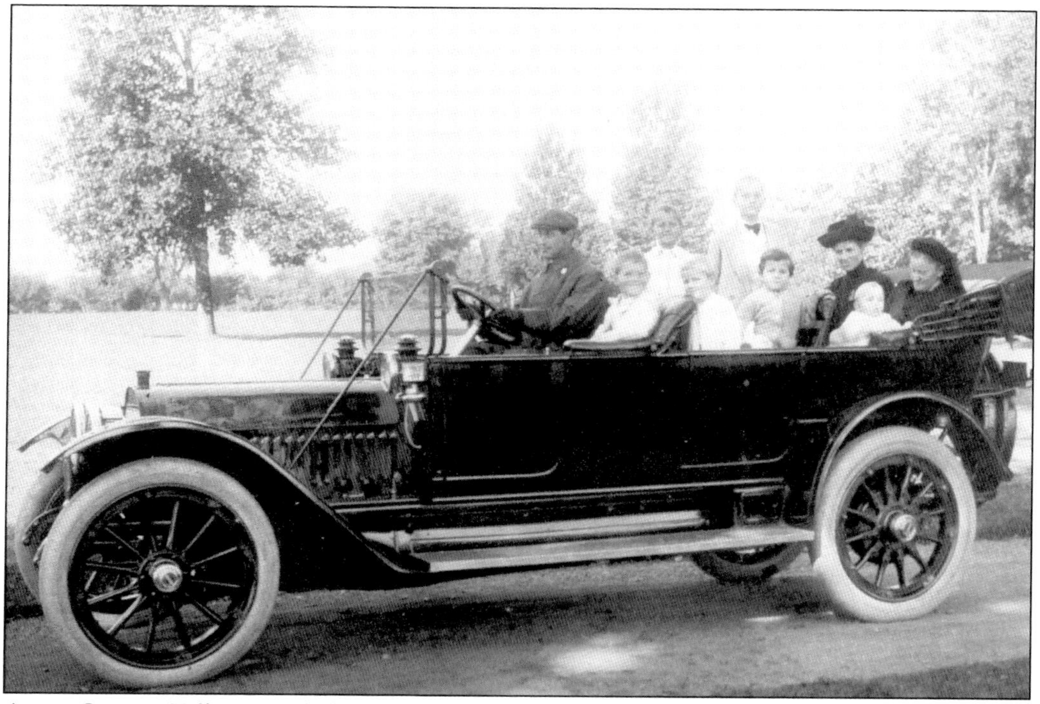

Annie Octavia Tiffany Mitchell, the daughter of Charles Tiffany, and Alfreda Mitchell Bingham are seen here dressed in full mourning attire three months after the death of Alfred Mitchell. Six of the seven sons of Alfreda and Hiram Bingham III are passengers in this 1910 Locomobile in the summer of 1911.

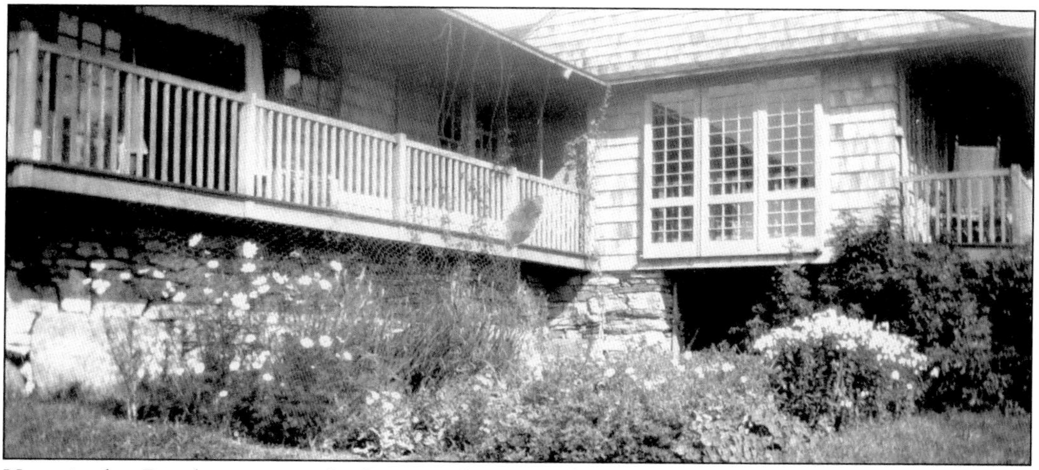

Here is the Bingham camp, built around 1903. This is one of the first houses of Japanese architecture in Connecticut. It was designed by Hiram Bingham III and reminiscent of his childhood home in Hawaii. Each room in the Bingham camp is dedicated to a particular son of Hiram Bingham III with photographs and memorabilia of each son and that particulars son's family. Weddings at the camp are remembered by a unique tradition of etching the initials of the newlyweds in the panes of glass of one window. With extended family, the Binghams number about 200. Besides wedding parties, many Bingham family members come here for reunions or simply to vacation. Though modest in presence, being adorned only by two large clamshells, the views are spectacular.

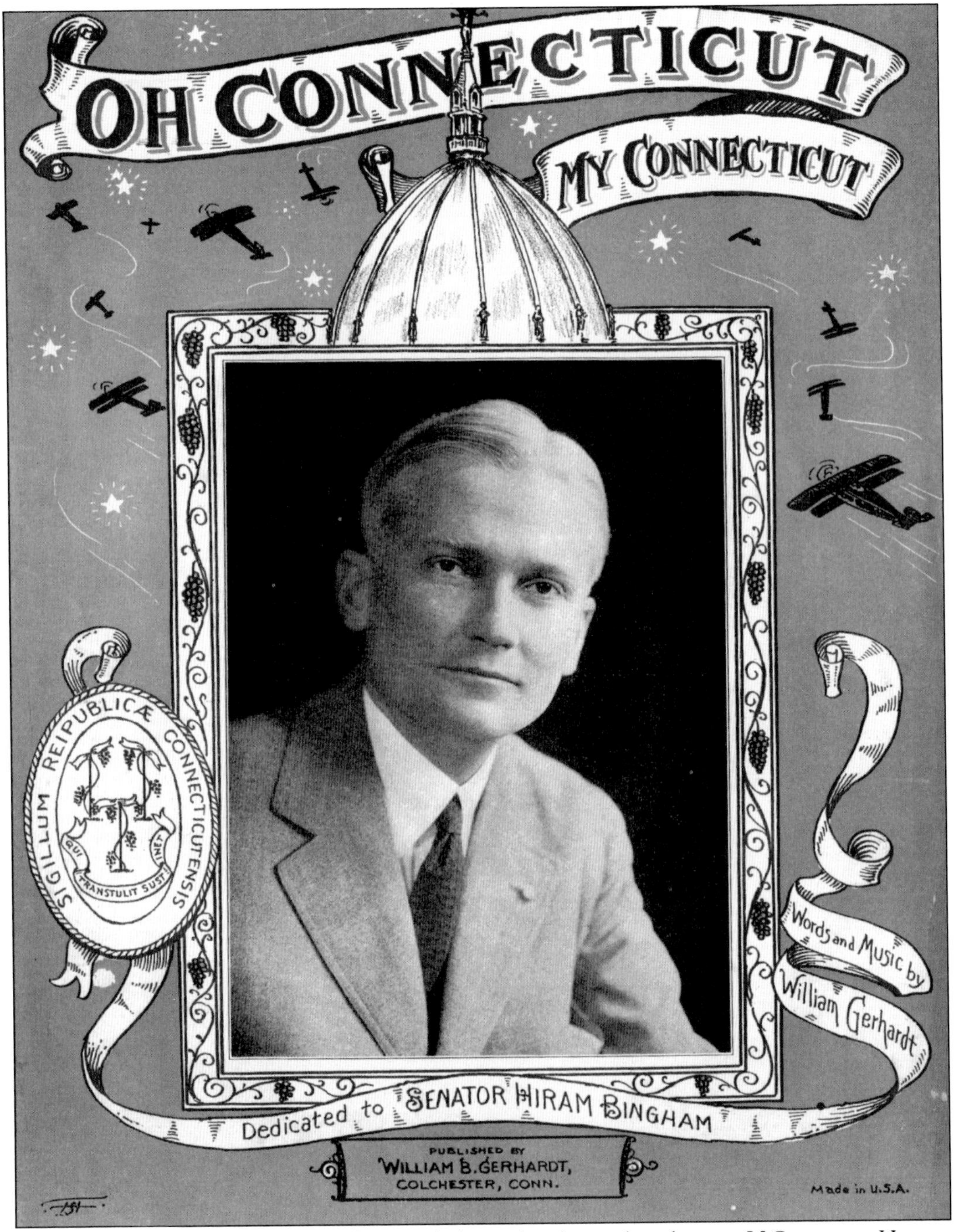

Hiram Bingham III had a piece of music dedicated to him when he was U.S senator. He was a professor at Yale and became a well-known explorer, having rediscovered Machu Picchu in Peru. He helped pioneer American investment in Latin America and wrote a guidebook for American business ventures in South America. He was elected lieutenant governor of the State of Connecticut and, in 1924, became governor for a day. Two days later, opportunity arose, and he ran for the U.S. Senate and won. Though most of his time was spent at his home in the Prospect Hill section of New Haven, summers were spent here in Salem at the Bingham camp.

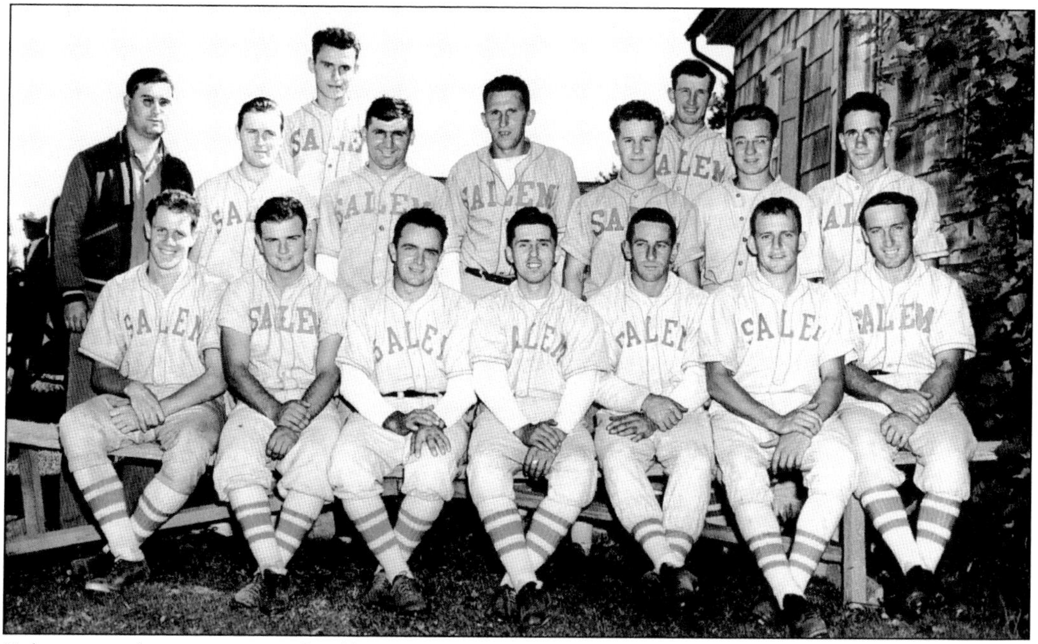

Salem won the pennant in the Shore Line League in 1940 after defeating Old Lyme at Bingham Field. Pictured from left to right are (first row) Fred Mitchell, Ernest Day, Paul Hudmya (Chesterfield), Paul Suchowirsky, Joseph Chynski, Edwin (Stubb) Coffeey, and Alfred/Albert Wickson; (second row) manager George Wickson, Richard Wickson, Louis Priolo (New London), Edward Prokop (Chesterfield), James Beebe Jr., Edward Dytko, and William Mitchell; (third row) Peter Suchowirsky and Charles F. Dimmock Sr.

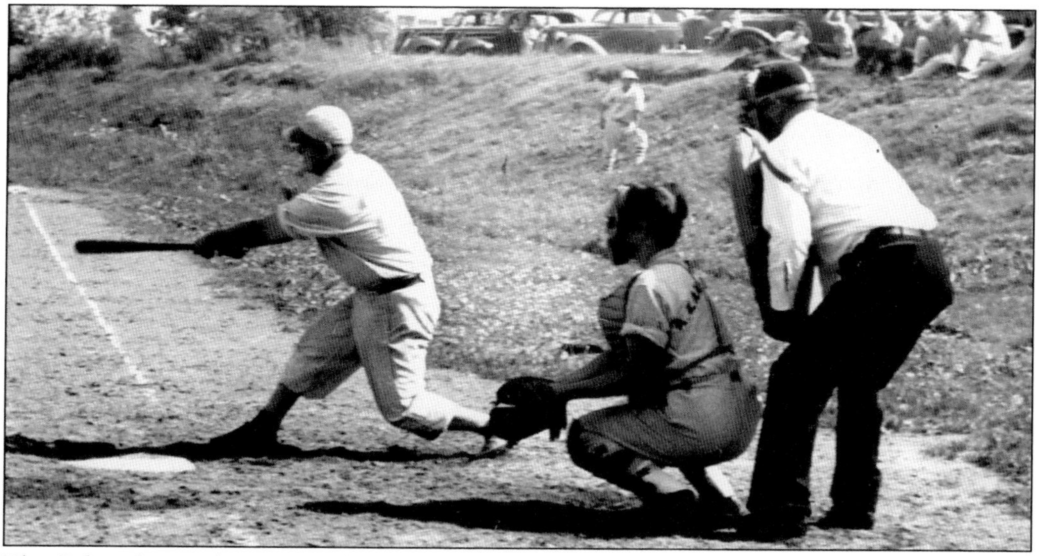

The Salem Bears play on Bingham Field behind the library around 1941. In the background is the Salem School. Senator Bingham donated the land for the school playground and town recreation field. During the 1950s, Salem had games of donkey baseball in which baseball players rode donkeys while playing baseball. The very first game was the Salem Firehouse dressed in costumes against Colchester Firehouse, who came wearing white hats and T-shirts. The score was 21-20, and the proceeds from this fund-raiser were split between the two teams.

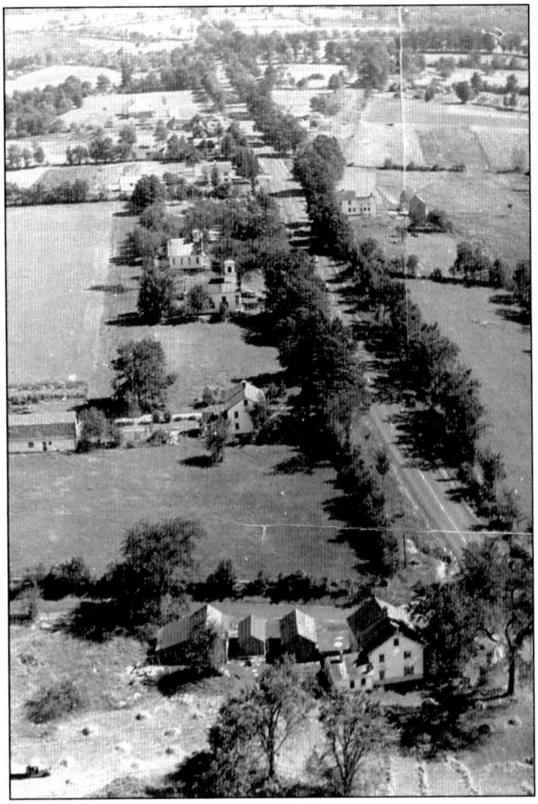

Taken around 1942, this is a view from north of Route 82 looking south on Salem Street from Round Hill Road. On the left are the Simon Ray house, original town hall before addition, church, Grange building, and town house behind the trees. The parsonage is hidden behind the trees. Next is Zemko's Lumber, then Mrs. Scovill's, the old library, Mrs. Chynski's (now owned by the school), and Salem School (three-room school) prior to additions with a circular driveway. On the right side of the road are the Beebe house across from parsonage and the Cannell house just before the school (across from Chynski's).

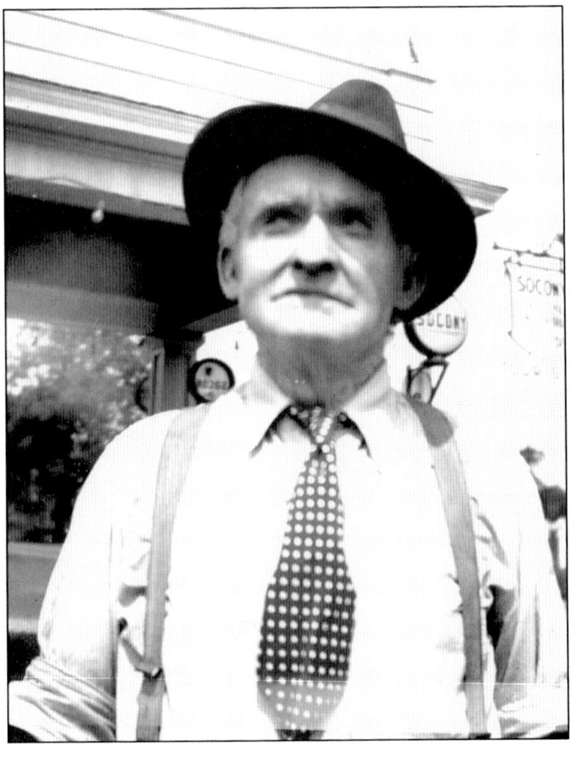

Pictured is Ed Hagen at 67 years old, taken around 1940. Hagen lived near Salem Four Corners, probably on the road that was named after him. He was a farmhand on the Mitchell farm, a sawmill hand, horse trader, and clerk in a country store, ran a livery stable, and could turn a six-horse team in a wagon shed with little effort. His claim to fame was that he drove a bandwagon in the Barnum and Bailey's circus for several seasons. Legend has it that one night after exhausting his wages in a New London saloon, Hagen was hoisted up into his wagon by the bartender. The bartender slapped the horse on the flank, and, unattended, the horse made the 12-mile journey back to Salem. The horse, spooked by something, made its way, wagon and all, into Horse Pond. Ed managed to hold onto the wagon until help arrived, but the horse unfortunately drowned. And this is how the pond acquired the name Horse Pond or Dead Horse Pond.

Nellie Way was just two and a half feet tall (30 inches) and weighed 42 pounds at age 40. She lived on route 354 near where the Suefert farm used to be. A well and foundation still remain there. She can be seen as a child in some of the schoolhouse pictures.

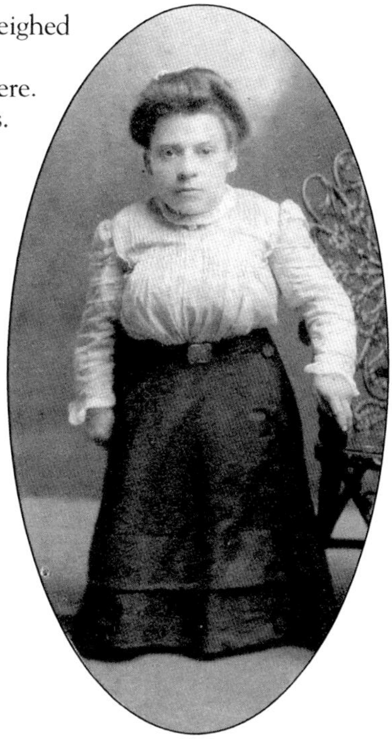

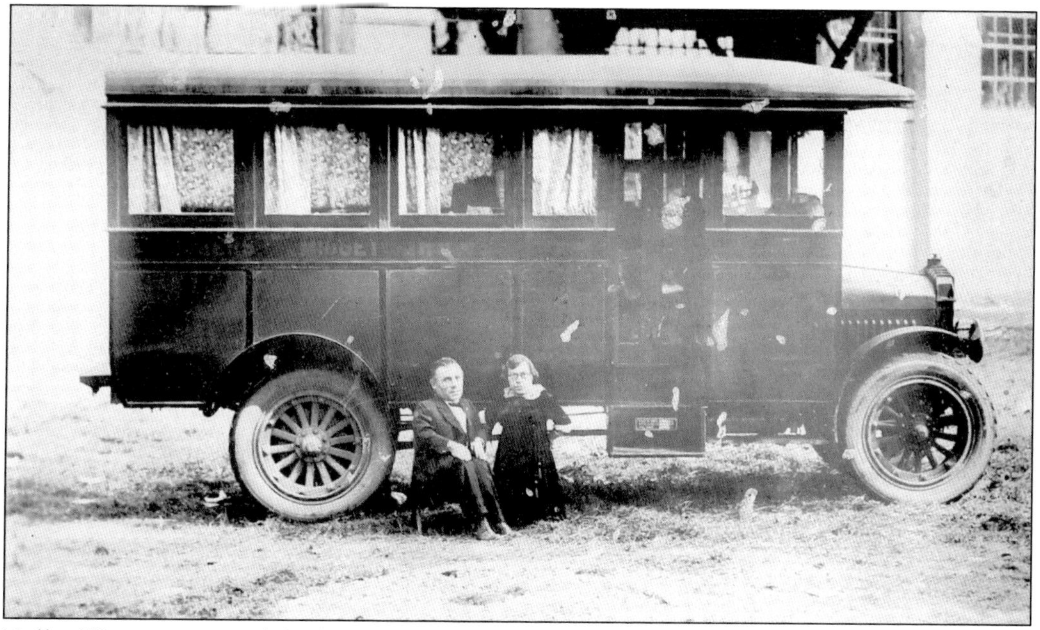

Nellie Way, an accomplished violinist and seamstress, married Maj. Stanley Jober of Warsaw, Poland, on April 14, 1920, at the Huntington Baptist Street Church in New London. He was 35 inches tall and weighed 56 pounds at 41 years of age according to one account. Another source states he was 42 inches tall. Together Nellie and Stanley joined a circus called the Mighty Doris-Col. Francis Ferrari Show, where Nellie became known as Princess Nellie. Here are the Jobers in front of their circus home on wheels.

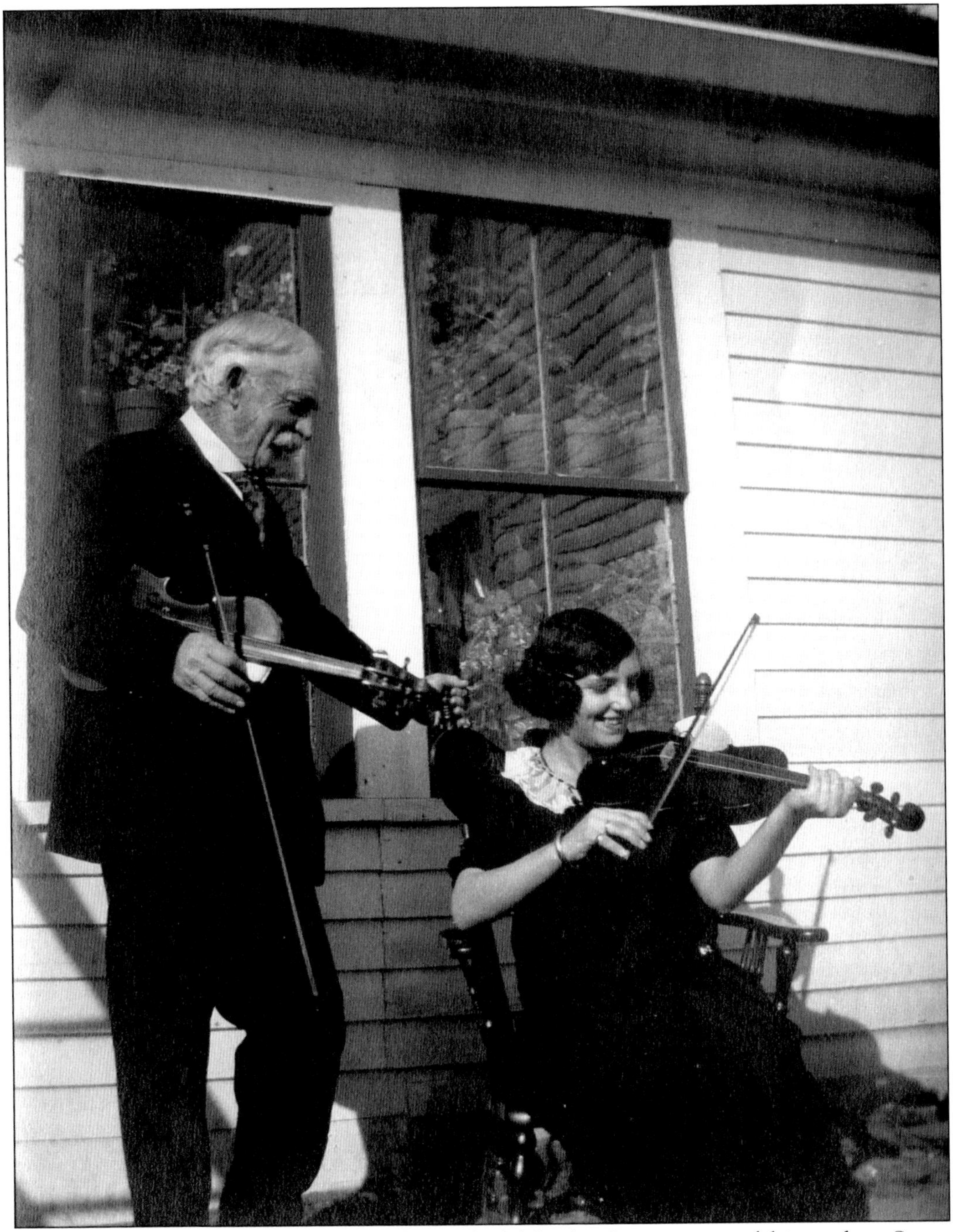

Henry Archibald Rogers of New London, a bashful schoolmaster, wooed his student Susan Bailey Tiffany of Salem with comical verse. Rogers was smitten, and Tiffany did not object to her status as favorite pupil. Four years passed before they were married and settled down in Echo Glen in Salem, where they took up farming. Both became judges of probate. Here they are playing violin together.

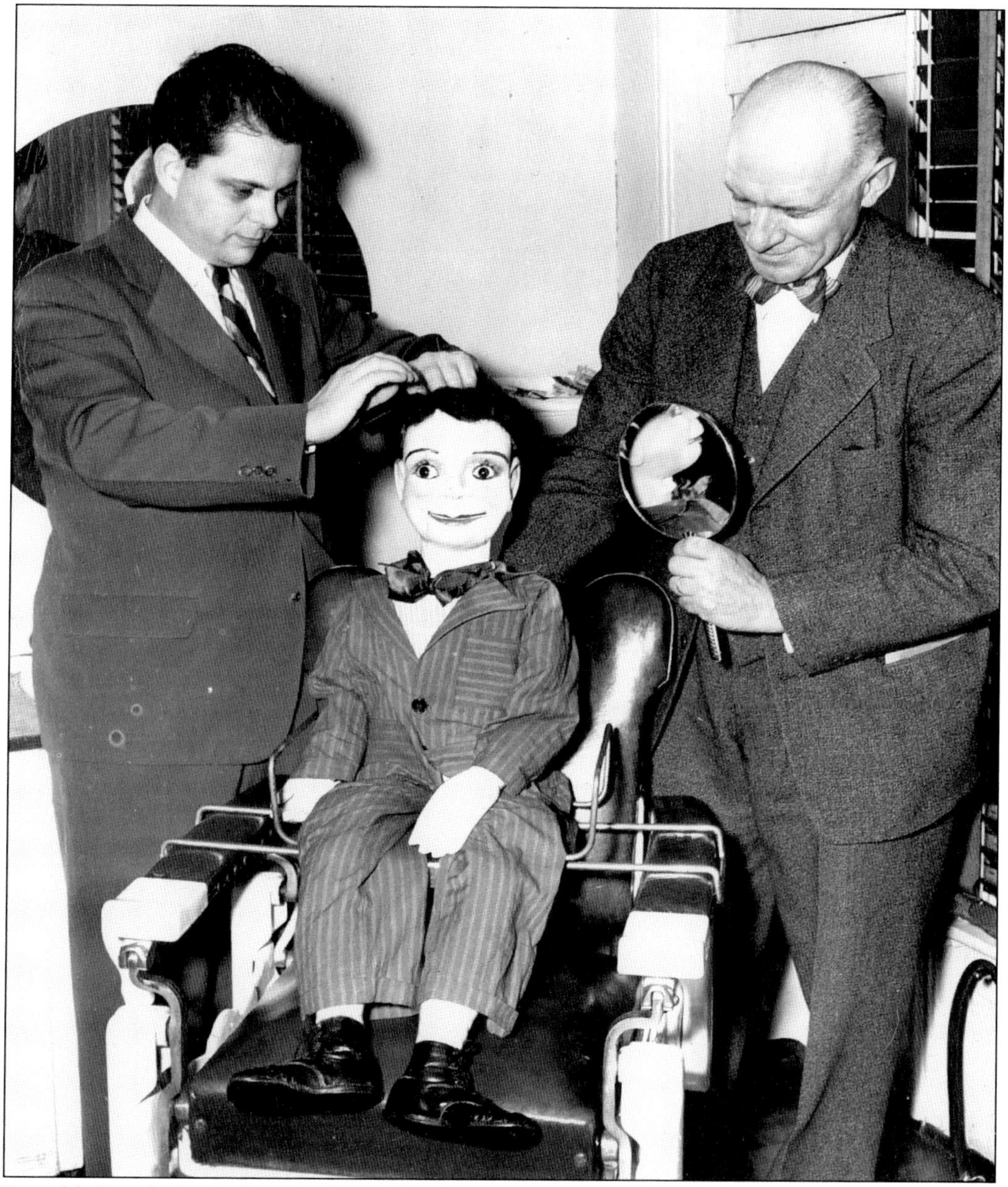

Donald (Don) Fraser Sr. (1895–1970) ran the Country Store or Fairy Lake Store from 1922 to 1946. It later boldly donned the name Don Fraser. Known for his civic and governmental involvement, he was sealer of weights and measures for New London County, served as U.S. marshal for the State of Connecticut, and was a tax collector for the Town of Salem, just to name a few. He was Salem's correspondent and feature writer for *The Day* for 40 years. He wrote stories about strange animals in Salem: Jonah the Swiss cheese–eating trout, the goofus "dillinger," a sea serpent that inhabited Horse Pond, the talking wumph, and the gallapaloozer. Also an artist and cartoonist, he was known best for his ventriloquist act with Elmer. It has been said that as state representative, often times Elmer accompanied Donald to these meetings. Someone once remarked that they did not know who was doing the voting, Elmer or Donald. Elmer is getting a haircut in this photograph with Donald to the right.

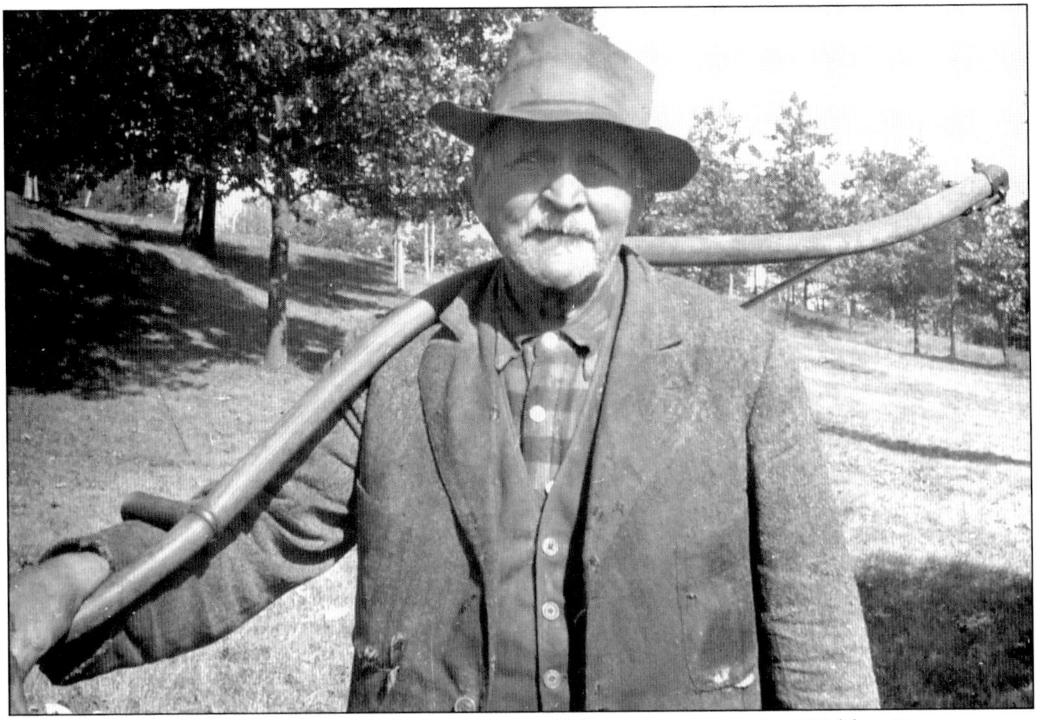

When Salem Land Trust acquired the preserve in Salem, they named it Walden Preserve, not only in reference to the name of the old dirt road that leads into the property but for Henry David Thoreau's *Walden* as well. This old farmer, named Asa Walden, is coming in from the fields with a scythe on his shoulder after cutting hay.

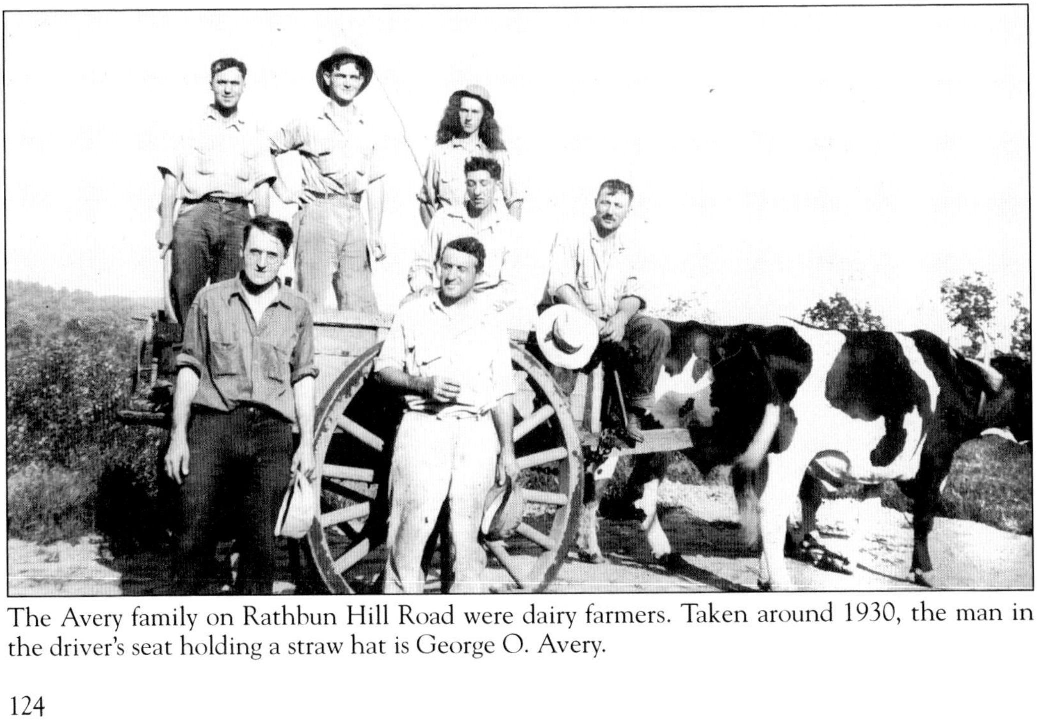

The Avery family on Rathbun Hill Road were dairy farmers. Taken around 1930, the man in the driver's seat holding a straw hat is George O. Avery.

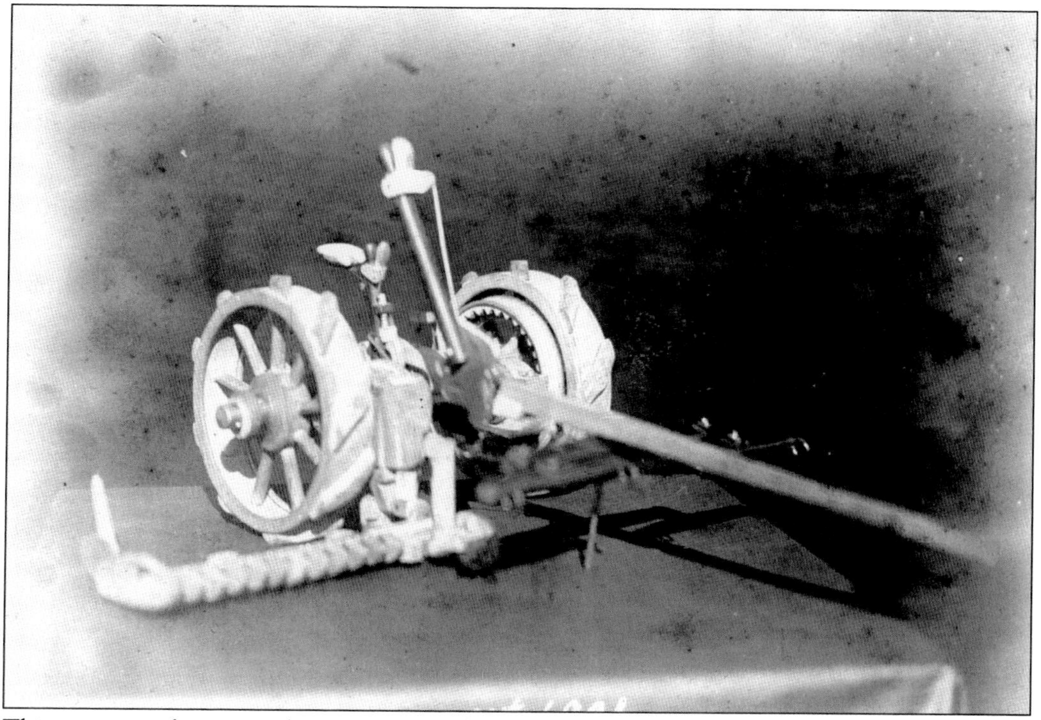

This apparatus for cutting hay was patented in 1901 by C. W. Harris. Harris was from a long line of farmers in Salem. Sometimes inventions and improvements on apparatus were brainstormed out of a need for faster or more efficient ways to achieve a desired goal.

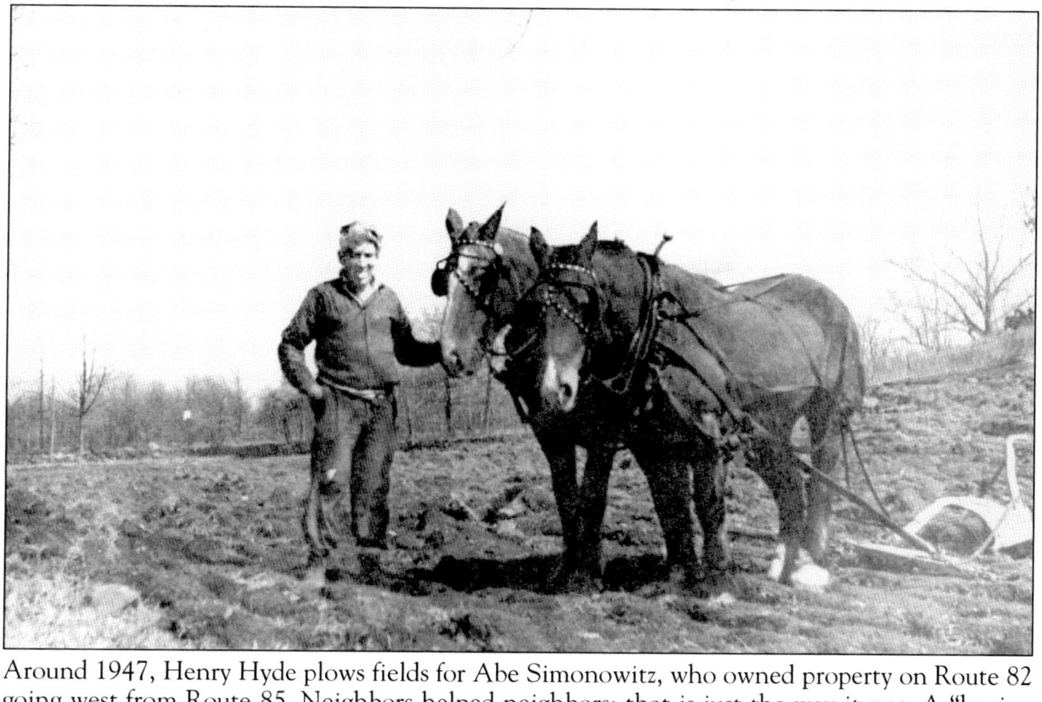

Around 1947, Henry Hyde plows fields for Abe Simonowitz, who owned property on Route 82 going west from Route 85. Neighbors helped neighbors; that is just the way it was. A "haying bee" might end after a day's work with a bean or chowder supper.

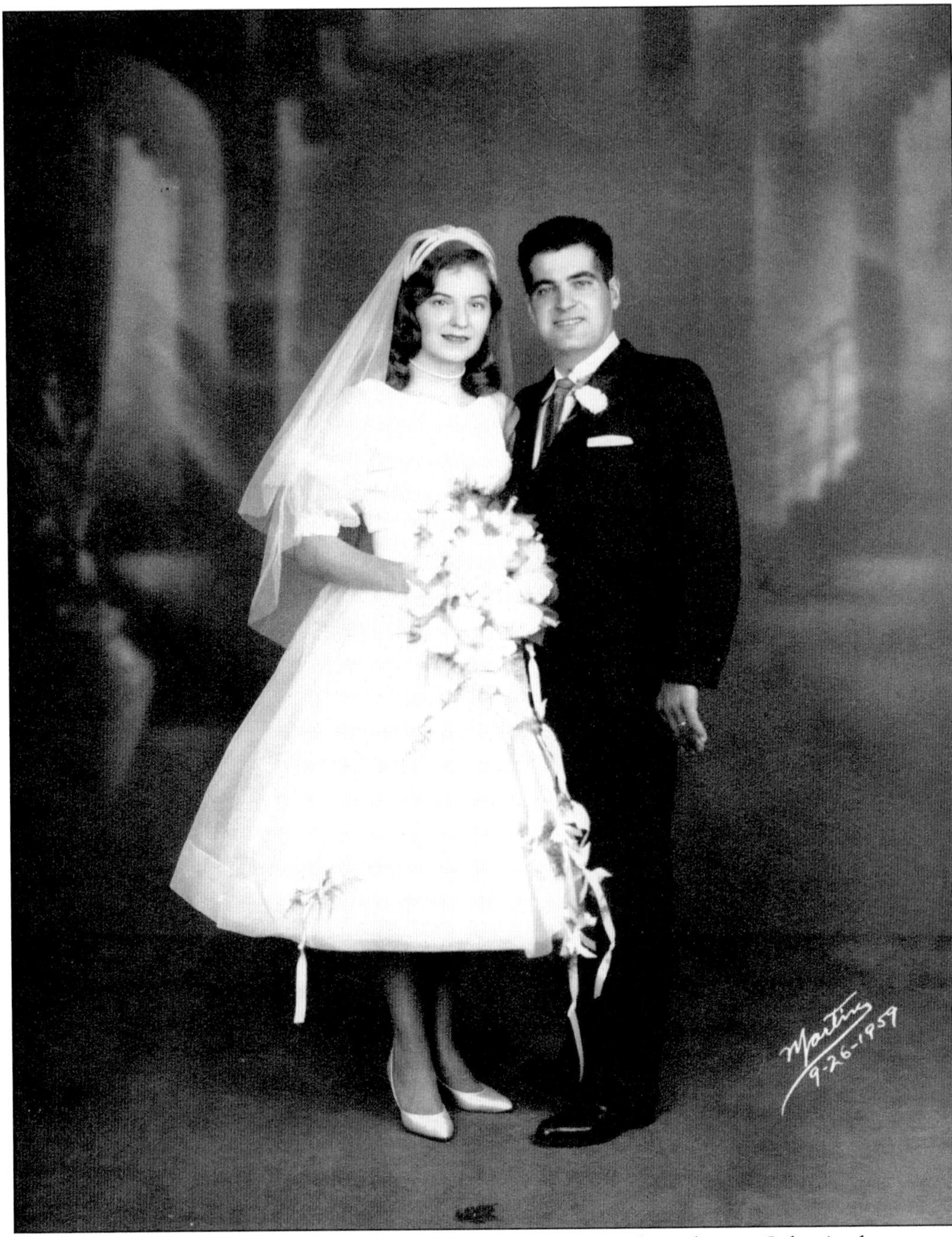

Deanna Moore St. Jean came to Salem in 1947, a second grader in Salem's three-room schoolhouse, Salem Elementary. She graduated Salem Elementary in a class of 14 students. As of 2005, St. Jean has been curator and historian of the Salem Historical Society since 1975 and municipal historian for the Town of Salem for the past 15 years. She has dedicated 30 years to the town of Salem in preserving its history and making it available to the public. Here she is on her wedding day, September 26, 1959, to Gerard St. Jean of Jewett City, who was a veteran of the Korean War. The St. Jeans settled in Salem and raised one daughter, Antoinette Marie.

Nine

EXCAVATIONS

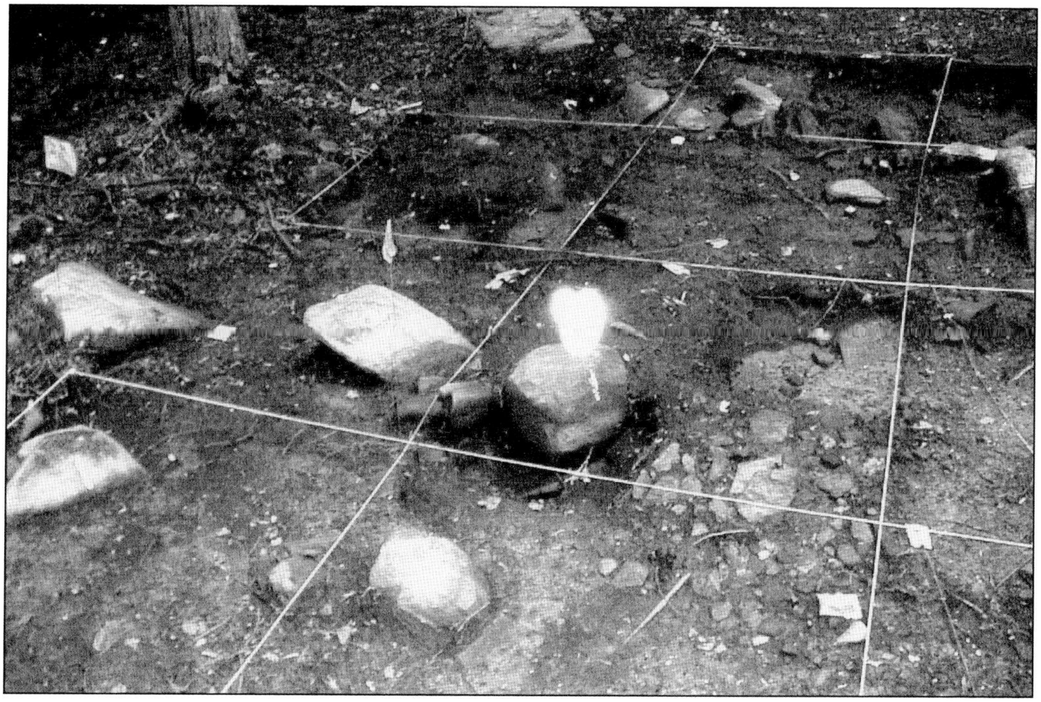

New England has a long history of profit made from slavery, just as much as did the South. The triangle trade consisted of rum, molasses, and slaves between New England, the West Indies, and Africa. There were 12–15 million survivors of the Middle Passage and the Atlantic Slave Trade. In 1774, there were 5,000 or more captives in Connecticut, with at least 2,000 African captives in New London County alone. Salem was just one of many towns in Connecticut that had the institution of slavery. Col. Samuel Browne, a wealthy merchant, purchased 4,000 acres and eventually amassed over 9,000 acres in Salem. Differing accounts state he brought 60 slaves or 65 families of slaves to work the land. He hired overseers to maintain his personal 4,000 acres and rented the other parcels. Here is a photograph of the gridded area being excavated by Dr. Warren Perry, Gerald Sawyer, and several Central Connecticut State University students. The sankofa, or the heart, an Akan symbol that, loosely translated, means "look to the past to know the future" appears in a photograph directly over this site on June 21, 2001. This particular day is also the summer solstice, World Healing Day, and the same day as the solar eclipse in Zimbabwe, Africa. It is also the symbol of the New York City African burial ground and the African diaspora.

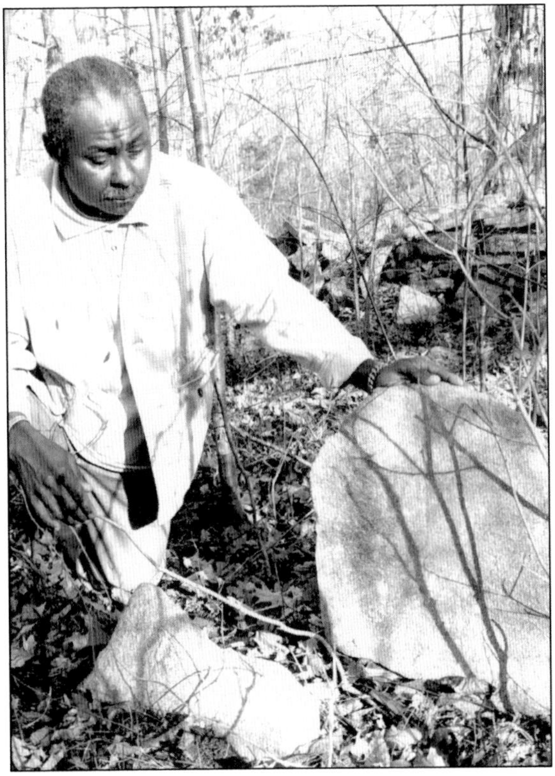

Abraham Abdul Haqq, local historian, studied at the University of Massachusetts in Amherst, where he started some black student organizations. In the 1980s, he moved to Colchester, where he began researching ancient burial grounds and the local history of people of color. He has given slide presentations and tours of local cemeteries of unmarked graves. He began a campaign to reconstruct a replica of one of the first African American schools in Connecticut, the Old District School House for Colored Children 1803/4–1848, and it is now listed on the Connecticut freedom trail. To elevate the replica to museum status, he formed the Concerned Citizens Committee of Colchester, in which he is chairman. Haqq showed Warren Perry his research, which initiated the archaeological excavations in Salem. As of 2005, he had two manuscripts ready for publication.

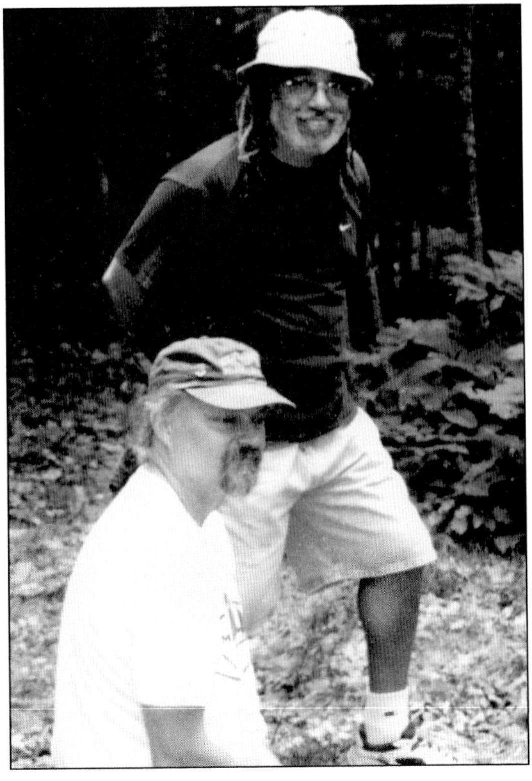

Gerald Sawyer (front) and Dr. Warren Perry are seen here at an archaeological site in Salem in 2001. Perry is associate professor of anthropology at Central Connecticut State University. He worked on the New York City African Burial Ground Project. Sawyer is a student who is using the two-and-a-half-acre site for his doctoral thesis. They investigated a dump site as well as cairns and structures in the area that may have been African captive related. They found the remnants of the dwelling of Tapheny, a Native American/ African healer and what may have been the gravestone of a slave named Pomp Henry. They also discovered shards of pottery and quartz used in burial customs native to Africa.